North and East Scotland Sea Kayaking

Doug Cooper

PESDA PRESS

WWW.PESDAPRESS.COM

First published in Great Britain by Pesda Press 2014

Tany y Bwlch Canol

Ceunant

Caernarfon

LL55 4RN

Wales

Maps by Bute Cartographic.
Printed in Poland, www.hussarbooks.pl

© Donald Thomson

Foreword

At last, a guidebook covering some of Scottish paddling's best kept secrets. Scotland is a world-class sea-kayaking destination, the Scottish Islands being rightly famous for the standard of paddling they offer. The north and east coasts are to some extent the Cinderellas of the Scottish coastline. They don't have as many islands as the west or north, but they will richly reward your efforts to explore their hidden nooks and crannies.

I've not given up paddling on Scotland's west coast and in the Western and Northern Isles, but I've made the effort to explore the north and east coast over the years and have not been disappointed. The north coast has some of Scotland's great headlands, and strongest tides. Treat the Pentland Firth with respect, plan well, and you will be rewarded with access to fascinating, now deserted islands.

My introduction to the far north east coast was with the local Pentland and Caithness clubs who passed on their in-depth knowledge of these waters and introduced me to many a small harbour with such names as Whaligoe and Lybster and their associated history. Further south in the Moray Firth my own club had an annual 'Dolphin Spotting' weekend, camping at Chanonry Point, and we were seldom disappointed as the country's most famous and studied dolphins strutted their stuff. The Fife coast was the location of the first expedition trip I led at the age of 19. It was only a three-day trip, but filled with much interest as we worked our way north from the Forth to the Tay via the many picturesque fishing villages of Fife, and of course the Isle of May.

The north and east coasts of Scotland do not have as many sheltered water options as you might get on the west or in the islands, and there is always some sort of swell, but if you make the effort you will be richly rewarded by stunning cliff and coastal scenery, numerous bird colonies and fascinating fishing villages, each with their own history and character. I recommend both the north and east coasts of Scotland and this guide. Enjoy investigating them by kayak. See you on the water.

Donald Thomson
Level 5 Sea Coach
Chairman North East Sea Kayakers

Contents

Foreword 3
Contents 4
How to Use the Guide 6
About the Author 8
Acknowledgments 9
Warning 9
Scottish Outdoor Access Code 10
Dolphins 11
East Coast Harbours 11

NORTH COAST 13

1	Cape Wrath	15
2	Faraid Head	21
3	Whiten Head	25
4	Eilean nan Ron	29
5	Farr Point	33
6	Strathy Point	37
7	Sandside Head	43
8	Holborn Head	49
9	Dunnet Head	55
10	Island of Stroma	61
11	Pentland Skerries	67
12	Duncansby Head	73

MORAY FIRTH – NORTH 79

13	Keiss Castle	81
14	Noss Head	85
15	Whaligoe	89
16	Lybster to Dunbeath	93
17	Dunbeath to Helmsdale	97
18	Tarbat Ness	103
19	North Sutor	107
20	Sutors Stacks	113
21	Chanonry Point	117

MORAY FIRTH – SOUTH 123

22	Burghead to Lossiemouth	125
23	Bow Fiddle Rock	129
24	Redhythe Point	135

25   Banff to Gardenstown 139
26   Troup Head 143
27   Kinnaird Head 147

ABERDEEN COAST 151

28   Rattray Head. 153
29   Bullers of Buchan 159
30   Port Erroll to Collieston 163
31   Cove to Stonehaven 167
32   Stonehaven to Inverbervie 171
33   Scurdie Ness 177
34   Bell Rock. 183

FIFE AND THE FIRTH OF FORTH. 187

35   St Andrews. 189
36   Fife Ness. 193
37   Isle of May 197
38   Anstruther to Elie 203
39   Inchkeith 207
40   Firth of Forth 211
41   Fidra 215
42   Bass Rock 219

THE BORDERS 225

43   Barns Ness 227
44   St Abb's Head. 233
45   Eyemouth 239

APPENDICES. 243

A   HM Coastguard and Emergency Services 243
B   Weather Information 243
C   Mean Tide Ranges 244
D   Glossary of Gaelic Words. 244
E   Trip Planning Route Card - Users Guide. 247

How to Use the Guide

To use the guide you will need an up-to-date tide tide table for the relevant area, the appropriate Ordnance Survey maps and the knowledge to use them.

Each of the forty-five trip chapters is set out into six sections:

Tidal & Route Information - This is designed as a quick reference for all the 'must know' information on which to plan the trip.

Introduction - This is designed to give the reader a brief overview of what to expect from the trip and to whet the appetite.

Description - This provides further detail and information on the trip including the coastline, launching/landing points, the wildlife and environment, historical information and places of interest to visit.

Tide & Weather – Offering further tidal information and how best to plan the trip which takes the tides, weather and local knowledge into consideration.

Map of Route – This provides a visual outline of the route's start/finish points, landing places, points of interest and tidal information.

Additional Information – This section provides further information (including Admiralty Charts and other useful maps) that will complement the trip, or be of interest if in the local area.

Using the Tidal & Route Information

Each route begins with an overview of pertinent details beginning with the following information: grade of difficulty, trip name, route symbols, and trip number.

Grade A | Relatively easy landings with escape routes easily available. Offering relative shelter from extreme conditions and ocean swell. Some tidal movement may be found, but easy to predict with no major tidal races or overfalls.

Grade B | Some awkward landings and sections of coastline with no escape routes should be expected. Tidal movement, tidal races, overfalls, crossings, ocean swell and surf may be found on these trips. They will also be exposed to the weather and associated conditions.

Grade C | These trips will have difficult landings and will have no escape routes for long sections of the trip. Fast tidal movement, tidal races, overfalls, extended crossings, ocean swell and surf will be found on all these trips. They will be very exposed to the weather and sea state, therefore require detailed planning and paddlers to be competent in rough water conditions. With this considered, the journey may require good conditions for the trip to be viable.

ROUTE SYMBOLS

Distance	Total distance for the trip.
OS Sheet	Number of Ordnance Survey 1:50,000 Landranger map required.
Tidal Port	The port for which tide timetables will be required to work out the tidal streams.
Start	△ map symbol, name and six-figure grid reference of starting point.
Finish	○ map symbol, name and six-figure grid reference of finishing point.
HW/LW	The high and/or low water time difference between local ports nearest to the trip and the tidal port.
Tidal Times	Location or area of tidal stream movement, the direction to which the tidal stream flows and the time it starts flowing in relation to the tidal port high water.
Max Rate Sp	The areas in which the tidal streams are fastest and the maximum speed in knots attained on the average spring tide.
Coastguard	Name of the relevant Coastguard Station.

MAP SYMBOLS

start & alternative start	major counter-current
finish & alternative finish	areas of counter-currents / eddies
landing places	areas of rough water / overfalls
possible escape	lighthouse & light
portage	lifeboat station
described route	ferry, passenger & car
alternative route	campsite
tidal stream direction	bird reserve
−0520 HW time relative to Tidal Port HW	town / buildings
7kn Sp Max Rate at Springs	Prohibited Zone prohibited area
High point	car park

How to Use the Guide

7

About the Author

Doug Cooper

Doug works at Scotland's National Outdoor Training Centre, Glenmore Lodge, where he is Head of Paddlesports. He works as a Level 5 Coach in Sea and White Water and has the fantastic job of taking people to remote and spectacular coastlines and rivers, then helping them improve their paddling skills and understanding. Many of these days are spent on the sea on the north or east coast of Scotland, which is a great office on work days and an even better playground on days off.

Doug also enjoys pushing his envelope or just having fun on personal adventures and expeditions. He has sea kayaked extensively around the world including Greenland, Alaska, Iceland, Norway, Ireland, Corsica, Croatia, Sardinia and Greece, and always has a new destination and adventure planned.

When not out on the water Doug can be found in the mountains at work as a Mountain and Ski instructor or at play in search of new crags or fresh powder tracks. He was also co-author of *Scottish Sea Kayaking* and author of *Sea Kayak Handling* and *Rough Water Handling*, all published by Pesda Press.

So if it involves discovering new remote parts of the world, having an adventure or helping friends and clients, then Doug will have a smile on his face and definitely be having fun.

📷 *Doug Cooper*

Acknowledgements

I would like to thank all those people with who I have shared a sea kayak journey on the north or east coasts of Scotland. Your company and enthusiasm will have shaped my feelings for these fantastic sections of coastline, and you will have no doubt shared some personal insights and knowledge along the way. In this you will have not only inspired me to write this guide, but also strengthened my passion for these coastlines which I hope have come through in the following pages.

The process of turning that knowledge and passion of a coastline into a guide book could not have happened without the constant support, enthusiasm and encouragement of my wife, Lara. We have paddled the majority of the trips together, and spent many a night staying in the van working on the day's photos and researching the next section of coastline.

Invaluable local knowledge was readily given by Ken Nicol, Alan Meikle and Donald Thomson; without this the guide would not be as comprehensive as it is and certainly would be missing that essential 'local' ingredient. Charlie Phillips, the Whale and Dolphin Conservation Society field officer, has been invaluable with his expert advice on the east coast bottlenose dolphins. A big thanks to all of you.

Finally, thanks are due to Franco Ferrero and his team at Pesda Press. Without their attention to detail and professionalism this book would not look as good as it does and certainly would have never have made it to your bookshelf.

Photographs

Thanks to Charlie Phillips for the fantastic dolphin photo on page 122.

All other photographs by Doug and Lara Cooper.

WARNING

Sea kayaking is inherently a potentially dangerous sport. The sea is one of the most committing and unforgiving environments. Conditions can change quickly and dramatically on the sea. When planning to venture out on any of the trips described in this book, ensure that your knowledge, experience, ability and judgement are appropriate to the seriousness of the trip. The author recommends acquiring appropriate training and advice from experienced and qualified individuals.

The information in this book has been thoroughly researched. However the author can take no responsibility if tidal times differ or if the information supplied is not sufficient to negotiate the conditions experienced on the day. The outdoors cannot be made risk-free and you should plan and act with care at all times for your own safety and that of others. The decision on whether to go out sea kayaking or not, and any consequences arising from that decision, remains yours and yours alone.

Scottish Outdoor Access Code

Access to the outdoors in Scotland is encouraged; visitors and locals have a right of responsible access. Scottish Natural Heritage (SNH) is responsible for promoting and publicising the Scottish Outdoor Access Code (SOAC).

Where you have access rights to is not shown on Ordnance Survey maps, or any other map in Scotland. The Scottish Outdoor Access Code deals with the land and freshwater access which is pertinent to the sea kayaker as you have to gain access to the sea over land or down a river and then again land to camp, walk or rest.

You are completely free to kayak on the sea, and there is no limit how far offshore you can travel. However, for safety rather than access reasons, the further you travel offshore during a crossing to an island, for example, the more reason there is to contact the Coastguard and let them know your plans.

The Scottish Outdoor Access Code is based on three key principles and these apply equally to the public and to land managers.

RESPECT THE INTERESTS OF OTHERS

Acting with courtesy, consideration and awareness is very important. If you are exercising access rights, make sure that you respect the privacy, safety and livelihoods of those living or working in the outdoors, and the needs of other people enjoying the outdoors. If you are a land manager, respect people's use of the outdoors and their need for a safe and enjoyable visit.

CARE FOR THE ENVIRONMENT

If you are exercising access rights, look after the places you visit and enjoy, and leave the land as you find it. If you are a land manager, help maintain the natural and cultural features which make the outdoors attractive to visit and enjoy.

TAKE RESPONSIBILITY FOR YOUR OWN ACTIONS

If you are exercising access rights, remember that the outdoors cannot be made risk-free and act with care at all times for your own safety and that of others. If you are a land manager, act with care at all times for people's safety.

GETTING MORE ADVICE AND INFORMATION

The Scottish Outdoor Access Code cannot cover every possible situation, setting or activity. Free information and advice on access rights and responsibilities, and on who to contact in your local authority, is available online at www.outdooraccess-scotland.com.

In addition to this, further information about responsible use of the environment while sea kayaking can be found on the Scottish Canoe Association's website (www.canoescotland.org/AccessEnvironment) and on Scottish Natural Heritage's website (www.snh.go.uk)

DOLPHINS

The east coast of Scotland is particularly lucky to be home to the most northerly population of bottlenose dolphins. These dolphins enjoy feeding and playing along the entire east coast, but Chanonry Point, the Kessock Narrows and the areas between the North and South Sutors are the best feeding sites in Europe. Bottlenose dolphins are rare in Europe and are protected by both UK and EU law as they are a European Protected Species. As sea kayakers we clearly have an amazing opportunity to see and enjoy dolphins. However we also have a similar opportunity to disturb, prevent feeding and harm dolphins. Please follow this agreed Code of Conduct for seeing dolphins while paddling on the east coast, in particular around the Moray Firth.

Be cautious and courteous; approach areas where there are dolphins with extreme caution.

Stay at least 50 to 100 metres away, and if they come to you that's fine but don't paddle towards them. When they depart do not try and follow them as this means the interaction remains under their control.

Be predictable and act in a sensible way, do not make sudden changes in speed or direction.

Approach from the side on a parallel converging course, not from the front or behind. Maintain a parallel course as you paddle past them. Try to avoid pointing your kayak at them as this may make them feel threatened (you'll look more like a predator).

Make sure the whole group paddles on one side. If you split up and 'surround' the dolphins they're likely to feel trapped or hemmed in.

EAST COAST HARBOURS

The east coast is characterised by its exposed coastline broken only by a few small bays or long expanses of unbroken sand. Launching and landing opportunities are limited, and these are often reliant on the local harbours. Many of these are run by harbour trusts, which at various stages over the last 200 years have been granted the right in law to build and operate a harbour, and to charge fees to support its construction and maintenance. Some of the smaller harbours only support one or two inshore lobster and crab fishermen, and see an ever-increasing leisure use of the harbour. With the constant need for repair and maintenance of these historic and important harbours, some Harbour Trusts (appropriately) charge fees for leisure as well as commercial usage. As sea kayakers we will be classed as leisure users in some of these harbours and will be asked to pay a launching fee. This could be in the form of an honesty box, or could be asked for by the harbour master. So whenever making use of a harbour please be mindful of this and look to see if a contribution is asked for. If it is please pay accordingly or choose to launch elsewhere. After all, if it were not for the harbours we would not have such easy access to this amazing coastline and losing them would be a real blow to the sea kayakers of the future.

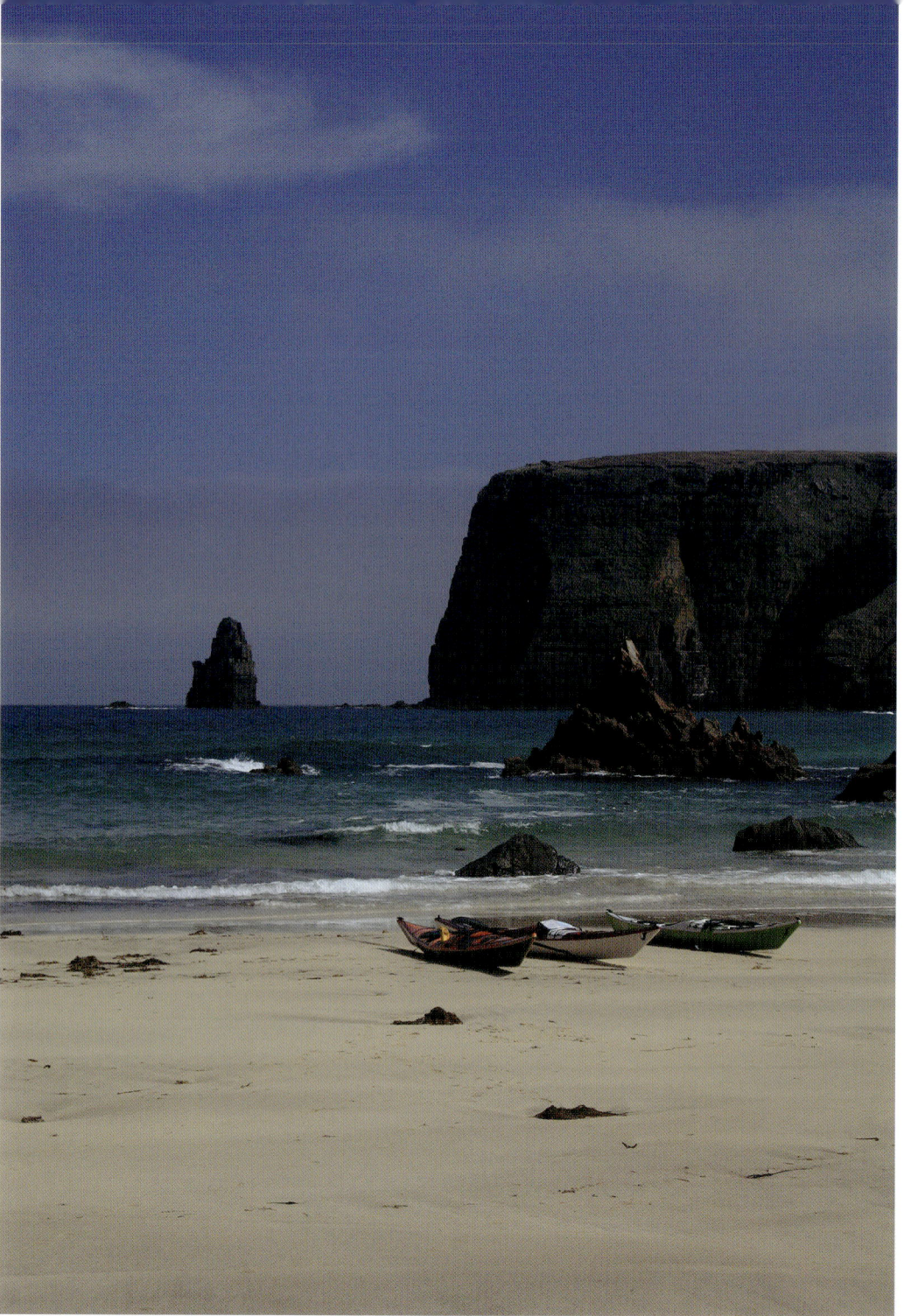

Stack Clò Kearvaig from Geodha na Seamraig, Cape Wrath

North Coast

Introduction

The north coast of Scotland is one of the most dramatic coastlines in the British Isles. With its exposure to the Atlantic Ocean and strong tidal flows it is also one of the most serious. In good conditions and with appropriate experience it offers some of the most spectacular and rewarding sea kayaking that Scotland has to offer.

For those who like to paddle around big headlands the north coast is made up of some of the biggest, with Cape Wrath at its western entrance and Duncansby Head at its eastern end. Between these two giants there are plenty more, including Britain's most northerly mainland point of Dunnet Head. This coastline is not just about committing headlands though; there are some unique islands to explore as well. The relative shelter of Eilean nan Ron, Eilean Neave and the Rabbit Islands are set amongst a landscape of pristine sandy beaches all overlooked by Scotland's most northerly Munro (mountain over 3,000 foot) of Ben Hope. To the west of these is Eilean Hoan surrounded by Ceannabeinne and Sango Sands, perhaps some of the most beautiful beaches in Scotland. In contrast to these are the exposed islands of Stroma, Swona and Muckle Skerry, situated in the heart of the Pentland Firth that has a fearsome reputation for its strong tidal flows and associated tidal races. All of these islands still have plenty of evidence of the unique history of the north coast of Scotland, a wild place where for generations people have strived to make a living. The north coast is also home to a lot of wildlife with numerous birds nesting on the cliffs and marine life enjoying the good feeding that the ocean and its tidal flows bring.

The north coast is an incredible location and with its remoteness offers a solitude and dramatic beauty that few other coastal destinations could match.

Tides and weather

The tidal streams of the north coast and in particular the Pentland Firth are formidable, with tidal flows, eddies, tidal races and overfalls unlike anywhere else. It has a justifiable reputation. That said, as with any tidal area, with good planning it is accessible to experienced sea kayakers. Perfect weather, neap tides and trips planned around slack water is the norm when starting to venture into the Pentland Firth. The use of tidal vectors, transits and GPS are all essential to maintain an awareness of the tidal movement effect.

To the west of Dunnet Head the extreme tidal flows of the Pentland Firth subside, and although there is tidal movement off all the headlands it becomes a lot easier to plan. Along with the tides the swell has a huge impact on the north coast. It is exposed to the Atlantic as well as the North Sea and the swell coming from any of these areas must be taken into account. Many of the landings along the coast involve beaches, rocky shores and reefs; with any swell these quickly become inadvisable.

There are few coastlines affected by wind, swell and tidal streams more than the north coast and this needs to be taken into account when planning any trips to this amazing area.

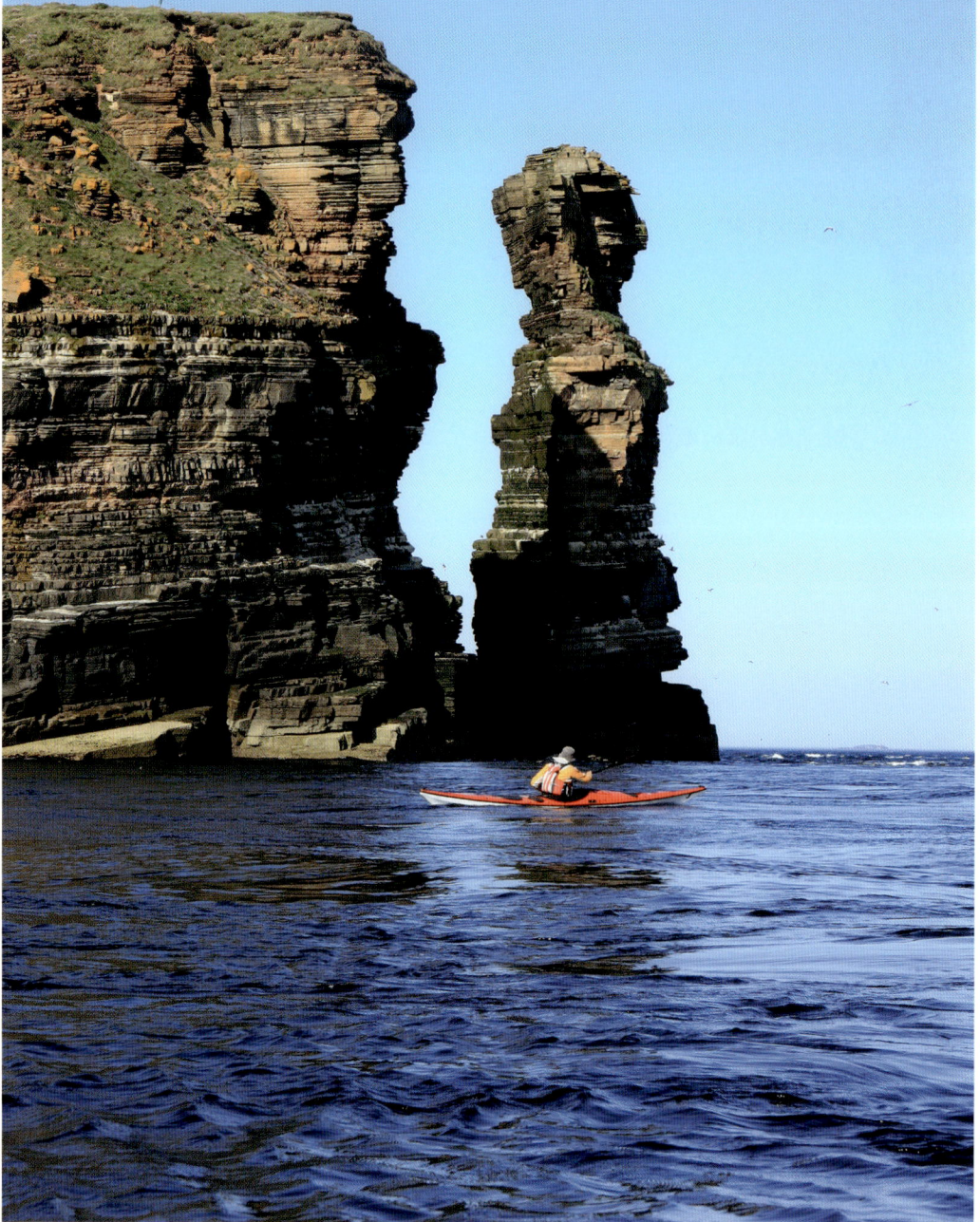

The huge sea stack and tidal waters on the approach to Duncansby Head

Cape Wrath ⬛⬛▨⬚

No. 1 | **Grade C** | **32km** | **OS Sheet 9**

Tidal Port	Ullapool
Start	△ Balnakeil Bay (NC 391 687)
Finish	○ Balnakeil Bay (NC 391 687)
HW/LW	HW/LW at Durness is around 3 hours and 30 minutes before Wick.
Tidal Times	From Stack Clo Kearvaig (NC 294 736) eastwards: The E going stream starts at about 2 hours and 20 minutes before HW Ullapool. The W going stream starts about 3 hours and 50 minutes after HW Ullapool.
	From Cape Wrath to Stack Clo Kearvaig: The E going stream starts at about 3 hours and 50 minutes before HW Ullapool. The W going stream starts at about 2 hours and 35 minutes after HW Ullapool.
Max Rate Sp	At Cape Wrath, expect rates of up to 5 knots. To the east, close in to the coast along to Stack Clo Kearvaig the rate is 3 knots. At An Garbh-eilean the rate is 3 knots. Close to the cliffs either side of Cape Wrath there may be eddies, on the east side this can form a continuous west going flow.
Coastguard	Shetland (E of Cape Wrath), tel. 01595 692976, VHF weather every 3 hours from 0710.
	Stornoway (S of Cape Wrath), tel. 01851 702013, VHF weather every 3 hours from 0710.

Introduction

Cape Wrath, the furthest north-west point of mainland Britain is a wild and stunning place. A lighthouse stands high above the caves and arches where the sea swirls and boils as it forces its way around the headland on its journey from the west coast of Scotland to the north coast and back again. The highest sea cliffs on the mainland are here at Clo Mor, 180 metres of towering vertical rock. In amongst this rugged coastline is an amazing beach at Kearvaig, its beauty will provide a respite from the rugged cliffs that surround you.

Description

Balnakeil Bay is a superb place to start this journey, the wonderfully clean, sandy beach stretches for two kilometres to the north and the water is crystal clear.

Leaving the stunning beach behind and setting off in the azure blue waters is a magical way to start, and the journey takes you across the entrance to the Kyle of Durness. While crossing you may just get a glimpse of the small passenger ferry that crosses the Kyle to the road that provides access for visitors to travel out to Cape Wrath by land. If you have non-paddlers in the group this is highly recommended, however getting there by kayak is going to be a far more dramatic journey. Once on the other side of the bay, the cliff scenery that will dominate the trip begins and the island of An Garbh-eilean will be clear to see. The area you are now paddling in is the only place in the Northern Hemisphere where NATO forces combine land, air and sea capabilities in assault mode for training manoeuvres. They will deploy up to 1,000 pound live bombs, and it is the rock that forms An Garbh-eilean that is often the unfortunate target. Paddling close to this island you will see the effect these bombs have had on the island, with remnants of the bombs sticking out of the rock face. Ensure you paddle this trip when there is no live firing; you do not want to become a new target for the bombs!

Paddling round Cleit Dhubh the spectacular view of Clo Mor opens up, and it is truly breath-taking with the immense 180 metre cliffs towering vertically up from the sea and stretching for more than three kilometres. These cliffs provide the highest sea cliffs on mainland Britain, paddling beneath them is an unbelievable experience and you will feel very insignificant in this 'on the edge of the world' environment. The impressive sea stack of Stack Clo Kearvaig marks the end of the mighty cliffs and just beyond this is the beautiful beach of Kearvaig. The sea stack itself is a popular place for breeding birds such as guillemots and razorbills. The stack is also known as 'The Cathedral' due to it having two spires and a natural window created by the fierce north-coast weather.

There will always be a certain amount of surf rolling into Kearvaig beach, so be prepared for a fun landing. At the back of the beach lies Kearvaig house which the Mountain Bothies Association have converted into a bothy, and this provides shelter for a lunch break, or maybe you could consider making this a two-day trip and spend a bit more time savouring this amazing location. After negotiating a surf launching from the beach the final section of coastline that leads out to Cape Wrath lies ahead. About halfway along look out for the old lighthouse jetty which can provide another possible landing. This was used by the lighthouse tender MV *Pharos*

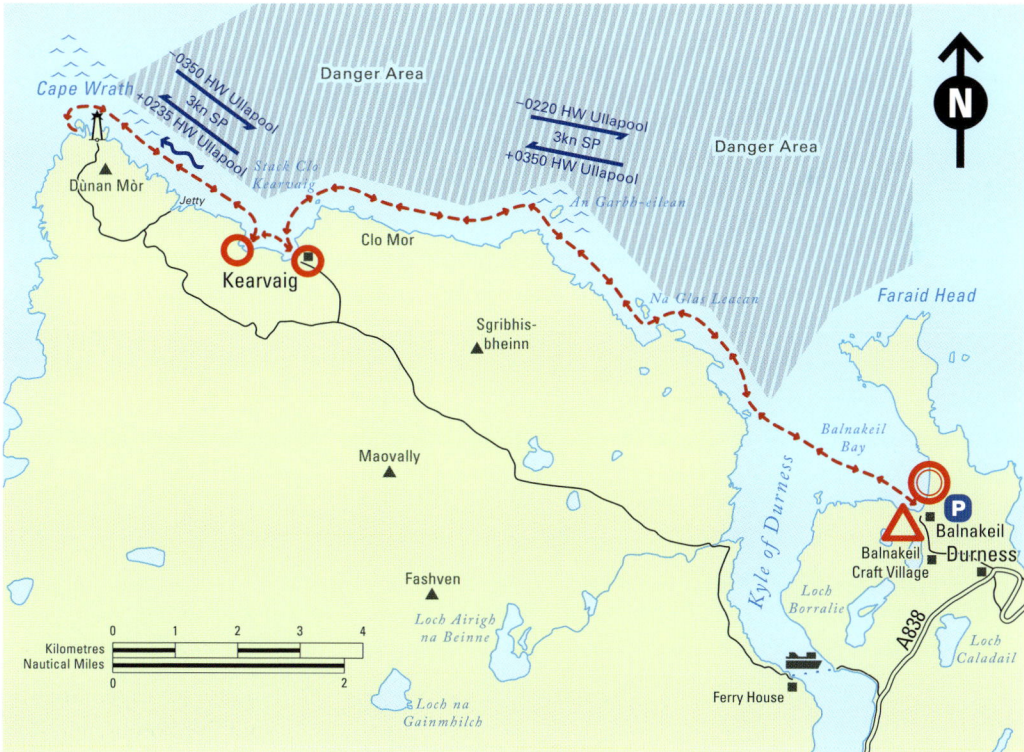

that brought supplies on an annual basis for the lighthouse keepers, a remote place indeed for these hardy men to live and work. Cape Wrath is as 'out there' as it gets on mainland Britain and with a lively ocean under you and soaring impregnable cliffs above you, it will feel like it! Underneath the headland are two large arches that you might be able to paddle through and 'circumnavigate' the headland. The tidal stream runs through these arches so there is no guarantee this will be possible, so care should be taken. Standing 121 metres above on top of the headland is the Cape Wrath lighthouse, facing out to the expanse of the Atlantic Ocean. First lit on Christmas day 1828 this light was built by Robert Stevenson and clearly marks this remote corner of Britain. The name Cape Wrath is derived from Old Norse 'hvarf' which means turning point, this is possibly due to the fact that the Vikings often used to turn around here and return back home. So if the mighty seafaring Vikings decided to turn and head for home at the Cape, it is time for us to return as well.

The trip back takes the same route as already paddled, however this time it is worth landing at Geodha na Seamraig to have a rest. This lovely beach provides an incredible view out to Stack Clo Kearvaig. Although paddling the same coastline, it is certainly no compromise as it just gives more time to take in these amazing cliffs. The views will be different as well, with some of the other dramatic headlands that reach out into the Atlantic being visible, Faraid Head initially and then Whiten Head beyond. Before long the expansive white sands of Balnakeil Bay will be clear to see and the crystal clear waters will lead you to a picture-postcard landing spot on the beach. You will feel that you have been to the edge of the world and back, and this will not be too far from the truth!

The last voyage of the Maggie from Hull

(from Cape Wrath Light: wreck log, 1897)

14 miles off the north-west tip
was no time to discover a hole in their ship

they tried for hours to bail and float
but they couldn't keep up – there was little hope

at 1am on December 13 the fishing boat foundered
filling with ocean its last bell was sounded

the crew had nought but a small rowing boat
and their love of life to keep them afloat

they sat caught, way out, in the Atlantic night
as their fair lass the Maggie slipped away out of sight

"row said the captain row for your lives
think of your children think of your wives"

"over yon is a beacon I see it flashing on and off
if I'm not mistaken that's the light of Cape Wrath!"

"come on pull – if we all pull together
and if Jesus and Mary sends us calm weather"

and they rowed and they rowed and they rowed through the night
always keeping the bow on the light

the swell it was boisterous and the wind it did blow
though they sweated and heaved, their progress was slow

the beacon was visible yet never seemed to get bigger
their resolution was tested, their mettle, their vigour

but in the early glimmering pink of the dawning
they could see the white tower as it heralded morning

and they knew in their hearts that somehow they survived
the currents of chance on the deep Atlantic tide

and as they got closer to under the cliff
hands blistered from rowing their shoulders stiff

within the next hour they had made it to shore
at 9am, the records show, they made their approach to the lighthouse door

and a welcoming meal from the keepers provided
the crew were exhausted but their spirit undivided

they set off on the road next day for Hull their home town
and sang songs all the way of how they survived

when the Maggie went down…

(Scottish Lighthouse Poems, Knotbrook Taylor, www.knotbrook.co.uk and Blue Salt Publishing, www.bluesalt.co.uk Working with the Scottish Lighthouse Museum, www.lighthousemuseum.org.uk)

Tides and weather

This is not a section of coastline to get caught out on. There are few landing spots, these often with the potential of big surf and challenging walk-outs. The headland of Cape Wrath is fully exposed to the Atlantic and rarely will there be a day without much swell, so whichever direction it comes from it will have an effect on how this trip goes. Ideal conditions are required, light winds and minimum swell.

The trip needs to be planned to make use of the strong tidal movement in this area. Timing the trip so that Cape Wrath is reached at the slack water at the end of the west going stream is essential, this being about 3 hours and 50 minutes before high water Ullapool. The few kilometres leading up to Cape Wrath will most probably be continuously flowing in a westerly direction due to the tidal stream and then eddy effect, this can be paddled against at the slack water time when it is recommended to arrive at the Cape.

Additional information

Cape Wrath is a live firing exercise area for the military. Check with the coastguard, look out in local papers, check at the shop in Durness and look to see if any red flags are flying before you set off. It is also possible to phone the range control on 0800 317071 to ask about the live firing. At Balnakeil there is a craft village that is worth a look and provides a café, Cocoa Mountain, which is highly recommended for a chocolate fix on completing the trip.

Variations

The obvious variation would be not to turn around at the Cape but continue on around to the west coast. If this is the case this will usually be a two-day trip and finishing at Kinlochbervie (NC 217 564) is recommended. To complete this trip further tidal planning will be required and the overnight stop would usually be either Kearvaig or Sandwood Bay. To help with the tidal planning look at Scottish Sea Kayaking, Fifty Great Sea Kayak Voyages by Doug Cooper and George Reid, and the appropriate tidal pilots.

Faraid Head ▦▦▨▨▦▦

No. 2 | Grade B | 10 or 25km | OS Sheet 9

Tidal Port	Aberdeen
Start	△ Balnakeil Bay (NC 391 687)
Finish	⬭ Sango Sands (NC 407 676)
HW/LW	HW/LW at Durness is around 3 hours and 30 minutes before Wick.
Tidal Times	Off Faraid Head: The E going stream starts about 2 hours and 20 minutes before HW Ullapool. The W going stream starts about 3 hours and 50 minutes after HW Ullapool.
Max Rate Sp	2-3 knots off Faraid Head
Coastguard	Shetland, tel. 01595 692976, VHF weather every 3 hours from 0710.

Introduction

Some of the most spectacular beaches on the Scottish mainland are found during this journey, landing on any one of them and taking in the scenery is a breathtaking experience. Allowing time to land on them all is highly recommended. The beaches, cliffs and impressive sea stacks around the narrow headland of Faraid Head make for a magical day out.

Description

The beach at Balnakeil Bay provides a stunning place to start this trip, and launching out in the crystal clear, azure blue waters on a sunny day will have you believing you are somewhere far more exotic than the north coast of Scotland. Park by the churchyard and remains of Durness Old Church, which was built in 1619 on the site of a much older church dating back to the Crusades in the 1100s. Within the old church you will find the skull and crossbones that mark the tomb of Donald Macleod. He was henchman to the chief of Clan Mackay and is said to have murdered eighteen people, disposing of their bodies down the waterfall at Smoo Cave (visited later in this trip). The churchyard also contains the mass grave of a ship that sank of Faraid Head with all hands in 1849, a sad story; however there can be few more spectacular resting places.

As you head out from the beach towards Faraid Head the scenery is both beautiful and ruggedly wild, and in this is so very Scottish. The sand dunes that form the backdrop to the two kilometre-long beach are some of the largest to be found in the British Isles, and where these finish the steep cliffs and coastline of Faraid Head begin. The headland forms a long narrow peninsula unlike any of the other headlands along the north coast, making it a lot less committing to paddle around. From the land this headland may appear to be lacking in grandeur, but once beyond the sight of the beach steep cliffs soar up from the sea along with the occasional cave and sea stack. These spectacular cliffs provide a home for plenty of nesting sea birds, including the comical puffin. Up on the headland itself there are Ministry of Defence buildings surrounded by high security fences. These days it is a control tower for the Cape Wrath bombing range but originally it was built as a radar station to monitor the north coast of Scotland. The view while paddling around Faraid Head is truly spectacular with Cape Wrath behind and the whole of the north coast of Scotland ahead. On a clear day you will see Whiten Head in the near distance and then beyond will be Strathy Point, Dunnet Head and the Orkneys; inland there will be Ben Hope, Scotland's most northerly Munro, looking down on everything below.

Leaving Faraid Head and continuing to Sango Bay the impressive sea stacks of Clach Bheag and Clach Mhòr na Faraid will be passed, the latter almost looking like a miniature version of Boreray out near St Kilda. Shortly after this Seanachaisteal (The Old Castle) is reached. This is thought to be an Iron Age fort, however little remains now as the Vikings reputedly destroyed it in 1265. As well as destroying the Castle, King Hakon and his Vikings also burnt twenty townships in the area before continuing to the Battle of Largs. In this battle they were defeated by the Scots, bringing an end to Norse domination of the Western Isles. On from the castle Sango Bay provides one of the most stunning beach landing spots there could be. This is where you will return to at the end of the journey, and a perfect landing place for those wanting a shorter day out. Chances are there will plenty of paddling time left in the day, so extending the trip is highly recommended as there are more beaches, islands and cliffs to explore.

If choosing to continue, head along the coastline that continues for a short while with the Lewisian Gneiss rock that has formed all the cliffs so far before turning into the narrow geo that leads to Smoo Cave. This unique feature is made from Durness Limestone and at the end of this long geo an impressive cave is found, the outer part being formed by the sea and the inner part by the freshwater stream running through it. Sadly it is not possible to paddle into the cave, but it is worth getting out of the kayaks and walking in for a look. Be prepared to be joined by a few tourists as this is a popular venue to visit along the north coast. From Smoo Cave head out around Eilean Hoan, this provides great views back to Faraid Head as well as on to Whiten Head. Unlike the surrounding landscape this island (a nature reserve) is a rich green colour with the vegetation benefiting from the island being made of limestone. The crofters of the nearby Sangobeg used to grow their potato crops out on the fertile island; nowadays it is the sheep that enjoy the rich grazing. Paddling around the island there will no doubt be seals out on the rocks joining you in enjoying the impressive surroundings. There is a landing spot in front of the small building on the south side of the island, this building can offer shelter if required.

From the island head across to Ceannabeinne beach, which is arguably the best of the day. The expanse of perfect sand, turquoise waters and incredible views from it across to Whiten Head make for a place you may never want to leave. In Gaelic this golden sandy beach is known as Traigh Alt Chailgeag that translates into Beach of the Burn of the Old Woman. Legend has it that an old woman was gathering peat to take home to her fire, as she stopped to drink from the swollen burn she slipped in. Her body was carried downstream to the beach where she was found the next day. It is hard to believe that such an inspirational beach in its stunning setting can be named after such a sad event.

The final part of this journey will take you back along the coastline to Sango Bay and provides some more truly breathtaking beaches, Sangobeg perhaps being the most memorable. Landing back at Sango Bay and reflecting on the day, it will be hard to believe that in such a short journey there has been such amazing variety, including an impressive headland with soaring cliffs, a remote island and some of the most spectacular beaches in the UK. All that is left is the short carry from the beach up to a rough car parking area, this is found by the stream to the west of the main tourist car parking area.

Tides and weather

This trip needs to be planned to make best use of the tidal stream that runs off Faraid Head. Arriving at the head to make use of the east going stream and using this tide to help the journey on to Eilean Hoan is recommended. Returning to Sango Bay the tidal stream in negligible close into the shore. This coast is affected by swell from the west, north and east, and as many of the landings are on beaches the swell forecast needs to be taken into account to avoid too challenging a landing.

Additional information

There are no amenities at Balnakeil Bay, although at Sango Bay and Durness there plenty. Ensure to plan a trip to the Balnakeil craft village where the café at Cocoa Mountain provides a well-deserved chocolate fix after a great trip.

Variations

The trip could be shortened by launching or landing at Sango Bay or Ceannabeinne Beach. The latter requires a long carry, which is possible but not recommended. Continuing on around Whiten Head makes a great two-day journey. If doing this it is worth considering using the bothy at Freisgill as an overnight stop.

Sea stacks off Whiten Head

Whiten Head 🛶🎣📷🪨🛶

No. 3 | Grade C | 27km | OS Sheet 9 & 10

Tidal Port	Ullapool
Start	△ Ard Neackie (NC 448 597)
Finish	⊙ Talmine (NC 586 627)
HW/LW	HW/LW at Loch Eriboll is around 3 hours and 10 minutes before Wick.
Tidal Times	Off Whiten Head: The E going stream starts about 2 hours and 20 minutes before HW Ullapool. The W going stream starts about 3 hours and 50 minutes after HW Ullapool.
Max Rate Sp	3 knots around Whiten Head.
Coastguard	Shetland, tel. 01595 692976, VHF weather every 3 hours from 0710.

Introduction

There can be few places in Britain that offer as remote and committing a day's paddle as Whiten Head. With next to no landings, the expanse of the Atlantic Ocean on one side and 250 metre cliffs on the other, it really is an amazing environment. There is little room for error on this trip, but that in itself makes it a paddle that has to be done.

Description

3

The starting point for this adventurous trip is the sheltered bay that is formed at the limekilns of Ard Neackie in Loch Eriboll. This intriguing feature, formed by a mound of land prevented from becoming an island by an umbilical cord of sand and shingle, was once the terminus for the Helium Ferry which was used to cross Loch Eriboll prior to the road. The four large limekilns that are situated on the water's edge along from the derelict ferry house were built in 1870 by Reay estate. The estate produced large amounts of lime here and on the nearby island of Eilean Choraidh and loaded it into ships for export. The journey up the east side of Loch Eriboll passes the navigation light that for us marks the start to a coastline that provides plenty of interest and surprises. Although not as grand as the cliffs to come there are plenty of caves and arches, along with dramatic waterfalls on route to Whiten Head. You may want to stretch your legs at Freisgill, which is a bothy that provides a unique resting spot. It is well worth having a rest along this section of coastline as once the headland is reached there may be no further opportunities until near the finish.

As Whiten Head is approached you will come across a huge arch alongside a cathedral of a cave that is formed by an almost yellow colour rock quite different to the rest of the coastline. If you are lucky enough to have the conditions to enter there are a choice of ways in and out, with the ceiling high above your head and the sea echoing around you. As you round Whiten Head the views are fantastic, ornate sea stacks rising from the sea around you, Cape Wrath along to the west standing proud out into the Atlantic Ocean and then the immense coastline of Whiten Head itself. One of the ornate sea stacks seen here is called The Maiden and is where the famous

Scottish climber Tom Patey sadly died in 1970 whilst abseiling. From here on you are paddling in as exposed a place as it is possible to get in the UK, the swell and tide will no doubt be lively under your kayak and there will a real sense of exposure. Soon the mountain-like Cleit an t-Seabhaig dominates the view alongside a cascading waterfall. As you pass it there will be plenty more sea stacks and tempting arches, but rarely is the sea calm enough to explore them.

Along the coastline you will see the steeply shelving pebble beach of Geodha nan Aigheann; in calm seas this gives the only possible landing place on this headland. Once ashore, imposing steep sides of rock and grass surround the inaccessible beach. The only things easily escaping from this area are the seabirds that circle above. As you leave the beach the dramatic cliffs will continue unrelenting in their magnitude, the rock and grass rising up to 250 metres all along this coastline. The rock walls are made up of metamorphic gneiss, and provide fantastic shapes and contortions amongst the rock features.

Not far beyond Geodha Brat, another possible landing is the beautiful sandy beach of Strathan. Although it is not far from here to the finish this beach provides an idyllic place to stop for a break. Around the corner from here you will be met with the fantastic view across to Eilean nan Ron, and then down to the Rabbit Islands with the Kyle of Tongue behind. It is opposite the Rabbit Islands that the sandy beach and harbour of Talmine provides as picturesque finishing point as you could ask for.

Tides and weather

Whiten Head is very exposed to swell from the west, north and east, as well as the wind. There are no easy landings and certainly no escape routes. Good weather conditions are essential, from both a safety and enjoyment point of view. There are relatively strong tidal streams off Whiten Head so the planning needs to take this into consideration. Starting the trip when the east going stream begins at 2 hours and 20 minutes before high water Ullapool gives plenty of time to make use of the tide.

Additional information

Talmine has a full range of local amenities including a pub that serves fine local seafood, including Loch Eriboll Scallops. There are no facilities at Ard Neackie. In this area under the cliffs VHF communication with Shetland Coastguard can be difficult.

Variations

The trip can be paddled starting from Talmine if the tides or weather makes that a preferable option. For a multi day trip it can be easily combined with either a trip around Faraid Head or exploration of Eilean nan Ron and the Rabbit Islands.

Eilean nan Ron

No. 4 | Grade B | 20km | OS Sheet 10

Tidal Port	Ullapool
Start	△ Skerray Pier (NC 660 637)
Finish	O Skerray Pier (NC 660 637)
HW/LW	HW/LW at Skerray is around 3 hours before Wick.
Tidal Times	Main stream on the outside of the islands and in Caol Raineach: The W going starts at about 3 hours and 50 minutes after HW Ullapool. The E going stream starts at about 2 hours and 20 minutes before HW Ullapool.
	Between the Rabbit Islands and Eilean nan Ron: The S going stream starts about 2 hours and 20 minutes before HW Ullapool and only runs for 3.5 hours. The N going stream starts at about 1 hour and 10 minutes after HW Ullapool.
	In Kyle of Tongue and around the Rabbit Islands: The outgoing stream starts about 1 hour and 10 minutes after HW Ullapool. The ingoing stream starts about 5 hours and 5 minutes before HW Ullapool.
Max Rate Sp	The tidal stream is at its fastest between Eilean nan Ron and the mainland, where it can reach 2 knots.
Coastguard	Shetland, tel. 01595 692976, VHF weather every 3 hours from 0710.

Introduction

This is a journey of contrasts. It offers committing exposed coastline with impressive cliffs and no landing, along with sheltered waters and sandy beaches. It has changing rock architecture and rock type around every corner. There are areas that used to be heavily populated now lying empty as a ghost town, and busy local fishing hamlets.

Description

Skerray harbour provides an easy launching place to start this trip. Leaving the shelter it is worth heading through Caol Beag and around Neave Island. You will soon pass a stunning sandy beach on the south-east corner, with maybe a lone seal sunbathing on it. The cliffs lead you around to an ornate arch on the northern tip of the island. Don't be tempted to cut across to Eilean nan Ron until you have discovered the large cave followed by a hidden arch inlet around the next couple of corners.

Mol na Coinnle is the main landing spot on Eilean nan Ron. There is a tiny natural harbour on the right as you enter the bay. At low water this has to be entered through a small natural arch and it then has steps leading up to the route to the settlement. In 1881 this settlement was at its largest with eight houses and seventy-three inhabitants. No one lives on the island these days; the final nine residents left in 1938. It is a National Nature Reserve with hundreds of grey seals breeding here in the autumn; about 350 calves are born each year. Moving on north from the harbour, you will soon pass a large natural arch leading into an open top cave. On the outside of the island, a sense of the exposure of the north coast will be felt as you pass an arch over a rock slab where the islanders used to dry their fish. It is worth continuing on around Meall Thailm for the rock architecture and bird life, or a shortcut to a landing spot is available between Mol Mor and Eilean Iosal up to about mid-tide when it dries.

For a shorter journey it is easy to head back from here although if time and energy allow the Rabbit Islands are worth a visit. Head to Sgeir an Oir and see if you can find the narrow natural arch which splits the island in two. On the calmest of days it is possible to paddle through this arch. This island's name translates into 'skerry of the gold', and supposedly a ship carrying gold to Charles Edward Stuart was wrecked here. If circumnavigating the islands take care on the shallow sandbars off the southwest corner, but a landing on the immaculate sheltered beach on the south side is a must.

From here it is worth exploring the mainland coastline on the way back to Skerray. If time allows head across to Skullomie. Here you will find a thriving little community on the hillside above a substantial hidden harbour. All too soon you will arrive at the harbour at Skerray, after a magic day out exploring a special cluster of islands.

Tides and weather

A good day's paddle will be possible in any reasonable weather conditions. The outside of the islands is very exposed to the swell and the weather so only commit to these areas (where there are no landings) in fine conditions. The tidal streams here are fairly complex yet even on spring tides they are never too fast. It is therefore possible to paddle this journey in any state of the tide, being aware that using natural eddies of the islands en route could ease the passage. It is quite easy to have the tide with you all the way. Use the last 2–3 hours of the west going stream to get

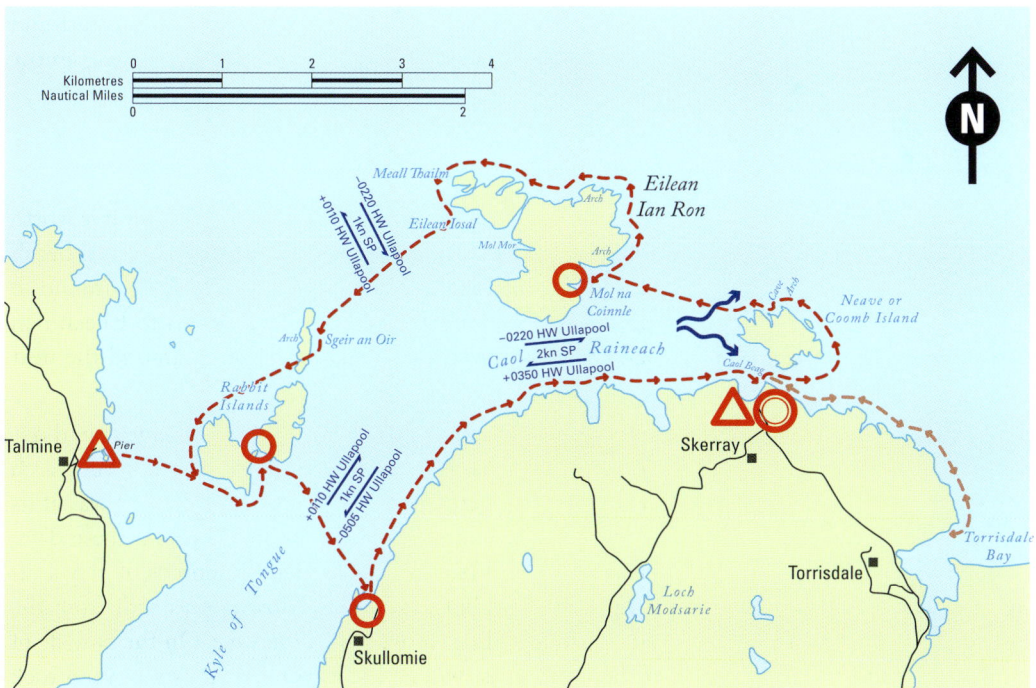

© Neave Island's fantastic beach

you to Eilean nan Ron to then pick up the south going stream to the Rabbit Islands that starts 2 hours and 20 minutes before HW Ullapool. Leaving the Rabbit Islands cross the Kyle of Tongue tidal flow and then use the east going stream through Caol Raineach to return, this starts at 2 hours and 20 minutes before HW Ullapool.

Additional information

There are no amenities at Skerray. Talmine, across from the Rabbit Islands, has local amenities and a nice pub. Tongue has similar amenities as well as a bank.

Variations

The beauty of this trip is that it can be a short or a long day out. Starting/finishing at Talmine is an additional option. Consider exploring the section of mainland coastline to the east of Skerray harbour as this provides some stunning caves and arches and is worthy of a trip in its own right. This could be done as an out and back, or you could consider paddling to the pier at Bettyhill (NC 700 619) or starting the Farr Point trip described next from Skerray.

Port a' Chinn

Farr Point ▦✖🚗🌀

No. 5 | Grade B | 18km | OS Sheet 10

Tidal Port	Aberdeen
Start	△ Bettyhill (NC 700 619)
Finish	ⵔ Port a' Chinn (NC 783 652)
HW/LW	HW/LW at Port a' Chinn is around 2 hours and 45 minutes before Wick.
Tidal Times	Off Farr Point: The E going stream starts about 2 hours and 20 minutes before HW Ullapool. The W going stream starts about 3 hours and 50 minutes after HW Ullapool.
Max Rate Sp	1-2 knots off Farr Point and Ardmore Point
Coastguard	Shetland, tel. 01595 692976, VHF weather every 3 hours from 0710.

Introduction

Nestled on the north coast between the imposing giants of Whiten Head and Strathy Point, Farr Point has a rugged beauty and charm of its own. Less committing than other headlands on this coast it provides a wonderful paddle along a very remote section of coastline that many a paddler could enjoy on the right day. Cliffs and sandy beaches are all around while views to islands and dramatic headlands make for a great day out.

Surfing at Farr Bay

Description

The old pier at the mouth of the River Naver is the start to this trip, with incredible views out across Torrisdale Bay. The beach here is one of the largest and most dramatic on the north coast, and with its exposure to the Atlantic it is rare that there will not be lines of surf crashing upon its shores. The mouth of this river once provided this area with a key source of income in the form of salmon fishing, and just along from the pier are the remains of the Bettyhill fishing station. Sweep nets were put out across the river to catch the salmon as they made their way upstream, once caught the icehouse and canning factory were used to preserve the fish for sale in distant markets. Sadly little remains of this important fishing station these days, and as with the original name for this community of Navermouth, it has all but disappeared. As you paddle out into Torrisdale Bay surf can often be a challenge, but the rip formed by the river mouth will usually provide a route to paddle out through without getting too wet. If the surf looks too awkward, leave this trip for another day as the rest of the coastline will be difficult to enjoy in these conditions.

The views of this dramatic section of coastline will start opening up as you make your way to the small headland of Creag Ruadh. The extensive sands of Torrisdale will be behind and then out to the west will be the cliffs and stunning sandy beach of Neave Island, with Ben Hope (Scotland's most northerly Munro) towering above the wild north coast mainland landscape. Once around this first small headland you should paddle in to the idyllic, smaller sandy beach of Farr Bay. This provides an easy landing opportunity or perhaps a spot to enjoy a bit of user friendly surfing if the swell is right. Along this coastline this beach offers some of the most consistent surf that is suitable for enjoying in a sea kayak. It is a popular spot though, so consideration for others will be required.

Clan Wars

In the 16th century the Mackays failed to appear in front of the queen consort of Scotland, Mary of Guise (the mother of Mary, Queen of Scots) and as a result the Earl of Sutherland was ordered to destroy the castle. A ship with fifty men and a cannon was sent to do just this, and although the castle had withstood many previous sieges the cannon proved too much. It was destroyed and the captain of the castle hanged.

After the castle was destroyed a force from Clan Mackay fought the Clan Sutherland at the Battle of Garbharry to try and avenge their previous defeat. Clan Sutherland was victorious and this was the last ever battle between these two great clans of the north. Paddling along this incredibly remote section of coastline it is hard to believe that it was the site of a major clan battle in years gone by.

After Farr Bay the rest of the coastline takes on a more inhospitable character with endless cliffs, numerous caves and many arches. Not long before Farr Point are two large caves, the first with a surprising through route not to be missed. As the point is reached there are incredible views of its two neighbouring headlands standing proudly out into the Atlantic in all their grandeur. Whiten Head and its towering cliffs is to the west and the long finger-like headland of Strathy Point and its lighthouse to the east. Soon an amazing arch will be reached, and through it lies a hidden landing spot. On the cliffs above stands the grass-covered mound that are the remains of Borve Castle. Originally thought to have been constructed by Vikings, it became the stonghold of the local Clan Mackay.

Head across to Kirtomy Bay from Borve Castle, and hidden behind the rocky island is a jetty and small fishing community. This provides another stopping opportunity, or an emergency get out if required. Cliffs, exposure and big views are the theme for the remainder of the paddle that will take you to the unique finish at Port a' Chinn.

Just before Ardmore Point is an arch that can provide a tight squeeze-through route. Beyond this more caves are easily explored in Port Mor. The bay at Port a' Chinn, nestled amongst steep sides and cliffs, is surprisingly sheltered and provides the finish for this trip. Unbelievably this is a fishing station and high on the hillside above the bay are the buildings where the nets are dried and cleaned. The fishermen have constructed an aerial cableway to get everything up and down between the shore and the top of the cliff, the bottom end of the cable being attached to a natural thread in the rock above the sea. It's yet another reminder of how it is to make a living on the north coast, and the lengths that the crofters and fishermen have go to in order to survive.

It's a steep and arduous climb to the road. A sturdy trolley for the kayak will make a difference. Even with the walk at the end, it will be well worth the effort as the rewards from this spectacular section of coastline will more than make up for it.

Tides and weather

Compared to the other headlands on the north coast this section of coastline is least affected by the tide and does not contain any rough tidal water. To make life as easy as possible it is still recommended to paddle this trip with the east going tide that starts 2 hours and 20 minutes before high water Ullapool, although it is possible to paddle against the tide with relative ease. The wind and the swell are the key considerations when planning this trip as it is very exposed to both, the start beach receiving a lot of surf from any swell from the west through to the north.

Additional information

Bettyhill has a good selection of local amenities including a swimming pool and campsite, but there are no other amenities available in this area of the north coast. There is limited parking a Port a' Chinn, please be considerate if leaving cars.

Variations

If time allows it is worth extending the trip by paddling the coastline out to the beach at Neave Island when leaving the pier at Torrisdale Bay. This section of coastline provides some stunning caves and arches, with the beach at Neave Island offering an idyllic stopping place to aim for before heading back across to Creag Ruadh. To avoid the steep carry at Port a' Chinn, continuing on around Strathy Point as described in the next trip chapter is an option, although this will double this distance and add an additional committing headland. This considered it does make an exceptional day out along the north coast. Paddling the trip starting at Port a' Chinn is preferred by many, thus carrying kayaks downhill and not up!

Strathy Point

No. 6 | Grade B | 15km | OS Sheet 10

Tidal Port	Ullapool
Start	△ Port a' Chinn (NC 783 652)
Finish	⭕ Portskerra (NC 878 663)
HW/LW	HW/LW at Portskerra is around 2 hours and 50 minutes before Wick.
Tidal Times	At Strathy Point: The E going stream starts about 2 hours and 20 minutes before Ullapool. The W going stream starts about 3 hours and 50 minutes after HW Ullapool.
Max Rate Sp	3 knots around Strathy Point.
Coastguard	Shetland, tel. 01595 692976, VHF weather every 3 hours from 0710.

Introduction

This is a fine quiet section of the Scottish coastline, where the chance of meeting another kayaker on the water is very slim. The rocky coast has some incredible caves and arches that will entertain any kayaker who has allowed plenty of time to explore them all. Along with this there is the finger-like headland of Strathy Point protruding out into the ocean and the beautiful beach at Strathy Bay, all making for a great day's paddling.

Description

Port a' Chinn is a unique launching place with a steep carry down from the road above. A sturdy kayak trolley can help a lot here. Leaving the port head out across Armadale Bay with it's beautiful beach. The coastline is surprisingly low-lying here and there is a possible landing spot at Geodh' Ruadh if the conditions are right, found below the unusually named group of houses called Brawl. Just beyond this is a magnificent arch that will no doubt have caught the eye. Paddling through it will provide an additional surprise in that it is not one arch but two! Not far from the arches, opposite the small yet steep-sided Boursa Island there is another landing at the improbable small fishing station seemingly in the middle of nowhere. Fishermen also used the next inlet known as Port Allt a'Mhuillinn. Look out for remnants of the mill that powered the stream here; if lucky you may even come across an old millstone.

From here to Strathy Point the cliffs rise is stature, and no doubt the numerous seabirds will be crying out to you as you pass below. There is another small bay to explore (NC 823 687) just after a group of rocky skerries, tiny islands and natural arch; this is used by fishermen and offers a landing in certain conditions and tidal heights. Beyond this the scenery is breathtaking, with huge caves, arches and cliffs, all overlooked by the lighthouse. There is a fantastic natural arch 500 metres before the lighthouse that can be paddled under, however in most states of tide it will not be possible to paddle all the way through. This is then followed by perhaps the largest of all caves on this trip, set amongst impressive vertical surroundings at the back of the final inlet before the point. As with so much of this coastline spend the time to explore every blind alley, as many will hold a worthy surprise.

Portskerra

Portskerra used to be a busy harbour that was used by many in the herring-fishing boom, and it was here in August 1918 that a severe gale from the north-west appeared without warning. Many men were out in their boats, as it was a calm evening before the storm caught them by surprise. Seven of the Portskerra fishermen lost their lives that night, and by the time morning came the sea was calm once more.

Paddling around Strathy Point itself you will no doubt have some lively water to contend with due to the tide racing past this headland that stretches so far out into the sea. No matter how bumpy the paddling gets, ensure you find a quiet bit to take in the impressive view. Here, on a clear day, you will have the Orkney Isles and Britain's most northerly point of Dunnet Head to the east and then back to the west the great headlands of Whiten Head and Cape Wrath. With this view and the wildlife that make this there home this truly is a magical place, and the lighthouse that sits proud atop of the headland overlooks it all. Strathy Point lighthouse was first lit in 1958 and is therefore a relative newcomer in comparison to the many lights that were built in the 1800s. It was the first all-electric station. As far back as 1900 requests were made for a lighthouse to be constructed here, and during World War II a temporary light was shown on the promontory.

Heading south from the point to the fantastic beach of Strathy Bay you will have the choice to stop at a couple of inlets, which again have been used as small relatively sheltered havens by

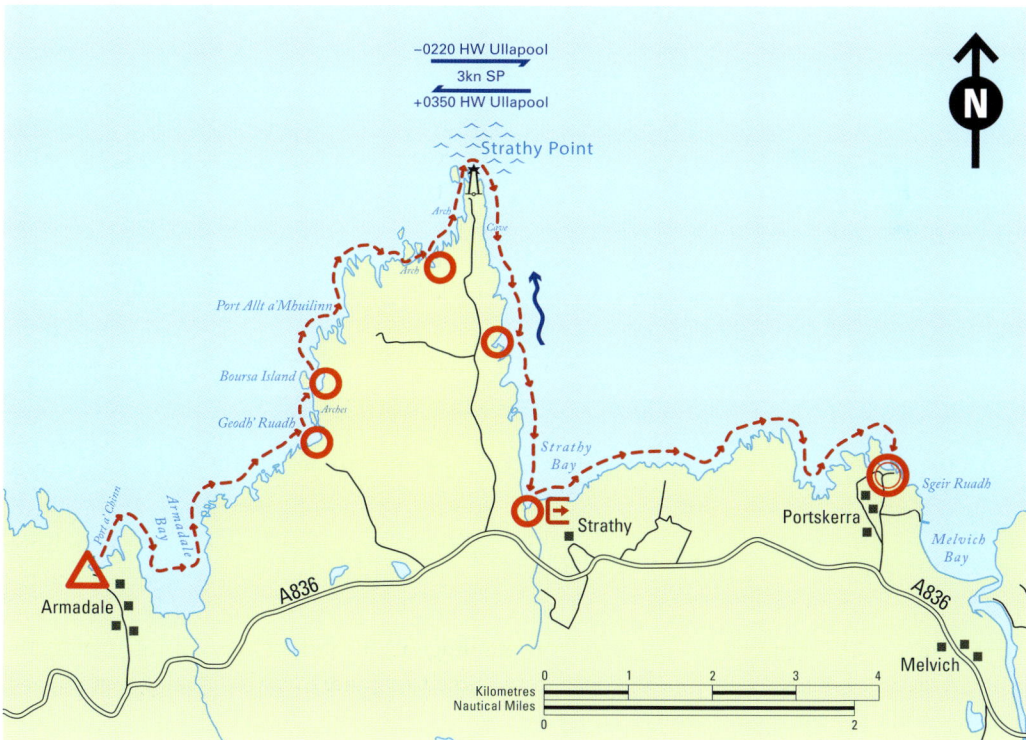

-0220 HW Ullapool
3kn SP
+0350 HW Ullapool

Strathy Point

N

Arch

Cove

Arch

Port Allt a'Mhuilinn

Boursa Island

Archer

Geodh' Ruadh

Strathy
Bay

Strathy

Sgeir Ruadh

Portskerra

Melvich
Bay

Poul a'Chinn

Armadale
Bay

Armadale

A836

A836

Melvich

Kilometres
Nautical Miles

0   1   2   3   4

0   2

fishermen over the years. If there is surf on the beach these will probably be preferable landing spots, however the beach is a spectacular place to land and enjoy if it is possible. The journey east from Strathy Bay provides cliffs of wonderful colour with plenty of caves to explore, along with hidden inlets that could provide an isolated landing spot. These cliffs all too soon lead to the finish at the fantastic natural harbour of Portskerra, which has a concrete slipway hidden at the back of it providing an easy landing.

Tides and weather

There are tidal streams up to 3 knots off Strathy Point, and therefore this trip needs to be planned to make best use of the east going tide. To arrive at Strathy with minimum flow aim to be there when the east going stream starts, paddling out to it during the final part of the west going stream is straightforward due to the eddy effect caused by the point. To the east of the point along the coastline that leads south to Strathy Bay there can be a continuous north going flow caused by the west going tidal stream and then the eddy formed on the east going stream. This can be paddled against but making use of close in micro eddies will assist. Swell and wind also have a big effect on this section of coastline and should be taken into account when planning, if necessary paddling the trip in the opposite direction.

Additional information

At both start and finish there is limited parking so please leave cars considerately. In Portskerra village there is a small shop and a pub for refreshments to finish the day. If wishing to walk out to

Strathy lighthouse then there is parking at the end of the public road and then an easy 15 minute walk out to the point along the old lighthouse road.

Variations

To shorten the trip starting or finishing at Strathy Bay is possible but it is quite a long and arduous walk with the kayaks. Starting at Torrisdale, as described in the previous trip chapter, can extend the trip; this will avoid the steep carry at Port a' Chinn. It is also possible to extend this trip by continuing on to Sandside Bay as described in the next trip chapter. Both these extensions provide a fantastic day out, as long as you allow plenty of time for exploration.

Scottish Primrose

The Scottish primrose (Primula scotica) is one of Scotland's rarer plants and is unique to the north coasts of Sutherland and Caithness, and Orkney. The plants are found in exposed locations where the grass is short cropped, along with no form of cultivation or exposure to the use of fertiliser. The plants are very small, yet sturdy to stand up to these exposed locations. They can live up to twenty years, yet may not flower until they are ten years old. The plants generally have between two and eight small purple flowers with a yellow throat. There are two flowering periods, the first being in May and then the main period in July. Strathy Point is one of the best locations to enjoy this rare plant on mainland Scotland.

41

Strathy Point lighthouse with surrounding rock architecture

Sandside Head ▰▰▰▰▰

No. 7 | Grade B | 11km | OS Sheet 10 & 11

Tidal Port	Ullapool
Start	△ Portskerra (NC 878 663)
Finish	⭕ Fresgoe Harbour, Sandside Bay (NC 958 660)
HW/LW	HW/LW at Portskerra is around 2 hours and 50 minutes before Wick.
Tidal Times	Off Sandside Head: The E going stream starts at about 1 hour and 40 minutes before HW Ullapool. The W going stream starts at about 4 hours and 20 minutes after HW Ullapool.
Max Rate Sp	0.5 to 1 knot off Sandside Head.
Coastguard	Shetland, tel. 01595 692976, VHF weather every 3 hours from 0710.

Introduction

This short yet very remote section of coastline starts at a rugged natural harbour and finishes at a picturesque sandy harbour. In between there are no easy landings, constant wave washed cliffs, skerries, and beautiful rock architecture. With the constant backdrop of the Orkney Isles across the Pentland Firth this short trip certainly packs it all in.

The 'Drowning Memorial'

The plaques read:

22-8-1918
ANGUS FRASER
HUGH FRASER
GEORGE FRASER
FINLAY MACDONALD
JOHN SINCLAIR
ALEXANDER MACDONALD
WILLIAM MACKAY

25-6-1890
JAMES MACDONALD
WILLIAM MACDONALD
HUGH MACDONALD
WILLIAM MACDONALD
HUGH MACDONALD
WILLIAM MACDONALD
GEORGE MACDONALD
HUGH MACINTOSH
JOHN CAMERON
HECTOR MACLEOD
WILLIAM MACLEOD

5-12-1848
JAMES SINCLAIR
JOHN SINCLAIR
EVANDER MATHESON
JAMES McLEOD
GEORGE SINCLAIR
ANGUS MACDONALD
WILLIAM MACINTOSH
DONALD MACKAY

THE PORTSKERRA DROWNINGS
ERECTED TO THE MEMORY OF THE MEN
WHO WERE OF THIS COMMUNITY AND WHO
PERISHED WITHIN SIGHT OF THEIR HOMES

Sandside Head

Description

The tiny natural harbour of Portskerra is formed by beautifully shaped and coloured rocks that provide shelter from the ravages of the Atlantic Ocean. It is a rugged and spectacular place to set out from. There is a concrete slip and stony beach that makes launching easy; parking is limited so please be considerate to the local users of this unique little spot.

Leaving the small harbour head along the coastline until reaching the more modern pier, from here there will be great views looking into the golden sands of Melvich Bay. This beautiful beach has a backdrop of large sand dunes, behind these on the banks of the Halladale river is the historic 'Bighouse Lodge'.

Memorial

Portskerra has always been a fishing community, and further along the coast overlooking the new pier it is worth visiting the Drowning Memorial. This monument commemorates the many fishermen from the village who have been lost at sea over the years. The stone includes a verse by the celebrated poet Hugh Macintosh, who was born in Portskerra in 1901. This monument should be a reminder to us all what an exposed and inhospitable place the north coast can be in less than ideal conditions.

Bighouse Lodge

The Mackays, the dominant clan of this north coast for many years, built this listed building in the 1760s. As well as the lodge there are other older buildings including barracks and an icehouse. The barracks are believed to have housed troops of clan Mackay during the 1745 Jacobite rebellion. In 1830 it was sold to Sutherland estates and was the last of the Mackay's houses and lands to go under the hammer; it was to be the "end of an auld sang" for the clan.

Paddling across the bay it will be impossible not to be drawn to the impressive cliffs ahead, with skerries below and a mass of seabird life covering them. The cliffs along this section of coastline are made from moine metamorphic rocks; this rock type with it the square cut ledges and water shaped features bring an added dimension to the cliff scenery. These ledges provide perfect nesting grounds for numerous guillemots, razorbills and fulmars that will keep you company for the trip. This area sees a lot of cetaceans, with the many tidal areas that stir up the water and provide good feeding. Whales, dolphins and porpoises have been seen, as well as some less frequent visitors, in particular the mighty killer whale or orca.

The coastline here provides constant interest with a maze of low lying skerries, sea stacks and inlets to weave between if the conditions allow, as well as the occasional cave to explore. Look out for the precarious sea stack perched high on a flat skerry quite early on in the trip. Dominating the view will be the Orkney Isles sitting majestically out to sea across the Pentland Firth, and on a clear day looking deceptively close. It will be the mighty west coast of the island of Hoy that you can see, and if you look carefully you may even be able to make out the famous sea stack, the 'Old Man of Hoy'. There are no easy landings along this coastline, just a wall of relatively low-lying cliffs plunging into the sea. If the conditions are very calm you may be able to land on the hidden stony beach at the head of an inlet behind some stacks (NC 919654). Beyond this, constant cliffs, stacks and a waterfall will soon bring you to Sandside Head.

One of the caves at Sandside Head is said to be the longest sea cave in Britain and, at 230 metres, one of the longest in the world. It would not be wise to explore the full length of this one by sea kayak, but it does give an insight into the hidden depths of the many caves passed. Paddling around the headland itself the low-lying cliffs overhang the sea and the view that will instantly overshadow all else will be the Dounreay Nuclear Power plant. Its massive infrastructure stands dramatically along the coastline beyond Sandside Bay, and the view is made all the more ironic with the new huge wind turbines that overlook Dounreay in the further distance.

The beautiful historic harbour at Fresgoe provides the finish to this trip; take care on the approach as there are a few hidden reefs that can give rise to the occasional rogue wave or two. The harbour was built in the early 1830s to encourage fishing and was also used on the north coast trading route. There are some grand fish stores overlooking the harbour and close to these was once the Fresgoe Inn (now called Fresgoe House). This was once a vibrant drinking spot being much frequented by the ships crews, many being French and Dutch, and was run by a French girl called Mary Moss who married a local man. Sadly the Inn is no more so you will have to settle for some alternative refreshments to enjoy on landing.

Tides and weather

Unlike much of this north coast there are no tidal streams of note on this section of coastline so when planning it is best to take account of the wind to make life easier. There may be a small amount of tidal movement off Sandside Head so timing the trip to take advantage of this is preferable but not essential. Due to the committing nature of this short trip and the lack of escape routes ensure the swell and sea state are appropriate for the group's abilities.

Additional information

There is limited parking at both harbours so please be considerate when leaving cars. There are shops and local amenities at both Portskerra and Reay, with the beaches at Melvich and Sandside well worth visiting.

Variations

Starting at Strathy Bay (NC 837 656) provides a longer trip with plenty of interest and minimal tidal movement to consider. This put on does require quite an arduous walk down to the beach however, which is too rough to make use of a kayak trolley. Alternatively the trip can be started at Port a' Chinn as described in the previous trip chapter. This provides a stunning day's paddle with the tidal streams of the dramatic Strathy Point to be enjoyed.

Peat for heat

While travelling around the north coast of Scotland it is hard not to notice the peat stacks, peat cuttings or on a colder day the unique smell of the peat being burnt on the open fires as a village is passed. Peat is an accumulation of partially decayed vegetation, of which one of the most common components is sphagnum moss. This decaying vegetation when dried out makes for a very effective fossil fuel, and along the north coast there is no shortage of it. Around the world peat makes up for around two percent of global land area, and for this reason it has been an important source of heat and energy for many generations, and not just in Scotland. Due to the lack of trees along the north coast of Scotland peat has been, and still is, the main traditional source of heat and energy. The crofts along the coastline will each have their own associated peat bank that they harvest for fuel. The peat is cut into brick like shapes using a purpose made tool called a tarisker, or peat iron, and then laid out in lines along the peat bank. Here it sits for a while drying, perhaps being turned over and placed against each other at this stage. After this initial drying period the peat is then gathered into large and well-constructed peat stacks. Here it stays for the summer further drying so it is ready to be brought in to fuel the fire for the winter. The other key use for the peat fires is the way it is used to dry the malted barley, thus giving malt whisky its unique flavour in certain areas.

Holborn Head

No. 8 | Grade C | 21km | OS Sheets 11 & 12

Tidal Port	Ullapool
Start	△ Sandside Bay (NC 958 660)
Finish	⊙ Thurso (ND 116 687)
HW/LW	HW/LW at Thurso is around 2 hours and 40 minutes before Wick.
Tidal Times	Off Holborn Head: The E going stream starts at about 1 hour and 40 minutes before HW Ullapool. The W going stream starts at about 4 hours and 20 minutes after HW Ullapool.
Max Rate Sp	2 knots off Holborn Head.
Coastguard	Shetland, tel. 01595 692976, VHF weather every 3 hours from 0710.

Introduction

This is a journey of contrasts, starting with a beautiful historic harbour followed by a huge nuclear power establishment, which is ironically overlooked by renewable energy wind turbines. An imposing section of cliffs, caves and sea stacks with a large headland, all being exposed to potential big seas and swell, make this a formidable trip.

Description

The historic harbour of Fresgoe overlooking Sandside Bay is as picturesque and idyllic a location to start a sea trip as you could ask for, quite unexpected set amid the often barren and inhospitable north coast of Scotland. The beach at Sandside provides a stunning backdrop to the start of this paddle, although the hidden environmental concerns that have been discovered on these beautiful sands have been well publicised, as these are radioactive nuclear fuel particles from the nearby Dounreay power establishment. You may well see the eight-wheel 'groundhog' vehicles out on the beach routinely monitoring it for further potential particles. This considered, enjoying the view of beach from the kayak may be a better option than building some sandcastles on it!

Across the bay the huge infrastructure of Dounreay dominates everything. This nuclear power development establishment was built in 1955 to develop nuclear reactors for power. The site was chosen by the government for safety in case of an explosion, being in the far north of Scotland and away from major cities. I'm not too sure the locals would agree with this reasoning! Over the years three nuclear reactors were developed at the plant, these have now all been shut down and the site is in the process of being decommissioned.

The next view to dominate the coastal landscape are the numerous renewable energy wind turbines, these being established as an alternative to nuclear energy for future power generation. The coastline along this section is very low-lying so these man-made structures provide the main interest. On a clear day the dramatic outline of the island of Hoy across the Pentland Firth will be visible. Soon Crosskirk Bay is reached and if stopping for a break here it is well worth the short walk to explore St Mary's Chapel situated on the south side of the bay. This 12th century chapel is now a ruin, but it still provides a great view of the coastline to be paddled along, with some ornate stonework and graves. After Crosskirk you come to the low-lying headland of Brims Ness. Do not underestimate this small headland as the reefs that surround it are notorious for producing surf with large waves and boomers. So much so that professional surfers from around the world have come to competitions held at Brims to test their skill on the fast, steep and hollow waves that form over the shallow flagstone rocks. There is a potential stopping place at the Port of Brims, where a deep-water channel leads into this relatively sheltered bay with a stony beach. Care needs to be taken finding this landing spot as it provides the last possible exit point before the finish at Thurso. The port is more of a sheltered inlet and is overlooked by a ruined farm building that was once Brims Castle.

The trip from here changes considerably in character, the man-made additions to the landscape disappear and nature provides its own dramatic scenery in the way of huge cliffs, caves and arches. The first small stack has a small cairn on the top of it and lies just beyond an old fort marked on the map which sits on the end of a small promontory. If conditions allow it is possible to find a secret landing spot at the back of the promontory. The views along this section of coastline are spectacular, with cliffs growing in stature as they lead towards Holborn Head. Beyond this the most northerly mainland point of the British Isles can be seen protruding far into the sea, this being Dunnet Head. In addition the island of Hoy and the Orkney Isles will become easier to see as the journey continues. Just beyond the Ness of Litter there is a huge cave to enjoy and next to that is a natural amphitheatre formed by a cirque of overhanging cliffs. This place will provide sensory overload with the scenery but in particular the acoustics of the sea echoing within the huge amphitheatre. Paddling on to Holborn Head the cliffs continue rising higher and higher out of the sea and just before the headland is turned there is a huge stack, more like detached area of cliff, to paddle around and explore.

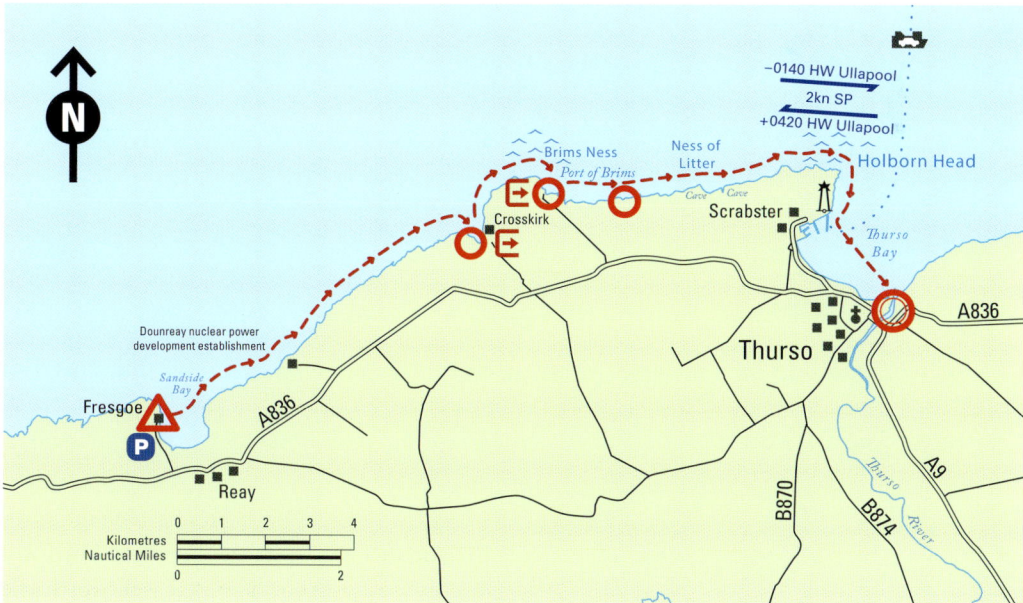

Once around Holborn Head chances are the sea will calm down and with that the feeling of complete commitment and exposure will start to subside for the paddler. Do not be tempted to cut across to the finish, but continue down the coastline to the lighthouse at Scrabster. This section of cliffs, although nowhere near as grand, is fantastically intricate with a mass of caves, geos and mini arches to explore. It will seem strange when approaching the lighthouse that it is not situated up on the main headland, there can be few lighthouses positioned half way along a headland, but it was used to provide light to guide ships safely into the port of Scrabster.

The finish is at the slip on the west side of the river mouth in Thurso, again care must be taken when paddling across to this as a reef break know as 'The Pipe' forms just to the west of the river and the famous 'Thurso East' surf break to the east. Even if there is a fair bit of swell there should be a surf free route paddling in directly up the river mouth to land at the slip.

Tides and weather

There is tidal flow off Holborn Head as well as some flow off Brims Ness, so this should be considered when planning the trip to make the most of any tidal assistance. This section is very exposed to swell from the west, north and east and in places this will create some potentially challenging or dangerous conditions for a sea kayaker due to the hidden reefs. Plan this trip for a day with minimal swell and light winds.

Additional information

There are toilet facilities at Sandside as well as amenities in the village of Reay, which is next to Sandside. In Thurso there is ample parking and toilets at the finish, as well as an excellent café.

Variations

To avoid the need for a shuttle, starting and finishing at Thurso works well. Paddling to the landing spot by the old fort or at the Port of Brims and back takes in the spectacular cliff scenery. You also get to enjoy it twice!

Skuas

In the north of Scotland there are two main types of skua that may be seen: the great skua and the Arctic skua. The larger of the two, the great skua, is indeed a force to be reckoned with and if you stray into their nesting territory, which is open moor/grassland, they will attack you with vigour from the air. These fearsome birds are known to many as the 'bonxie' and are most definitely the pirates of the bird world. They attack other birds to steal what they have just caught or even to kill the bird for a meal, and are also regularly seen preying on young chicks. The Arctic skua is a slighter more tern-like bird, with a distinctively shaped tail. These are rarer than the great skua and well worth looking out for. They are one of the fastest and most elegant sea birds when in the air, and although they are also pirates when it comes to surviving, they are less aggressive then the great skua. The Arctic skua has two plumage patterns or phases, all dark or with a lighter chest.

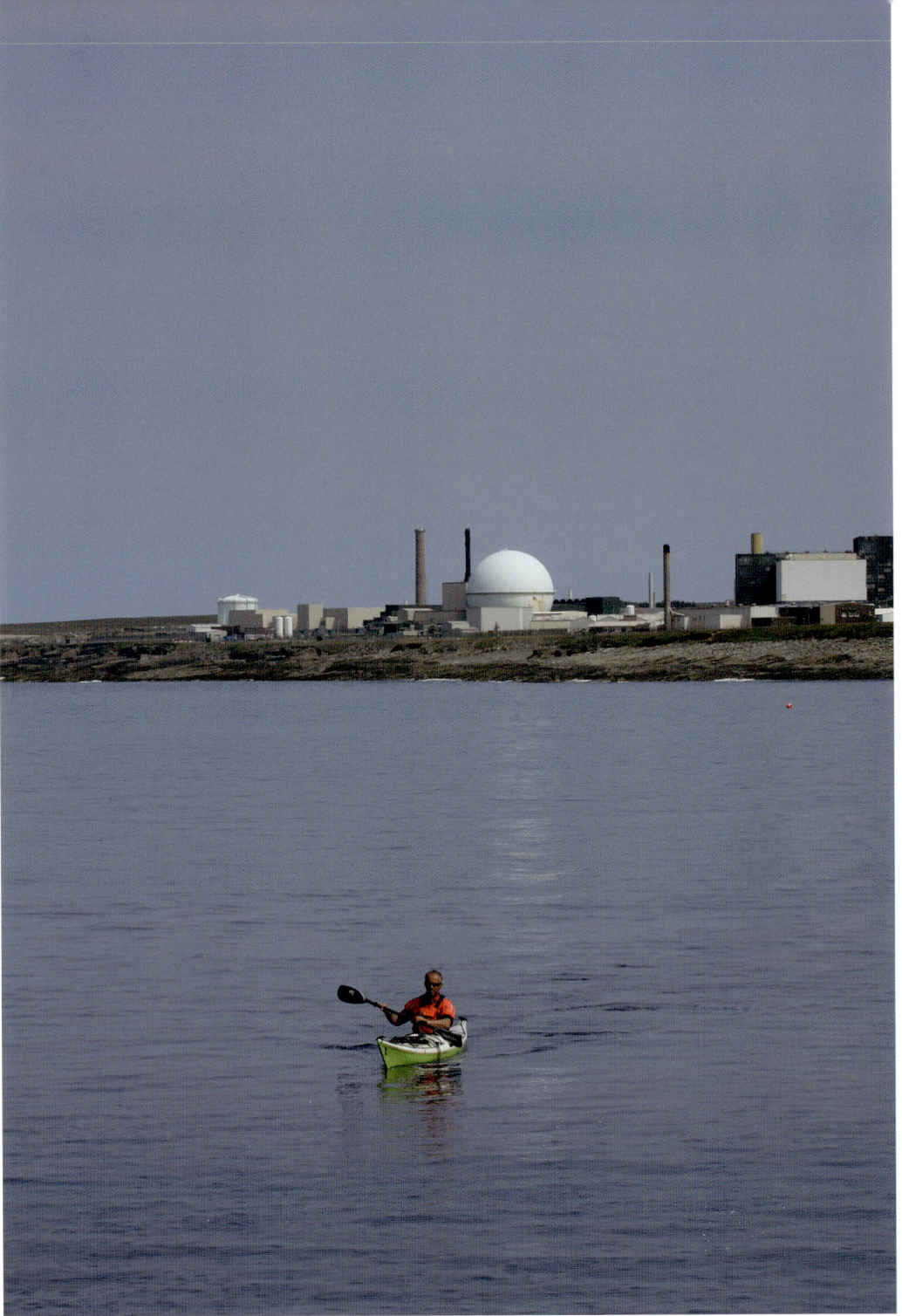

Dounreay nuclear power development establishment

Dunnet Head

Dunnet Head ⬛⬛◿⬛

No. 9 | Grade C | 25km | OS Sheet 12

Tidal Port	Aberdeen
Start	△ Dwarwick Pier (ND 206 713)
Finish	○ Gills Bay (ND 327 728)
HW/LW	HW/LW at Gills Bay is around 1 hour and 55 minutes before Wick.
Tidal Times	Off Dunnet Head: The E going stream starts at about 2 hours and 40 minutes after HW Aberdeen. The W going stream starts at about 3 hours and 20 minutes before HW Aberdeen.
	Off St John's Point: The E going stream starts at about 5 hours and 15 minutes after HW Aberdeen. The W going stream starts at about 1 hour and 50 minutes before HW Aberdeen.
Max Rate Sp	3 knots off Dunnet Head. 7 knots on the W going tidal stream off St John's Point. 5.5 knots on the E going tidal stream off St John's Point.
Coastguard	Shetland, tel. 01595 692976, VHF weather every 3 hours from 0710.

Introduction

This is a spectacular day out for any sea kayaker. It starts by venturing around the mighty cliffs and exposed waters of mainland Britain's most northerly point at Dunnet Head, and then continues

Approaching the 'Merry Men of Mey'

into the heartland of Britain's most notorious tidal waters, including the infamous Merry Men of Mey tidal race at St John's Point. This is the north coast at its best; cliffs, tides and wildlife all set amongst stunning scenery.

Description

Dwarwick Pier provides a surprisingly grand pier and parking area to start this trip from the west side of Dunnet Head. The Royal Family used to make use of this pier when visiting the Queen Mother at her highland residence The Castle of Mey just along the coast, hence the pier's good condition. Paddling out to Dunnet Head the cliffs will gradually rise in grandeur, reaching up to 100m in height at their highest. The cliffs are made of sandstone and provide plenty of interest, along with some waterfalls cascading down them into the sea below. These layered sandstone cliffs also provide perfect nesting sites for numerous seabirds including guillemots, razorbills, kittiwakes and everyone's favourite, puffins. On a calm day you may well find yourself paddling through great rafts of these seabirds. As you approach they will often dive beneath the surface and if lucky you will see them swimming under your kayak. Dunnet Head is now managed by the RSPB and sitting atop its impressive cliffs lays mainland Britain's most northerly lighthouse, built in 1831 by Robert Stevenson. Alongside the lighthouse there are some World War II fortifications that were built to protect the naval base at Scapa Flow across in the Orkneys.

Dunnet Head is Britain's northernmost extremity and marks the entrance into the Pentland Firth, notorious for its tidal waters. The views from this headland are about as good as they get; the Orkneys and in particular the spectacular west coast of Hoy with the huge sea stack 'The Old

Man of Hoy' will be clearly visible. To the east the view into the heart of the Pentland Firth and the tidal islands of Stroma and Muckle Skerry will tempt you on, and then behind on the clearest of days you will see the entire north coast all the way to Cape Wrath. Continuing on though the cliffs will lead you to the slipway at Brough, or if wanting to cut the corner perhaps head to the small harbour at Scarfskerry known as The Haven; either of these is a good landing spot. The slipway at Brough was used to land stores for the lighthouse and a large stack called the Clett shelters the bay, so if time allows it is worth a visit.

Scarfskerry is the most northerly settlement on mainland Britain, and its name comes from the Old Norse for 'cormorants' rock'. This is a perfect place to have a rest and ensure that the timings are correct for paddling through the mighty tidal race known as the Merry Men of Mey. Just on from Scarfskerry there is another small slipway at Wester Haven, and this is the last chance to pull ashore before the tide will take you around St John's Point. Set back from the low lying rocky coastline the Castle of Mey stands proudly looking out to sea.

St John's Point and the Merry Men of Mey will no doubt arrive quicker than expected with the tide sweeping you along. This tidal race demands a lot of respect and on the west going stream it can extend all the way across to Tor Ness on the Orkneys and reach flows in excess of ten knots. So for the sea kayaker, paddling on the east going stream is sensible, and arriving at the end of this tidal flow is advisable. Whenever you arrive it will be exciting; take care with the many submerged rocks that the race flows over and head for the sheltered pier and landing place just around the corner from St John's Point (ND 312 752) for a well earned rest. This small old harbour is known as 'The Bocht' and was built during the herring fishing days, and on the hilltop above there are the overgrown remains of the walls of a fort.

The last part of the journey takes the relatively benign coastline to the ferry terminal at Gills Bay. Scotland's Haven provides a large natural harbour that becomes almost cut off by rocks at low tide. This is a popular place for the resident grey seals to hang out and is a great place to

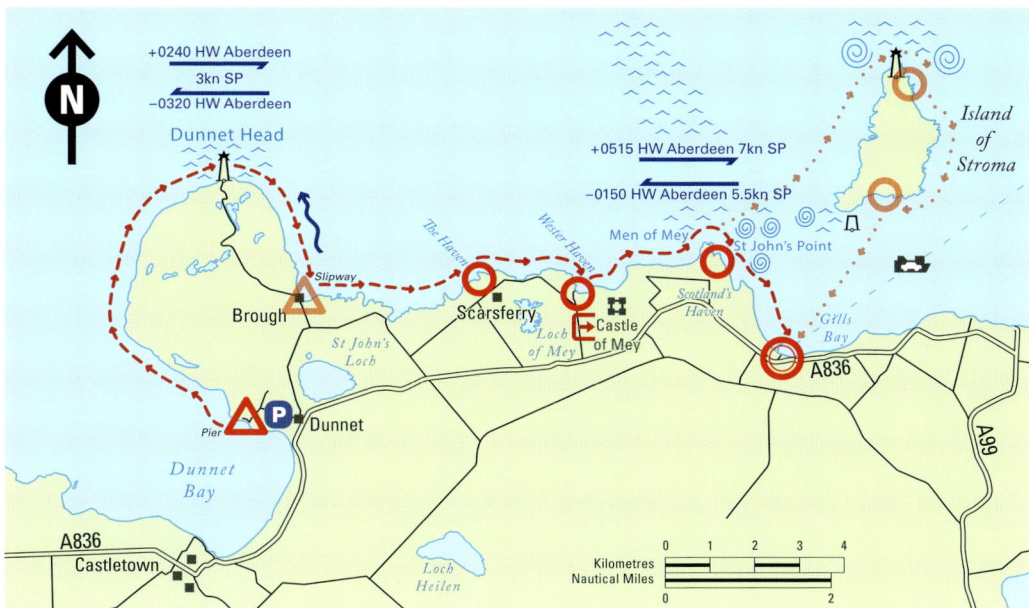

© Dunnet Head lighthouse with Hoy iin the background

wildlife spot before finishing the trip. The landing at Gills Bay is on the rocky beach outside the harbour walls on the east side. Not the most scenic place to finish but considering the scenery enjoyed during the paddle you can't complain too much.

Tides and weather

There are significant tidal streams on this trip and it's recommended that it's undertaken on neap tides if possible. The east going stream needs to be used throughout this trip and the Men of Mey tidal race at St John's Head should be arrived at in the last hour of this tide to avoid the worst of the tidal race. Arrive at Dunnet Head about 2–3 hours before this to allow time to enjoy the coastline, have some stops and be at St John's Head at the right time (leaving Dwarwick about 2 hours after the east going stream starts will allow for this). There will be an eddy flowing northwards on the east side of Dunnet Head, this can be paddled against by staying in very close or choosing to cut the corner can help make the paddling a bit easier.

Swell and wind will also have a large effect on the sea state of this very exposed paddle, there are numerous offshore reefs that can cause challenging breaking waves if there is a northerly swell running. Plan to do this trip in good conditions only.

Additional information

There are no amenities at Dwarwick, however in Dunnet there is a good pub that serves food. At Gills Bay there is a small café in the ferry terminal, or there are alternative cafés and pubs just up the road towards Mey. There are plans agreed to develop a lot of tidal power generators in the

Inner Sound of the Pentland Firth and off Duncansby Head. Work on these is due to start in the near future which will no doubt have an effect on paddling in this area.

Variations

For a shorter trip that avoids the Men of Mey and St John's Point, using the slipway at Brough provides an ideal finish to a great paddle around Dunnet Head and it is not too far to walk back to the Dwarwick to collect the vehicle. This shorter trip around Dunnet Head can be paddled in either direction. To extend the trip continuing from St John's Head to the north tip of the Island of Swona and going down the east coast of Swona, using the west going tide to return to Gills Bay makes for a great trip. This does involve paddling through some extremely tidal waters and it would require appropriate planning. The following trip chapter will help and it would be worthwhile using the 1:50,000 *Admiralty Chart 2162 Pentland Firth* and the *Orkney and Shetland Islands Admiralty Tidal Streams Atlas NP 209*.

Castle of Mey

This castle was originally built in 1566 by the Earl of Caithness, but fell into disrepair during the 1900s. In 1952 the Queen Mother was visiting friends after the death of King George VI, and it was during this time she noticed that the castle was for sale and then proceeded to buy it. She fully restored the castle and made it into a welcoming northern home for herself. The castle is open to the public and maintained the way the Queen Mother had it when it was her home.

9

Dunnet Head

Dunnet Head

Swilkie Point lighthouse, Stroma

Island of Stroma

No. 10 | **Grade C** | **15km** | **OS Sheet 7 or 12**

Tidal Port	Aberdeen
Start	△ John o' Groats (ND 379 735)
Finish	○ John o' Groats (ND 379 735)
HW/LW	HW/LW at Stroma is around 1 hour and 10 minutes before Wick
Tidal Times	In the Inner Sound: The E going stream starts rabout 4 hours and 35 minutes after HW Aberdeen. The W going stream starts about 1 hour and 50 minutes before HW Aberdeen.
	For Swilkie Point, Stroma; and the Tails of Tarf, Swona: The E going stream starts about 5 hours and 5 minutes after HW Aberdeen. The W going stream starts about 1 hour and 20 minutes before HW Aberdeen.
	For North Head, Swona: The E going stream starts at about 4 hours and 25 minutes after HW Aberdeen. The W going stream starts at about 1 hour and 55 minutes before HW Aberdeen.
Max Rate Sp	5 knots in the Inner Sound. 9 knots off Swilkie Point and the Tails of Tarf. 6 knots of the North Head.
Coastguard	Shetland, tel. 01595 692976, VHF weather every 3 hours from 0710.

Introduction

This trip takes a sea kayaker into some of the fastest tidal streams in the British Isles, which guarantees a day that will keep you on the edge of your kayak seat. Do not underestimate this coastal area, but plan carefully and enjoy a unique experience.

Description

The tourist circus of John o' Groats is a far cry from where this journey takes you, but it does provide plenty of parking and a launch site at the pier. Heading across the Inner Sound and aiming for the east side of Stroma, the focus will be on the appropriate ferry glide angle so as not to miss it! With a west going stream this should not give any rough water, but be aware that it still moves deceptively fast. The Island of Stroma aptly translates from the Gaelic meaning 'island in the tidal stream' and you will be constantly reminded of this as you circumnavigate it. The great headland of Duncansby will soon come into view, and out to the west is Muckle Skerry where tides of 16 knots have been recorded. Muckle Skerry's lighthouse stands tall, warning ships of the rocks and the fact they are about to enter the Pentland Firth. This was originally named Pictland Firth from when the Picts were thought to have first settled on Orkney.

Aim to arrive at the low lying rocky coastline on the east side of Stroma just beyond Tree Geo. This will allow you to follow the coast with the tide along to Nethertown Pier, which is the original landing site for those living on Stroma. The pier is guarded by a large community of grey seals. Landing here will provide an opportunity to stretch the legs and walk out to the lighthouse as well as explore some of the many deserted buildings. In the past Stroma had a population of

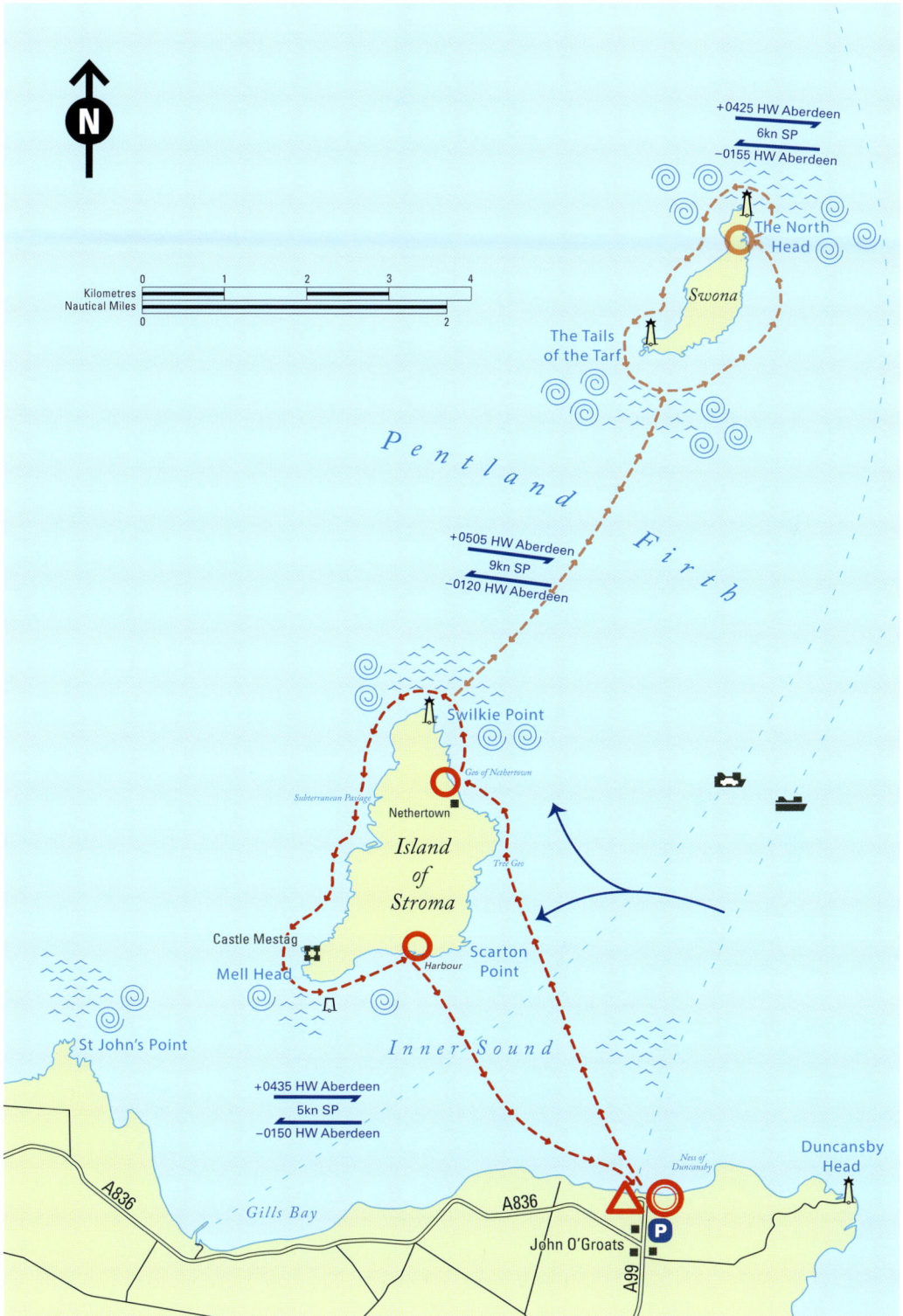

N

+0425 HW Aberdeen
6kn SP
−0155 HW Aberdeen

The North
Head

Swona

The Tails
of the Tarf

Kilometres
Nautical Miles

0 1 2 3 4
0 2

P e n t l a n d   F i r t h

+0505 HW Aberdeen
9kn SP
−0120 HW Aberdeen

Swilkie Point

Geo of Nethertown

Subterranean Passage

Nethertown

*Island
of
Stroma*

Trie Geo

Castle Mestag

Mell Head

Harbour

Scarton
Point

St John's Point

I n n e r   S o u n d

+0435 HW Aberdeen
5kn SP
−0150 HW Aberdeen

*Ness of
Duncansby*

Duncansby
Head

A836

A836

Gills Bay

John O'Groats

A99

© Nethertown Pier

about 550, which by 1901 had reduced to 377. The last residents left in 1962, which co-incidently was shortly after the new harbour had been finished on the south end of the island. The island has an eerie feel about it, and although somewhat resembling a ghost town it is a very real reminder of the island's past. Keep an eye on the time as the infamous tidal race called 'The Swilkie' is to be negotiated next and this is best done at slack water when it is resting!

The Swilkie can be one of the more violent tidal races in the Firth at certain states of the tide and runs off the north tip of the island overlooked by the lighthouse. Viking legend has it that the whirlpool that can form here is caused by a sea-witch turning the mill wheels that ground the salt to keep the seas salty. The name is thought to derive from a Norse term that means 'the swallower'. Whether these legends are true or not this place demands respect, and close to slack water is the time to enjoy it when it is relatively benign and there is no chance of being swallowed!

Leaving The Swilkie behind the sandstone cliffs of the west coast are soon to be seen. The vertical rock architecture provides some spectacular paddling, overlooked by the many guillemots, razorbills and kittiwakes that make this place their home. Soon you will reach the subterranean passage of 'The Gloup'. This is a mind-blowing place to look at, but take care if venturing in as this narrow passage funnels and enlarges the slightest swell quite violently. At Mell Head there are plenty more caves to explore. Just before the Mell Head look out for the sea stack on which Castle Mestag used to be situated. This old fort was once accessed by a bridge out onto the stack and must be one of the few fortified sea stacks around. Just below this there is a reminder of why the Pentland Firth has such a reputation – in the form of a shipwreck. Look out for the iron bridge over the geo that the locals used to access the wreck and retrieve things; this wreck is one of about sixty around the island of Stroma. The tide will be picking you up as Mell Head is passed. There is an old beacon marking the skerries here and the water can often be a bit rougher as you paddle through on the way to the new harbour for another rest.

Leaving the sheltered water of the harbour a final bit of careful navigation back to the finish is required. The tidal conveyer belt that runs through the Inner Sound will be picking up speed now and care is required to ensure it does not extend your journey out towards Norway as opposed to you finishing as planned at the harbour at John o' Groats. Just remember it is better to arrive too far upstream of the finish than downstream, and then all being well you should soon be back joining the tourists at John o' Groats for a well deserved ice cream.

Tides and weather

Due to the exposure to swell, the tidal streams and the committing nature of the route, this trip is not recommended in any other than perfect weather conditions and is best done on neap tides.

The trip requires careful tidal planning with the second half of the west going tide being used to reach Stroma. Swilkie Point must be paddled around when the water is at its slackest, just before the east going stream starts at about 5 hours and 5 minutes after HW Aberdeen. The tidal streams pick up speed very quickly, so do not leave it too long after this otherwise it will not be possible to get around. The east going stream will take you back towards John o' Groats from the south of Stroma.

The west going tidal stream splits around the island about halfway up the east coast, so when heading out to the island be aware of this and aim to arrive north of Tree Geo to avoid an opposing flow.

Additional information

There is plenty of parking and amenities at John o' Groats. In planning this trip using the 1:50,000 *Admiralty Chart 2162 Pentland Firth* is worthwhile as well as the *Orkney and Shetland Tidal Streams Atlas, NP209*. There are plans to develop tidal power generators in the Inner Sound of the Pentland Firth and off Duncansby Head. Work on these is due to start in the near future, and they will have an effect on paddling in this area.

Variations

If the tidal timings mean heading out to the island on the second half of an east going tide would be preferable, then starting at Gills Bay (ND 326 728) makes this possible. In this case using the eddy on the east coast to arrive at Swilkie Point just before the start of the west going tidal stream is easier than trying to go up the west coast.

If you have the tidal paddling experience, then crossing the Pentland Firth to Swona is a fantastic addition. In this case cross to Swona with slack water timed for the centre of the crossing from Stroma, or work out the tidal vector to cross in the first hour of the tide. There is a good landing spot on the north east coast of Swona at 'The Haven'. Spend 4–5 hours enjoying the island of Swona on foot and then return to Stroma during the next slack water period of the tide, again timing slack for the centre of the crossing or working out an appropriate vector for the last or first hour of the tide. With the spring rate at 9 knots in this area and tidal races off both islands do not underestimate the planning required for this very worthwhile yet challenging paddle.

Heading out to Muckle Skerry

Pentland Skerries

No. 11 | Grade C | 35km | OS Sheet 7

Tidal Port	Aberdeen
Start	△ Gills Bay (ND 327 728)
Finish	◯ Gills Bay (ND 327 728)
HW/LW	HW/LW at the Pentland Skerries is around 20 minutes before Wick.
Tidal Times	In the Inner Sound: The E going stream starts about 4 hours and 35 minutes after HW Aberdeen. The W going stream starts about 1 hour and 50 minutes before HW Aberdeen.
	Off Swilkie Point, on the Island of Stroma: The E going stream starts at about 5 hours and 5 minutes after HW Aberdeen. The W going stream starts at about 1 hour and 20 minutes before HW Aberdeen.
	At the Pentland Skerries: The E going stream starts at about 5 hours and 5 minutes after HW Aberdeen. The W going stream starts at about 2 hours and 20 minutes before HW Aberdeen.
Max Rate Sp	5 knots in the Inner Sound.
	9 knots off Swilkie Point.
	12 knots off the Pentland Skerries.
Coastguard	Shetland, tel. 01595 692976, VHF weather every 3 hours from 0710.

The wreck of 'Ben Barvis' on Little Skerry

11

Pentland Skerries

Introduction

This trip takes you into the heart of the Pentland Firth. Here the tidal streams run at their fastest, the waters are always confused and can be very rough. There is no room for error on this trip and it is certainly not for the faint hearted. Experience of tidal water paddling and planning is a must, along with perfect conditions.

Description

Setting off from the ferry terminal at Gills Bay to head out to the Pentland Skerries you will be experiencing both excitement and apprehension. This really is an 'out there' trip into Britain's fastest tidal waters. The waters will be calm and the weather will be settled, if it isn't you should not be starting this trip. This is one to only undertake in perfect conditions and on neap tides. It is also worth considering carrying extra equipment, including enough for an unplanned night out; anything can happen in these tidal waters and failing to plan for all eventualities is as good as planning to fail!

Use the east going tide to paddle out to the Island of Stroma and follow the east coast up to Nethertown Pier. On the way up to this easy landing spot you will come across the large colony of Atlantic grey seals that make this area their home; on a calm morning you can often hear them bellowing long before you see them. Landing at Nethertown will allow you to have a stretch of the legs as well as ensure that you leave at the perfect time to arrive at the Pentland Skerries in the last hour of the east going stream.

Leaving from the north end of Stroma means that the tide will provide some assistance, transits and GPS will be required to ensure that you don't get taken off course. It is amazing feeling the power of the tide whisking you towards the skerries. A glance at the GPS will reveal your 'speed over the ground'; this is a conveyer belt like no other. As you draw closer the impressive cliffs of this skerry will come into view along with the outer Pentland Skerries of Little, Louther and Clettack Skerry. There is a double lighthouse on Muckle Skerry because it needed to be differentiated from its neighbouring lights in the Pentland Firth and was built before the age of characteristic flashes. Enjoy exploring the cliffs of Muckle Skerry's north coast whilst heading around to the only possible landing at Scartan Bay. Keep a constant eye out for the wildlife as the confused waters here provide good feeding for marine life; killer whales are regularly seen in this area as well as the seabirds and seals.

Do not expect an easy landing at Scartan Bay, it is no more than a rock slab and can provide a bit on a challenge. It is worth the effort though as there are not many people who have been fortunate enough to explore Muckle Skerry on foot. Keep a close eye on the time and ensure you are back on the water to escape the skerries in the first hour of the west going stream.

If leaving the Muckle Skerry near slack water, head out to Little Skerry before making the crossing back to the mainland. Here you will see the wreck of the fishing boat 'Ben Barvis' that ran aground in 1964. It is in this area that the Pentland Firth's fastest tidal water is recorded, with speeds up to 16 knots. In the days of sail the mariners feared this bit of water so much that it was known as 'Hells Mouth'. Head towards the unmistakable cliffs and lighthouse of Duncansby Head. The west going stream will assist you, however keep a close eye on transits and the GPS, and consider using tidal vectors for this section as you will be crossing this tide slightly and it is possible to be swept in a northerly direction. When approaching Duncansby Head don't go in

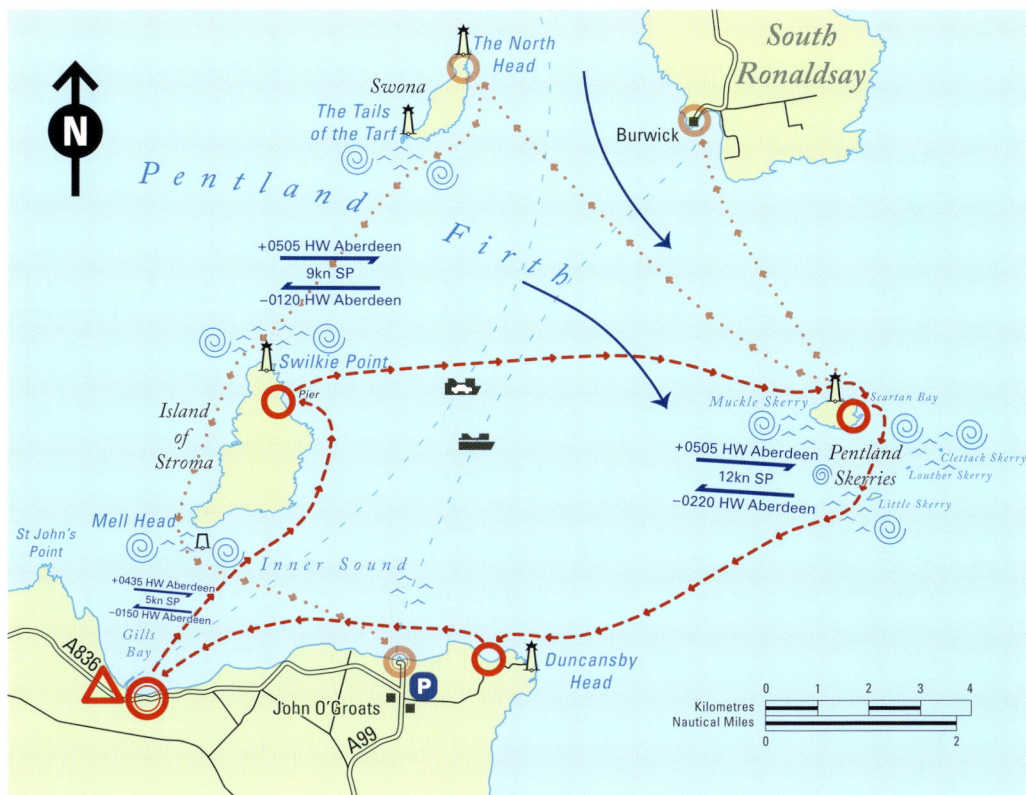

Pentland Skerries

too close but make use of the tide funnelling into the Inner Sound so as to get back to the finish at Gills Bay. If a stop is preferred, the beach at the Bay of Sannick provides a beautiful spot to land and an ideal place to relax after the tidal waters just negotiated. Arriving back at Gills Bay you will probably experience elation at having completed an incredible journey, along with relief that it went to plan!

Muckle Skerry Lighthouse

The rock slab and the track up to the lighthouse was used to land and transport supplies to the lighthouse keepers until 1972, since when helicopters were used. It is hard to imagine what it was like for the lighthouse keepers living here, but what is common in all accounts is that they required courage and initiative. There are numerous stories of these brave men leaving the relative safety of the lighthouse to carry out daring rescues for the crew of floundering ships off the surrounding rocks and skerries. The lighthouse was built in 1794 to open up the Pentland Firth to shipping, prior to that the ships used to take the longer route around Orkney. The Stevenson family are well known for their long history of building lighthouses around Scotland's coastline, and this light is notable in the fact it was the first that Robert Stevenson built for the lighthouse board. Try and allow time to discover one of Scotland's loneliest graves on the outer south wall towards its eastern end. The single headstone built into the wall remembers the seven crew of the '*Vicksburg*' who drowned as their ship was wrecked, as well as two children of a lightkeeper.

Tides and weather

The seriousness of this journey cannot be stressed enough, as well as the need for a lot of tidal paddling experience along with the planning skills required. Perfect weather will be required and a period on neap tides. Like a fine malt whisky, this is one of those trips that can take many years of waiting for all the correct ingredients to come together and make it possible.

Using the second half of the east going flow to get out to the Skerries, and landing there in the last hour of this tide is required. Towards the Skerries the tide sets strongly to the south, be aware of this to ensure they are not missed. Slack water at the Skerries is a fleeting moment and perhaps never really happens, however there is least movement at about 2 hours and 20 minutes before HW Aberdeen, or conveniently, HW Dover. Ensure the Skerries are left within the first hour of the west going tide, do not allow the tide to build too much out here or else getting back to the mainland could be a problem.

Additional information

There is a small café in the ferry terminal at Gills Bay but no other amenities. There are shops, cafés and pubs at John o' Groats or at Mey. Both Stroma and Muckle Skerry are uninhabited. In planning this trip using the 1:50,000 *Admiralty Chart 2162 Pentland Firth* is worthwhile as well as the *Orkney and Shetland Tidal Streams Atlas, NP209*. There are plans agreed to develop tidal power generators in the Inner Sound of the Pentland Firth and off Duncansby Head. Work on these is due to start in the near future and they will have an effect on paddling in this area.

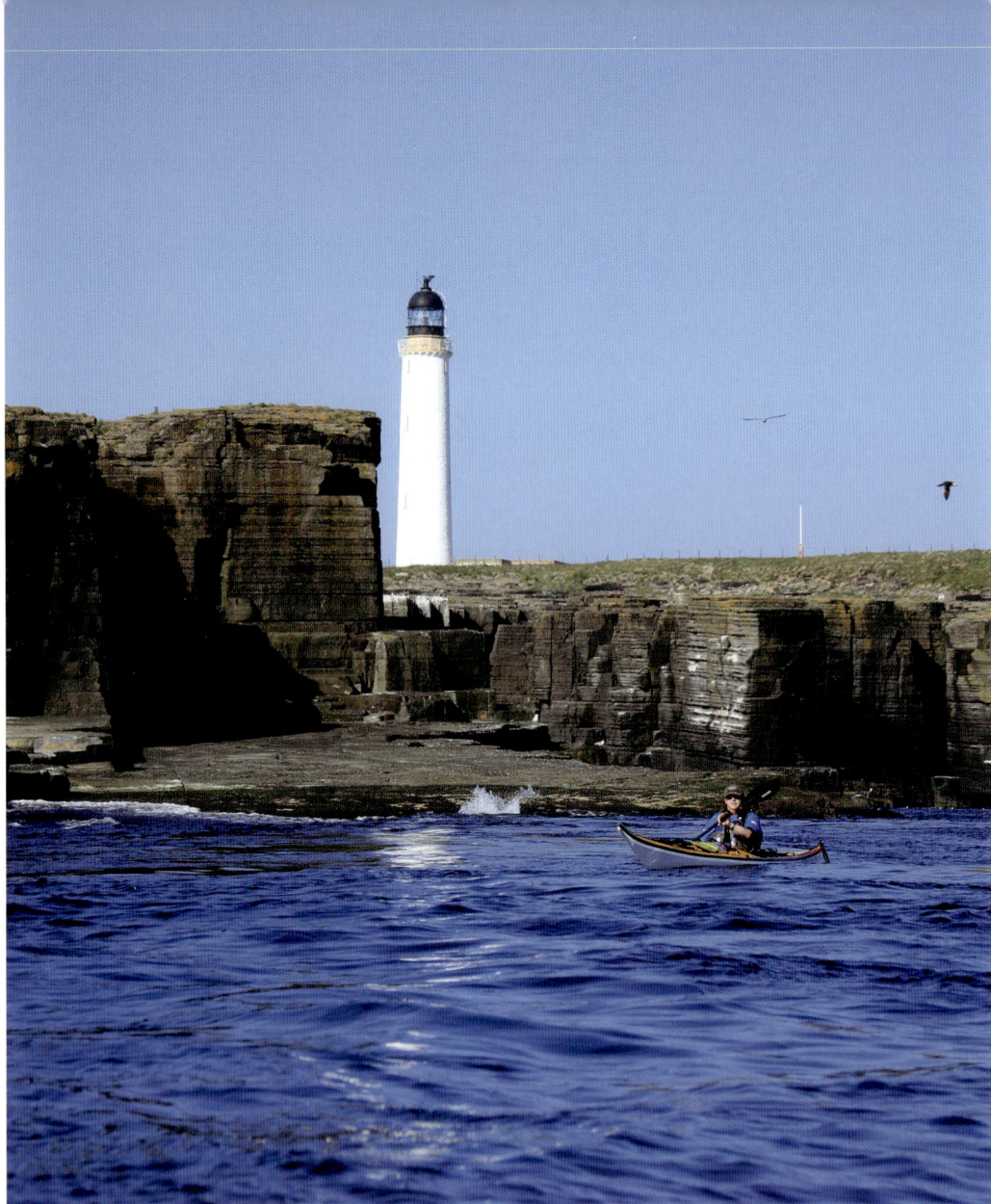

© Muckle Skerry and its lighthouse

Variations

Possibilities include continuing across to Burwick on South Ronaldsay and getting the ferry back to John o' Groats, or continuing on to Swona and then returning to Gills Bay via Stroma (known as the Pentland Triangle). Both of these trips involve negotiating extremely challenging tidal waters, particularly in the Liddel Eddy area. Complex tidal planning is required and they are rarely undertaken sea kayaking trips.

Duncansby Head ▨▨▨▨▨▨

No. 12 | **Grade C** | **10km** | **OS Sheet 12**

Tidal Port	Aberdeen
Start	△ Skirza Pier (ND 386 680)
Finish	○ John o' Groats (ND 379 735)
HW/LW	HW/LW at Duncansby Head is about 1 hour 10 minutes before Wick.
Tidal Times	For Duncansby Head: The N and then W going stream starts about 1 hour and 5 minutes before HW Aberdeen. The E and then S going stream starts about 5 hours and 5 minutes after HW Aberdeen.
	In the Inner Sound: The E going stream starts about 4 hours and 35 minutes after HW Aberdeen. The W going stream starts about 1 hour and 50 minutes before HW Aberdeen.
Max Rate Sp	8 knots around Duncansby head, between 'The Knee' and the mainland it can reach speeds in excess of this.
Coastguard	Shetland, tel. 01595 692976, VHF weather every 3 hours from 0710.

Introduction

This journey takes you along some of the most dramatic sea cliff scenery that Scotland has to offer, giant geos, stacks and caves a-plenty; all lined with an abundance of birdlife. Beneath these

Stacks of Duncansby with The Knee in background

Duncansby Head

12

amazing rock features the tide races by, producing eddy lines, boils and turbulent water as it squeezes in and out of the Pentland Firth. In the right conditions this has got to be one of the most spectacular paddles that can be found.

Description

The trip starts at the tiny sheltered pier of Skirza which is only used by small creel boats. The house beside it was owned by the last Pentland Firth pilot who used to navigate ships through the notorious waters that lie just around the corner. Hopefully you will have put plenty of time into planning this trip, as the pilot is no longer available to help out!

The low lying Skirza Head will soon be reached, here the sea will start to feel alive with tidal movement and this sets the tone for the day ahead. This initial small tidal flow subsides to give calm seas leading on to the Stacks of Duncansby. From here on the fantastic sandstone cliffs start to build, and the mass of caves and geos that line this entire route will begin to appear. The first of real note is the dramatic 'Wife Geo', which offers a huge, steep sided inlet with caves around it; the stack in the middle of this geo at the back is 'the wife'. Continuing on from this impressive geo you will get great views of the dramatic coastline ahead as well as the tall white double lighthouse of the Pentland Skerries to the north-east. The most prominent aspect of this view will undoubtedly be the Stacks of Duncansby. As you draw closer to these impressive rock features their grandeur will become ever more apparent. The Great Stack is over 60m high and rises above the summit of the adjacent cliff which in the early summer will be lined with many nesting seabirds. There are a number of stacks and they all have a narrow pyramid-like shape.

74

Having explored the stacks continuing a short distance further brings you to Thirle Door, the arch that marks the start of the stony beach, a good place to take a break.

Ahead lays the most spectacular section of cliffs and the fast moving waters and tidal races of Duncansby Head. A huge sea stack marks the start of these cliffs and as you approach this you will feel the water starting to move you along; this is the start of the tidal conveyer belt that leads into the Pentland Firth. If you do not like the look of the tidal race that can form here, give it a wide berth and stay out from the cliffs, this will give you a less lumpy ride around to Duncansby Head. Unfortunately by doing this some of the best caves are missed, so if confident in the moving water and feeling brave it is worth heading for the breakout behind the stack known as 'The Knee'. This stack stands just twenty metres away from the vertical sandstone walls of Duncansby Head and the boily eddy may give an opportunity to rest and take in the surroundings. The tide is squeezed through the gap between the stack and the main cliff at fantastic speed and it is a great place to watch in awe or even play! On leaving the eddy behind The Knee the tide will swiftly take you along the base of the cliffs that tower above; while on this conveyer belt make sure to break out into the Geo of Sclaites. This geo is an awesome place to explore, and after the tidal waters it provides a tranquil place to spend some time and fully appreciate the surroundings. You will not be alone as there will be plenty of seabirds nesting on the horizontal sandstone ledges that surround the geo and if they dive into the water then you may well see them swimming

Duncansby Head

under your kayak with the water being so clear. As you leave the geo you will have the option of heading out through the narrow arch to get back into the tidal waters.

As the lighthouse of Duncansby Head is reached, so is the most north-easterly point of mainland Britain. The dramatic scenery that surrounds this major British headland will not disappoint, the Pentland Skerries will be visible out in the fastest tidal part of the Pentland Firth, the Orkney Isles will look surprisingly close to the north and the Island of Stroma will be just the other side of the tidal race known as the 'Boars of Duncansby'. As the lighthouse is passed the cliffs soon start to abate and the beautiful sandy beach of the Bay of Sannick is reached. This provides an idyllic stopping place if time allows, before the final short paddle to the finish at John o' Groats.

Arriving at John o' Groats provides quite a contrast to the trip just paddled, it will also provide a well-earned ice cream to finish off the day. There will undoubtedly be plenty of tourists to watch you land in the sheltered harbour; some of these may have just finished the 876-mile journey from Lands End.

Tides and weather

Due to the exposed nature of this part of the world, the tidal streams and the committing nature of the route, this trip is not recommended in any other than perfect conditions. Careful planning of the tides is required and it is recommended to carry out the trip on neap tides. Making use of the north and west going tide is required to complete this trip and starting when the north going tide starts works well, but does give faster flows off Duncansby Head. It is possible to use the eddy that forms on the east going tide and therefore leave Skirza before the north going tide starts which allows arrival at Duncansby Head during the early part of the west going tide to avoid the worst of the strong tidal flows. An eddy forms after Duncansby Head, but it is possible to paddle against it for the short distance to John o' Groats without too much problem.

Additional information

There is limited parking at Skirza near a resident's house, so park courteously with as few vehicles as possible. It is also possible to launch at the beach in Freswick Bay if required. There are cafés and shops at John o' Groats but no amenities at Skirza. In planning this trip the 1:50,000 *Admiralty Chart 2162 Pentland Firth* could be useful. There are plans agreed to develop tidal power generators in the Inner Sound of the Pentland Firth and off Duncansby Head. Work on these is due to start in the near future and they will have an effect on paddling in this area.

Variations

This trip can be paddled in the opposite direction but this will involve less tidal assistance due to the eddy forming south of Duncansby Head. The trip can be extended by either continuing on to Stroma, or by starting at Keiss. Both of these are excellent additions and well recommended. Continuing on to Stroma requires careful tidal planning and details of both these extensions are found in this book.

Duncansby Head

Looking towards Duncansby Head

Moray Firth – North

Introduction

This often overlooked section of coastline contains some of Scotland's best 'hidden gems', when it comes to coastal paddling. This area starts where the coastline turns south at Duncansby Head, where the extreme tides of the Pentland Firth quickly subside, as does the exposure to the Atlantic Ocean. What does not subside however is the cliff scenery, which continues in dramatic fashion all the way to Helmsdale. This area is without doubt one of Scotland's best kept secrets, with arches, caves and sea stacks around every corner and only the wildlife to share it with. The wildlife realised long before sea kayakers that this more southerly facing coastline offers relative shelter and warmth, making it the perfect home. The sandstone cliffs provide endless ledges and caves, so the sea birds can be found in their thousands. Cetaceans make this area their home as well, with whales often being seen to the north of the area and the resident Moray Firth dolphins enjoying the more sheltered tidal waters to the south.

There is plenty of human history to enjoy with the dramatic castles of Keiss, Sinclair, Dunbeath and Dunrobin, along with the herring fishing stations of Staxigoe, Lybster and the incredible Whaligoe. To the south of the area evidence of more recent human history can be observed from the sea kayak, with the world war military defence installations at the Sutors guarding the entrance to the Cromarty firth, alongside the modern day oil rigs lined up for repair. The lighthouse at Tarbat Ness stands tall and proud above the Moray Firth and the light at Chanonry Point overlooks the modern city of Inverness.

Along this coastline there are also plenty of picturesque fishing villages with good pubs and eating places to enjoy after a day's paddle.

Tides and weather

There is very little tidal flow to be concerned about in this area, the only two exceptions being at the mouth of the Cromarty Firth and off Chanonry Point. The main consideration when visiting the area should be the wind and the swell. Although swell coming from the east is rare, in the north of this area northerly swells will wrap around into the firth and have a big effect. Any wind from the east through to the south-west affects this coast, and will often provide a more lively sea state than expected for a relatively sheltered area. In these conditions care should be taken on any of the trips north from Helmsdale as landings are few and far between with the cliffs continuous for long distances.

Noss Head lighthouse

Keiss Castle

Keiss Castle

No. 13 | Grade A | 10km | OS Sheet 12

Tidal Port	Aberdeen
Start	△ Skirza Pier (ND 386 680)
Finish	○ Keiss Pier (ND 351 609)
HW/LW	HW/LW at Skirza Pier is around 1 hour before Wick.
Tidal Times	Between Skirza and Keiss: The SSW going stream starts at about 5 hours and 15 minutes after HW Aberdeen. The NNE going stream starts at about 55 minutes before HW Aberdeen.
Max Rate Sp	0.5 knots off Ness Head.
Coastguard	Shetland, tel. 01595 692976, VHF weather every 3 hours from 0710.

Introduction

This is a fantastic short section of coastline that really packs a punch with its caves, castles and arches. Unlike the trips to the north this one has no strong tidal steams to contend with so you get all the spectacular coastal scenery without the challenge of the tidal races.

Description

13

Keiss Castle

Freswick Bay is where this trip starts and within this the small pier of Skirza provides a great launch site. Freswick Bay is well known for its surf, and many boarders will travel to enjoy its breaks, so choose a day when the swell is small to avoid the surf and enjoy the great caves. Crossing the bay, the steep rocky headland of Ness Head will draw your eye, and give a taste of what is to come. Beautifully sculptured sandstone cliffs along with the cries from the many guillemots that have made this cliff their home will greet you as you arrive. At the base of the cliff are some small sea arches but sadly these will not allow you to kayak through their rocky narrows. Continuing down the coastline you will arrive at Castle Geo and the first castle of the trip. As you paddle into the geo you will see the castle perched on the precipitous finger of rock and wonder how it was constructed. This castle dates back to 1140 when it was originally known as Lamaborg and built by a notorious pirate and robber. What you see today is a rebuilt version of the original castle renamed Bucholie Castle. It was built and used by the Mowat family until 1661, after which it fell into disrepair.

The next section of coast offers some of the best cliffs, caves and sea arches on this trip, so spend time exploring every nook and cranny, as there will be plenty of hidden surprises. The area marked on the map as Black Score has some particularly spectacular caves and arches and if you have chosen a day with little swell then you will not be disappointed exploring in close here.

There is a convenient place to stop for a break at Nybster. Here you will discover a small half natural, half man-made harbour which provides a perfect landing spot. As you enter look carefully for the engraved stone indicating the harbour may have been built in 1901. It is worth allowing time to walk up behind the harbour where you will find the old winch that use to haul up the boats and fish, proof of how busy this harbour used to be. Nybster is also well known for its Broch that has been recently excavated in 2011, this is a short walk from the harbour and worth the effort. A broch is an Iron Age building that is unique to Scotland and this great example of one was probably built between 200 BC and AD 200. Along the coastline from the hidden harbour of Nybster the coastline continues with plenty of interest, and hopefully there will be a few grey seals hauled out and relaxing on the low lying rocks. Although the cliffs are not as spectacular as previously, there are still plenty of narrow inlets and rocks to weave in and out, as you head to the second castle of the day.

Keiss Castle is perhaps one of the best-known and most visible castles in Caithness, and seeing it from a kayak while sitting below its precipitous walls is by far the best way to admire it. It is situated dramatically on top of sheer cliffs looking straight out into the North Sea. It is believed that the 5th Earl of Caithness constructed this great building sometime in the late 16th century. This castle marks the end of the trip, as a kilometre down the coastline will bring you to the finishing harbour of Keiss. Two more brochs are passed along this final section, although these are not really visible from the sea. It was 1831 when the fine harbour of Keiss was built, being made up of an inner and outer harbour. On entering you will not be able to miss the large fish

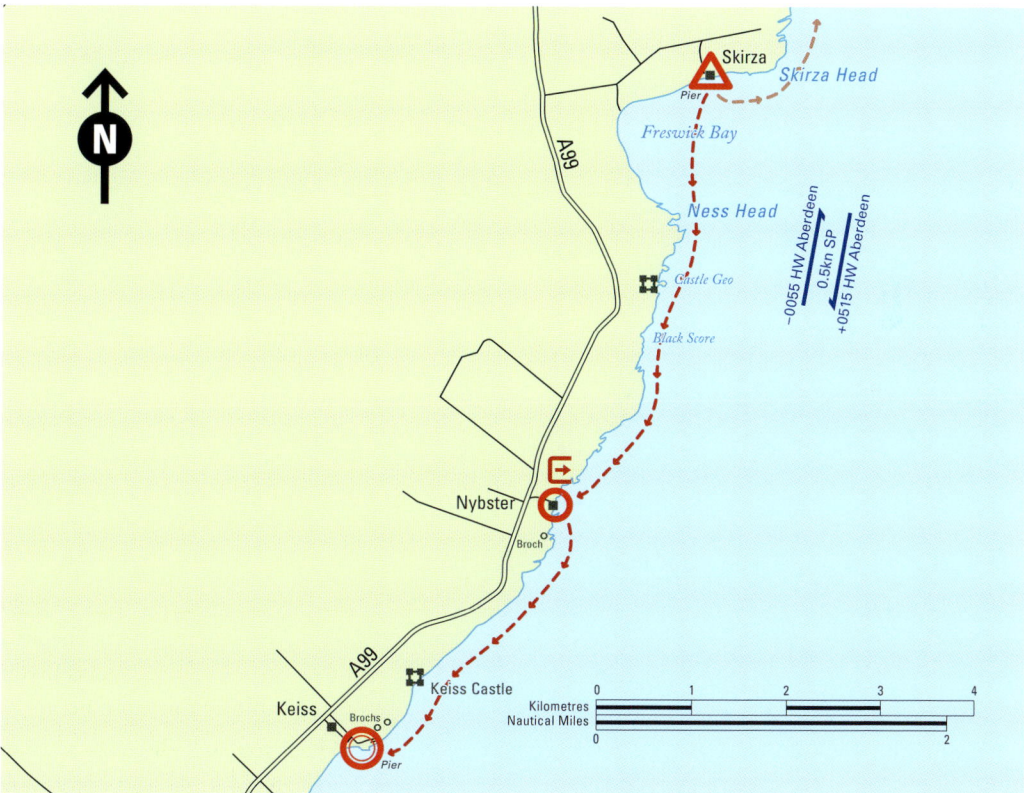

Keiss Castle

13

store that overlooks the harbour, but be sure you look carefully along to the right of this where the small icehouse still stands as well. There is parking available at the harbour close to the slip that makes for an easy landing.

Tides and weather

The tidal streams along this section of coastline are relatively weak; therefore the wind should be the main factor in the planning. This coastline is exposed to any swell from the north or east and the trip is best avoided if there is any noteworthy swell forecasted.

Additional information

There are no facilities at Skirza and limited parking at the pier. Please park considerately here as it is next to a residential house. There is alternative parking and launching down at the beach in Freswick Bay if required. At Keiss there are shops and facilities. If interested in the brochs in this area it is worth visiting the Caithness Broch Centre in Auckengill. www. caithnessbrochcentre.co.uk

Variations

The trip can be paddled in either direction. If you would like a longer trip and are happy with the associated tidal streams then continuing on around Duncansby Head makes for a spectacular day out.

Noss Head 🔲🔲🔲🔲🔲

No. 14 | Grade B | 6km | OS Sheet 12

Tidal Port	Aberdeen
Start	🔺 Ackergillshore (ND 358 545)
Finish	⭕ Staxigoe (ND 385 525)
HW/LW	HW/LW at Ackersgillshore is about 2 hours and 20 minutes before Aberdeen.
Tidal Times	Between Ackergillshore and Noss Head: The tidal stream sets in a continuous easterly direction.
	Off Noss Head: The S going stream starts about 5 hours and 30 minutes after HW Aberdeen. The N going stream starts about 40 minutes before HW Aberdeen.
Max Rate Sp	2 knots off Noss Head.
Coastguard	Shetland, tel. 01595 692976, VHF weather every 3 hours from 0710.

Introduction

This fantastic little trip provides a lot of interest for its short distance, taking a dramatic route around one of the most prominent headlands of the east coast. With views to the north of the Pentland Skerries and the Orkney Isles, and the coastline itself being guarded by castles and caves, it is a great little adventure.

Description

14

Noss Head

The small harbour at Ackergillshore overlooks Sinclair's Bay, for many years a safe anchorage for shipping waiting for the appropriate conditions to travel through the Pentland Firth. Now it provides the backdrop to the start of this great little paddle along with Ackergill Tower, the castle that overlooks the harbour. Legend has it that in the early 15th century a beautiful young woman who had been abducted threw herself from the highest tower to escape her abductor's advances. Supposedly her ghost is still seen wearing a long red ball gown looking from the tower. These days the castle is an exclusive five star hotel and business venue.

Take care of the surf that often breaks over the low lying skerries as you head to the cliffs that lead out to Noss Head. A pillbox and a gun platform, the remains of some World War II defences, can be seen above the shoreline. The beach at Sinclair's Bay was one of Britain's largest minefields in this era, showing what a strategic section of coastline this was. As soon as the cliffs start there are arches, stacks and caves to explore before you reach the dramatic castles of Sinclair and Girnigoe. These castles share the same spit of land that was obviously chosen for its ease of defence, the first being built in the mid to late 15th century. The Sinclair family, later to become the Earls of Caithness, occupied these castles. During this time they were also Earls of Orkney with a castle in Kirkwell as well as having a castle at Rosslyn outside Edinburgh, which shows what a powerful family they were in this period. If you go east of the castles you will find a hidden inlet, at the back of which you can land and explore the castles. The way the first stones of the castle walls are laid down and join into the bedrock is very impressive, and paddling under these walls gives a real insight to this amazing workmanship. There is not much left of the older Castle Sinclair, but Castle Girnigoe still has high walls, windows and doorways.

Noss Head is guarded by a cave and arch amongst its imposing cliffs. The name of this headland derives from the old Norse word "Snos" – a nose. After the relative shelter of the bay you may well start to feel some tidal movement as you round the headland, as well as a rougher sea state. The impressive lighthouse that was first lit in 1849 looks down on you as you paddle along this rugged coastline. The unemployed poor of the area who were paid seventeen and half pence a day built the long road from Wick that provides access to the lighthouse.

Staxigoe was the first port in Europe to 'salt the herring' during the herring fishing golden years, and it was the largest herring station in Europe for a while. Nowadays it provides a quiet and idyllic landing spot to finish a great little trip.

Tides and weather

There is a continuous east flowing tidal stream that leads out to Noss Head and off the headland itself the tidal streams are noticeable but do not form a tidal race of note. Time this trip to make best use of the south going tidal stream. The headland and low-lying skerries are exposed to the swell, and these skerries can produce boomers and awkward conditions, so it is best to avoid this paddle if there is a noteworthy swell forecast. Picking a safe route into Staxigoe Harbour through these boomers requires care and experience.

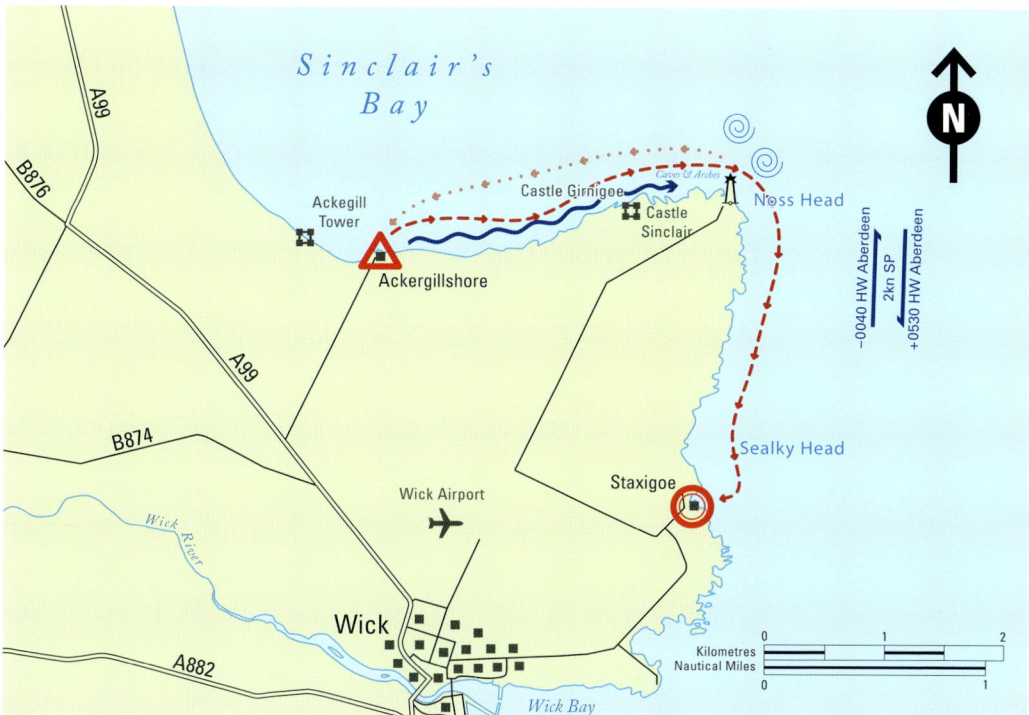

Additional information

There are no amenities at either the start or the finish, however nearby Wick will have everything you may need. There is limited parking at Ackergillshore so please drop the boats off but do not park in the turning area at the end of the road.

Variations

To avoid rougher conditions off the headland, or if there are strong winds from the south, paddling out to Noss Head and back from Ackergillshore provides a good option.

To Noss Head Light

As sweet to me as light of moon or star,
Is thy bright gleam, old trusty friend Noss Head
And doubly sweet, when o'er wide ocean far
The ray benignant on my course is shed
Blest be the hand that raised your steadfast tower
And he who trims you never-falling light
For oft when round me midnight tempests lower
Hope's pulse had failed, but for thy flash so bright
My gallant boat, though scare inch-thick her planks
Flies livelier on the track that heads her home
And dips her prow, as if in grateful thanks
When first your welcome ray reveals the billows foam
Long were the nights and weary were my watch
If from the lively deck thy flame I did not catch.
(Poem hanging in the light room).

Whaligoe ▨▨▨▨

15

No. 15 | Grade B | 24km | OS Sheets 11 & 12

Tidal Port	Aberdeen
Start	△ Staxigoe (ND 385 525)
Finish	◯ Lybster (ND 244 348)
HW/LW	HW/LW at Lybster is around 2 hours before Aberdeen.
Tidal Times	Between Noss Head and Wick: The SSW going stream starts about 5 hours and 30 minutes after HW Aberdeen. The NNE going stream starts about 40 minutes before HW Aberdeen.
	At Lybster: The SW going stream starts about 6 hours after HW Aberdeen. The NE going stream starts about 20 minutes before HW Aberdeen.
Max Rate Sp	1.5 knots off the small headlands of this section of coast.
Coastguard	Shetland, tel. 01595 692976, VHF weather every 3 hours from 0710.

Introduction

This is a truly stunning area of east coast scenery, in fact enough to make some diehards, who say the west coast is the only place to paddle, 'eat their hats'. With steep cliffs for the majority of the journey, many caves and huge arches, teeming with bird life in the spring and summer,

15

and a few seals, this is a trip worth keeping for a special day. On a calm day you will be able to paddle into more of the caves, through the arches and find somewhere to land more easily.

Description

Staxigoe harbour provides a perfect starting point for this trip. Driving down into the harbour you will clearly see the rock stack which gives Staxigoe its name (in Norse "Stakkr" translates as stack and "Goe" as an inlet). You may also have noticed the unique pole with a barometer attached and wind vane on top, which was erected in the 19th century to help fishermen predict the weather and was known simply as 'The Pole'. Take care as you paddle across Wick Bay as there will be many boats going in and out of the harbour, mainly fishing boats but also service and exploratory ships for the offshore oil industry. Before reaching the Castle of Old Wick you will see the outdoor sea water swimming pool set up on the flat sandstone rocks. On a summers day you may well see it being used, a testament to the hardy locals! The presence of Vikings in this and many other parts of Scotland is well documented, and the castle you paddle by could easily have been used by Saint Rognvald, Earl of Orkney, known for his part in creating the Cathedral of St Magnes in Kirkwell, Orkney. The castle itself stands on a precipitous neck of rock that has a protective ditch on the approach from the land. It was probably built in the 12th century making it one of Scotland's oldest castles.

From the castle the cliff scenery continues all the way down to Lybster and beyond. The calmer the sea the better the opportunity will be to explore the geos, caves, arches and stacks that litter this section of coastline. The cliffs are sheer for most of the route and around forty-five metres high. After some impressive caves and arches you will reach the only real possible escape route and relatively easy landing place on this trip. This is at 'The Haven' situated below the village of Sarclet, where you will find the remains of the fishing port that was heavily used for landing herring in the 19th century. On from The Haven the impressive cliff architecture will continue and the nesting birds will be there in abundance to cry out to you as you pass. Soon you will arrive at the fishing harbour of Whaligoe, which is most definitely without comparison. A series of 350 flagstone steps zigzag their way down a steep cliff to a narrow geo that forms the tiny natural harbour. This harbour was built in the 18th century, and once saw the harvest of many barrels of herring laboriously carried up the steps by the women of Whaligoe. All that remains today of that important industry are the ruins of a house at the bottom of the steps and evidence of winding gear that very cleverly managed to pull boats inward with the help of a pulley system attached to the back wall of the geo. Carrying the many barrels of herring up the steps must have been a back-breaking experience for the women, just imagine what it was like if you decide to scale the steps. Visiting this hidden gem will perhaps suggest the magnitude of the lure of the herring, almost a 'gold rush' of sorts. To create a fishing station at such a difficult location must reflect the lack of easier sites along the cliff-ridden coast and a huge desire to be involved in the profitable harvest of herring. Don't be fooled into thinking that because Whaligoe was a fishing harbour that it will provide an easy landing or even be a place to come ashore a cut short the trip. The landing can be tricky if any waves are coming into the geo, and

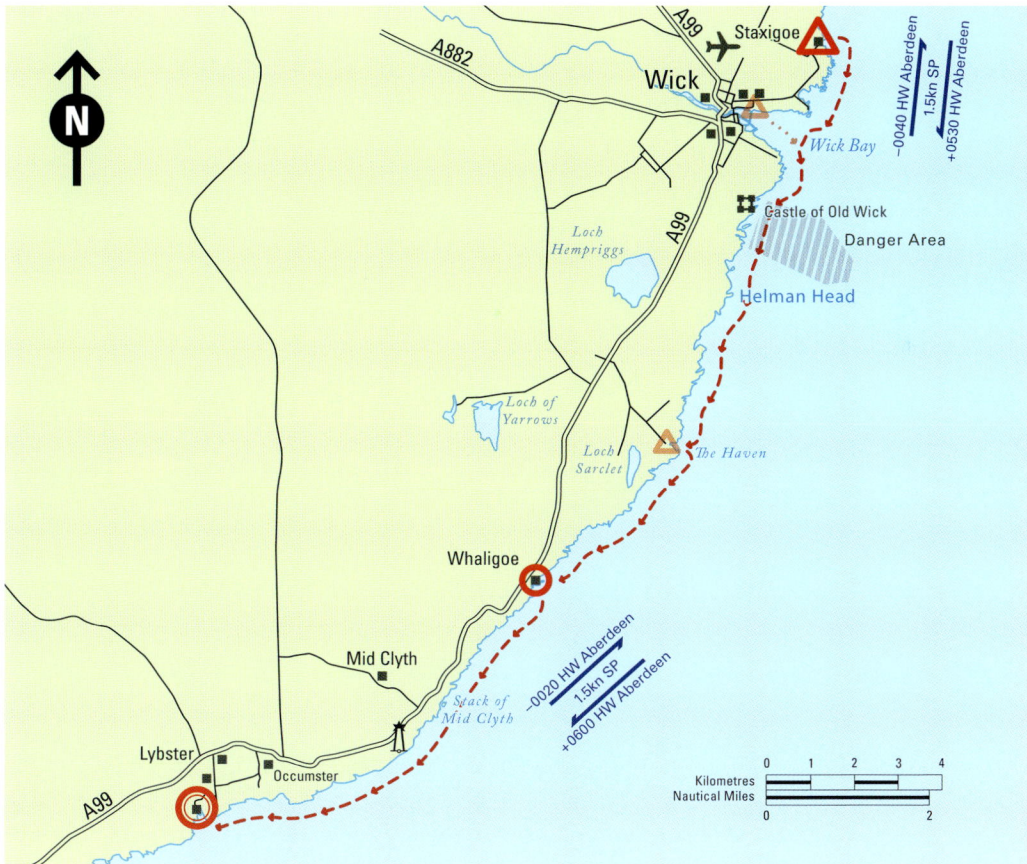

to cut the trip short would involve carrying boats up the 350 steps which would be too hard a task, even for the women of Whaligoe!

The cliffs, caves, stacks and arches continue on in unrelenting fashion all the way to Lybster. The impressive Stack of Mid Clyth is of particular note, and beyond this you may see some climbers scaling the vertical cliffs at the popular climbing venues of Mid Clyth and Occumster. Above the first of these venues sits a small lighthouse atop of the cliffs, built in 1916 by David Stevenson and perhaps one of his smallest lighthouses. Mid Clyth is best known to most people for its 200 standing stones that radiate outward in two separate fans, well worth a look if driving by at the end of the trip. The finishing harbour of Lybster will emerge suddenly as it is set back in a small bay forming a rare break in the cliffs. Hopefully you will have discovered the small stack with a narrow route you can squeeze through surrounded by fine coloured rock, about 600m before the harbour. Lybster Harbour was built in 1810 to service the herring boom, and in more recent times it was used in the making of the film *The Silver Darlings*. This film was based on the book by famous Scottish novelist Neil Gunn, who wrote about the herring boom and how the locals adapted to harvesting the 'Silver Darlings' after the clearances. If it is relatively calm and the best place to land is on the pebble beach just to the left of the harbour walls, right next to the car park and perfectly situated café.

Tides and weather

Although there are no particularly strong tides along this section of coastline, the trip is made easier if you leave with the start of the south-west going tide. The coastline provides a lot of shelter from north-westerly winds, however if from the south-west or north-east then plan the trip with the wind at your back. Due to exposed coastline and exposure to swell that can wrap around from the north as well as more obviously affecting from the east, plan to avoid paddling when there is going to be swell.

Additional information

The rifle range and the associated danger area marked on the 1:50,000 map just south of Wick is used by the Territorial Army. Phone Shetland Coastguard if you want to check if any danger exists on the day you plan to paddle this trip. At the top of Whaligoe steps there is a fine café/restaurant that is well worth the walk, you could even plan a convenient lunch stop around it. There is also a café at Lybster as well as a shop up in the village. There are no amenities at Staxigoe.

Variations

The large harbour of Wick does provide an alternative launch site on the north side of the river basin at ND 367 509. This is useful if you want to use the local bus for the shuttle. It is also possible to start or finish at The Haven below Sarclet, although this does require quite a long carry with the boats so it is not for the faint hearted.

Lybster to Dunbeath ▦▨▩▧▦ 16

No. 1 | Grade B | 10km | OS Sheet 11

Tidal Port	Aberdeen
Start	△ Lybster (ND 244 348)
Finish	⭕ Dunbeath (ND 166 293)
HW/LW	HW/LW at Lybster is around 2 hours before Aberdeen.
Tidal Times	Between Lybster and Dunbeath: The SW going tidal stream starts at about 6 hours and 5 minutes after HW Aberdeen. The NE going tidal stream starts at about 20 minutes before HW Aberdeen.
Max Rate Sp	1 knot along the coastline.
Coastguard	Shetland, tel. 01595 692976, VHF weather every 3 hours from 0710.

Introduction

Latheronwheel is a fantastic little harbour to enjoy half way along this magic little trip. It hides between small cliffs that provide plenty of opportunities to explore caves and arches. This is a great short day out with plenty of interest as well as never being too far away from an easy landing in a picturesque old harbour that was built in the herring fishing years.

16

Description

Lybster was once a busy place. In 1838 it had 101 boats working from it and was the third biggest herring port in Scotland. It will undoubtedly be a quieter place nowadays as you start off on the trip, however with its convenient car park, café and visitor centre showing off the local heritage you will feel welcomed in this lovely place. On leaving the pebble beach you will also be welcomed by the seabirds that will be looking down from their nests on the steep little sandstone cliffs that line the harbour entrance. The first half of this trip paddles the steep rock and grass coastline along to the smaller harbour of Latheronwheel. Not far along this coastline you will see the constant burning flame of the onshore drilling rig that belongs to Caithness Oil, sitting on the hillside overlooking the sea. The steep-sided grass and rock coastline continues and there is a possible landing spot at Achastle-shore. This rocky beach is overlooked by an impressive promontory to the east, which was once the site of Swiney Castle. All that is left here now are the earth mounds as this castle dates back to Norse times.

The attractive little harbour of Latheronwheel hides amongst the steep grass and rock cliffs that surround it and provides a perfect mid way stopping place on this trip. It was built in 1840 with salmon originally being the main catch, prior to the arrival of the herring; when at its peak it sheltered fifty boats. Nowadays it has been made into a beautiful place to come and visit, with picnic tables and a BBQ for all to use. There is also a reminder of how this coastline used to be accessed prior to the current A9 road; the fine old bridge that can be seen crossing the river dates back to around 1726 and was used by the old road that followed the coastline more closely.

Immediately on leaving Latheronwheel the small yet vertical cliffs provide a mass of caves, arches and through routes to explore. The calmer the better here as this really is a magical section for sea kayakers to wander amongst the fantastic natural rock architecture. While doing so you may well come across some rock climbers enjoying the vertical rock walls, as this is a popular place for climbing, being south facing and often getting some shelter from the wind. The cliffs abate for a bit, though there may well be some seabirds and seals for company, as well as great views up and down this remote and inaccessible section of coast that lines the outer reaches of the Moray Firth. Before long the sandstone rock architecture will return, with it bringing more stacks and caves to explore. Cleit Mhor offers some particularly spectacular stacks, and further on ensure you make the time to explore every nook and cranny of the beautifully sculptured little caves that lead to the end of the trip at Dunbeath.

Dunbeath harbour provides a convenient finish for the trip; the harbour slip itself can often be awkward to land on but there is a sandy beach before the harbour that can sometimes make things easier. The harbour area is well maintained and the old fishing stores are clear to see. The striking statue of 'Ken and the Salmon' commemorates Scotland's most acclaimed 20th century novelist Neil Gunn, who was born and raised here. His two most acclaimed works *Highland River* and *The Silver Darlings* were both inspired by this amazing landscape and the local economy, in particular the fishing.

Tides and weather

There is very little tidal stream movement along this coastline, so it is best to plan this trip making best use of any wind that may be of assistance. The coastline is affected by any swell from the east, and a strong south-westerly wind can produce a reasonable sea state to be aware of.

Additional information

The visitor centre and café at Lybster is open from May until October, generally from 11am until 5pm. There are no amenities at Latheronwheel or Dunbeath harbours. In Dunbeath village there is a good heritage centre that is worth a visit, www.dunbeath-heritage.org.uk

Variations

To avoid a shuttle, starting at Latheronwheel and paddling to either Dunbeath or Lybster and back can provide a good day out.

Oil

The Lybster oil field was first opened in 2008 and has been extended since. While on test it has produced 2,000 barrels of oil per day. This well is now on long-term production test with produced oil being exported by road tanker. As the drilling all takes place on the land it provides a cheaper and more environmentally friendly form of oil drilling than the oil rigs at sea. While paddling underneath it you will see its offshore counterparts out on the horizon. This is one of the few places in the UK where you can see offshore oil rigs in production from the mainland.

Dunbeath to Helmsdale

No. 17 | **Grade B** | **21km** | **OS Sheet 17**

Tidal Port	Aberdeen
Start	△ Dunbeath (ND 166 293)
Finish	◯ Helmsdale (ND 030 152)
HW/LW	HW/LW at Helmsdale is around 1 hour and 50 minutes before Aberdeen.
Tidal Times	Off Dunbeath Bay: The SW going tidal stream starts at about 6 hours and 5 minutes after HW Aberdeen. The NE going tidal stream starts at about 20 minutes before HW Aberdeen.
Max Rate Sp	1 knot along the coastline.
Coastguard	Shetland, tel. 01595 692976, VHF weather every 3 hours from 0710.

Introduction

This is a long, remote and exposed section of coastline that only has one sheltered landing spot, at the tiny, river mouth harbour of Berriedale. On this remote journey the paddler will be kept company by thousands of sea birds in the early summer months and be rewarded with exceptional cliff scenery with the grandfather of all sea arches to paddle through. It will be an unforgettable experience.

South of Dunbeath

Description

Dunbeath harbour offers plenty of parking and toilet facilities, along with a choice of easy launch sites from the harbour slip or beach alongside. On the other side of the bay the impressive Dunbeath Castle dominates the view. The castle guards the cliff edge looking out over the Moray Firth, its bright white colour ensuring it will not be missed. What you see today is the result of many generations of extensions to the castle, in particular during the 19th century, and it is a far cry from its origins as a Norse tower in the 13th century. Paddling directly underneath you can weave in and out of the skerries while marvelling at how the walls of the castle cling so precariously to the edge of the cliff. There are some great caves just around the corner, and in calm conditions some interesting through routes may be found. As this first section of caves finishes the eye will be drawn to the next great sea stack to paddle around, and beyond that is the incredible sea arch at An Dun.

An Dun is a tall narrow headland that sticks out into the sea and its is joined to the mainland by a giant sea arch that is tall, narrow and deep. As you approach this amazing feature the towering cliffs that lead into it provide perfect nesting ledges for thousands of seabirds, the noise they make drowning out the sound of the sea as it pushes up against the base of these giant walls of rock. This huge sea arch has to qualify as one of the largest in Britain! As you paddle through it you will experience the illusion of paddling steeply downhill, this is caused by rock strata not being horizontal but dipping down into the sea as you paddle through. Coming out the other side of the arch feels like entering a different world as impenetrable cliffs almost surround you.

As the coastline continues to the unique little harbour of Berriedale there is plenty on offer. A cascading waterfall lies around the first vertical headland beyond An Dun and then just before Berriedale at Traigh Bhuidhe there are yet more caves to explore. A spur of rock that protects the river mouth provides a tiny natural anchorage and forms the harbour at Berriedale. It is hard to spot, yet on the hillside above you will see the two giant leading towers that look like great chessmen. These two towers are known as the 'Duke's Candlesticks' after the Duke of Portland financed them in the 19th century. A pebble beach leads into the river mouth entrance to the harbour and the old fisher cottages that line the beach are currently being renovated. The harbour itself is a magical place and you should spend the time to enjoy it, perhaps taking a walk over the small swinging suspension footbridge to access the fisher cottage beach. On the spur of rock forming the harbour and immediate surrounds at least five brochs have been found, showing how key this natural harbour has been over the years. In addition to this the faint remains of Berriedale Castle can be seen on top of the spur. This has stood here since at least the 1300s and is reputed to be the site known as Beruvik in the Viking Orkneyinga Saga.

The journey continues along the remote and wild feeling section of coastline that leads to Helmsdale. Steep rock and grass slopes will tower above as you paddle along and there are stacks and caves of interest as well as steep-sided streams cascading into the sea below. There are views into the heart of the Moray Firth with plenty of the wildlife that make this remote area their home. Not far from the finish at Helmsdale, Ord Point will be passed and this marks the boundary between Caithness and Sutherland into which you now paddle. The steep coastline above will be some of the highest on this trip, and the route above it that the A9 now uses has had a fearsome reputation for travellers. In the 18th century the route followed the cliff top and there

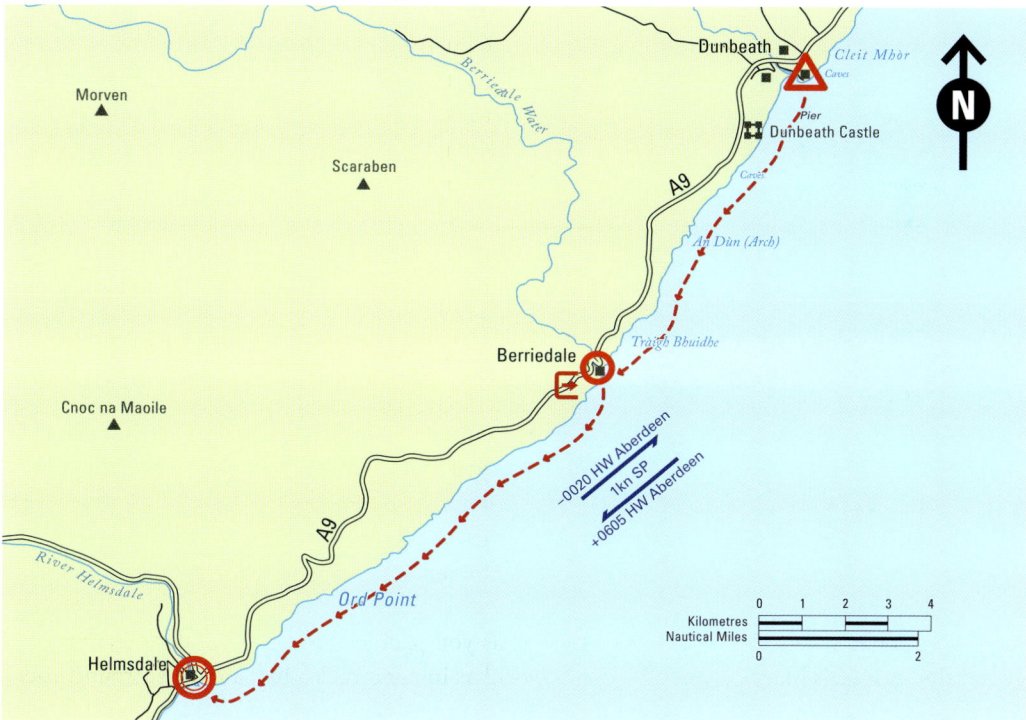

are many grim tales of travellers being blown off the road and falling to a sorry fate, and if the weather did not get them then the Ord robbers would. Even in more recent times the Ord has caused a challenge to many a traveller with the winter snowstorms it attracts.

The modern village and harbour of Helmsdale was planned in 1814 to accommodate local families that had been displaced as part of the Highland Clearances. As with so many east coast villages these locals then prospered from the salmon and the herring fishing that followed. The harbour today provides an ideal place to land at the end of this fantastic trip. Look out for the haunting sculpture known as 'The Emigrants Statue' that overlooks the harbour. This statue commemorates the tens of thousands displaced during the Highland Clearances in the 19th century.

Tides and weather

There is very little tidal stream movement along this coastline, so it is best to plan this trip making best use of any wind that may be of assistance. The coastline is affected by any swell from the east, and a strong south-westerly wind can produce a reasonable sea state to be aware of.

Additional information

There are plenty of local amenities to be found in Helmsdale including a choice of pubs and cafés. At Dunbeath there are toilets at the harbour, the village is situated on the hillside above the harbour and has a shop. The harbour at Berriedale can be accessed down a private estate road, but should be used only as an emergency exit point.

THE EMIGRANTS

COMMEMORATES THE PEOPLE OF THE HIGHLANDS AND ISLANDS OF SCOTLAND
WHO, IN THE FACE OF GREAT ADVERSITY, SOUGHT FREEDOM, HOPE AND
JUSTICE BEYOND THESE SHORES. THEY AND THEIR DESCENDANTS WENT
FORTH AND EXPLORED CONTINENTS, BUILT GREAT COUNTRIES AND
CITIES AND GAVE THEIR ENTERPRISE AND CULTURE TO THE WORLD.
THIS IS THEIR LEGACY.

THEIR VOICES WILL ECHO FOREVER THRO THE EMPTY STRATHS
AND GLENS OF THEIR HOMELAND.

UNVEILED BY THE FIRST MINISTER OF SCOTLAND, RT HON ALEX SALMOND MSP, 23 JULY 2007

Highland Clearances

The highland clearances form a key part of Scottish history, shaping the landscape and culture of Scotland to such an extent that the effects from this period can still be seen and felt today. During the 18th and 19th century tenant farmers and crofters were forced from their homes and lands by hereditary aristocratic landowners. They were driven from lands where they had lived and made a living for generations in order to make room for the more profitable farming of sheep. Having been forced from their homes they had little choice other than make a new start trying to survive along the coastal areas, or in other inhospitable areas where sheep could not easily be farmed. The majority of the beautiful fishing harbours and villages that we enjoy visiting by sea kayak in the north of Scotland, originated from families who had lost their homes in the clearances. At its most brutal it was not uncommon to see evictions at the rate of 2,000 families in one day, with many of these starving and freezing to death where their homes had once been. As well as the families fleeing to the coasts, many emigrated further afield, with a significant number leaving for North America. Nova Scotia ('New Scotland') in Canada is estimated to have had 25,000 Gaelic speaking Scots arriving as immigrants between 1775 and 1850. By the beginning of the 20th century the number is believed to have reached 100,000 in Cape Breton, Nova Scotia alone. Whilst enjoying the villages of the north of Scotland, take the time to spare a though for its sad and brutal history. The memorial found in Helmsdale is a permanent reminder of the families affected by the clearances, with this area of Sutherland being one of the worst affected.

The incredible sea arch of An Dun

Variations

To avoid a shuttle, starting and finishing at Dunbeath and paddling a return trip to Berriedale makes a great day out. This allows some spectacular cliff scenery to be enjoyed including the great arch at An Dun.

Tarbat Ness 🚌🚉🚗

No. 18 | Grade B | 21km | OS Sheet 21

Tidal Port	Aberdeen
Start	△ Portmahomack (NH 915 843)
Finish	⬤ Balintore (NH 864 754)
HW/LW	HW/LW at Portmahomack is around 1 hour and 30 minutes before Aberdeen.
Tidal Times	Between Tarbat Ness and Balintore: The SW going stream starts at about 4 hours and 35 minutes after HW Aberdeen. The NE going stream starts at about 1 hour and 20 minutes before HW Aberdeen.
Max Rate Sp	0.5 knots along the coastline.
Coastguard	Aberdeen, tel. 01224 592334, VHF weather every 3 hours from 0730.

Introduction

Tarbat Ness is a finger of land that projects out into the heart of the Moray Firth with a spectacular lighthouse at its tip. Stunning views of the Firth, plenty of wildlife and some beautiful fishing villages make for a perfect day out.

Portmahomack

Description

The trip starts in the beautiful fishing village of Portmahomack that is an idyllic place to start this journey. The harbour has a lovely sandy beach that is a perfect place to launch. These days the harbour is relatively quiet unlike during the white fish boom in the early 20th century when it was packed with scores of boats. As you make your way up to the headland of Tarbat Ness the sea will start to become a little more lively. Paddling along this relatively low lying rocky coastline you get a real sense of exposure as you look out of the Firth into the North Sea. There are also great views to the north of the Sutherland hills and coastline. You should be able to pick out Dunrobin Castle where the Duke of Sutherland lived and the monument on the hills above built to commemorate his life. To this day the monument causes much controversy due to the Duke's role in carrying out the Highland Clearances where thousands of tenants were forced out of their homes in the early 1800s.

The spectacular lighthouse of Tarbat Ness marks the tip of the headland as well as some slightly bouncier water. Look out for the seals which may well be resting on the rocks or many of the sea birds that use this area as a resting point. Although the headland itself is relatively low lying and unspectacular, its position and the stunning lighthouse more than makes up for it. The Tarbat Ness lighthouse was another one of Robert Stevenson's designs. It was the loss of sixteen vessels in the Moray Firth during a November storm in 1826 that called for the building of the light that was finished in 1830. Standing forty-one metres high Tarbat Ness is the second tallest land-based lighthouse in Scotland, North Ronaldsay being the tallest. Not far past the headland look out for a hidden slipway that will give the first easy opportunity for a break.

Continuing down the coastline the views will change as you look to the south side of the Moray Firth, with the Cairngorm Mountains in the distance. The coast is steep with grass and gorse covered slopes, a blaze of yellow colour in the summer. The next point of interest is the small village of Rockfield that clings to a small slither of land along the edge of the sea and is backed by steep slopes. This provides another landing opportunity, and an alternative start or finish point. Between Rockfield and Balintore there is a long and remote section, with few easy landings. The coastline continues steeply and your only company will be the wildlife or perhaps an occasional local fishing boat out checking on the creels. The first sign of civilisation is the village of Cadboll. This name is of Norse derivation and comes from Katter-bol or Cat Stead as the cliffs were the haunt of wild cats. In 1843 a 150-ton schooner called *Linnet* was wrecked and all life was lost, and this had such an effect on the village that in the history books time is referred to as pre or post *Linnet*. Cadboll joins the village of Balintore that provides the finish point. At higher tides there is a sandy landing in the harbour, or at lower tide the sandy beach of Sandwick may be easier. Balintore is another fishing village with plenty of interest, but perhaps most importantly a pub for the weary sea paddler.

Tides and weather

The tides are generally fairly weak, but the wind and swell should be the main consideration. Tarbat Ness is exposed to winds from most directions and any swell from a north or easterly direction will have an effect. Consider doing the trip in the other direction if the winds are from the south-west.

18

Tarbat Ness

Additional information

There is plenty of parking at Balintore and Portmahomack, as well as places to eat. It is well worth making time to eat at the Oyster Catcher in Portmahomack that does fantastic local seafood.

Variations

If the weather dictates or you just want to paddle around Tarbat Ness, the trip can be made shorter and the shuttle a lot easier by starting or finishing at Rockfield. There is next to no parking here however, so please consider this when planning the trip so as not to inconvenience the local community. There are no shops or places to eat in Rockfield.

Port Mo Chalmaig

Portmahomack's name derives from the Gaelic 'Port Mo Chalmaig', which means 'Haven of My (i.e. Saint) Colmoc', and it has a rich history. It was the site of the first confirmed Pictish monastery dating back to around AD 550 and the subject of one of the largest archaeological investigations in Scotland between 1994 and 2007. Many pieces of Pictish sculpture were found and some of these can be seen in the village's restored parish church of St Colmoc. This is now the museum and visitor centre managed by the Tarbat Historic Trust.

North Sutor

North Sutor ▣▣▣

19

North Sutor

No. 19 | Grade A | 10km | OS Sheet 21

Tidal Port	Aberdeen
Start	△ Balintore (NH 864 754)
Finish	◯ Nigg Ferry (NH 797 687)
HW/LW	HW/LW at Nigg Ferry is around 1 hour 30 minutes before Aberdeen.
Tidal Times	Between Balintore and North Sutor: The SW going tidal stream starts at about 4 hours and 35 minutes after HW Aberdeen. The NE going stream starts at about 1 hour and 20 minutes before HW Aberdeen.
	In the entrance of the Cromarty Firth: The ingoing stream starts at about 6 hours and 5 minutes after HW Aberdeen. The outgoing stream starts at about 1 hour and 5 minutes before HW Aberdeen.
Max Rate Sp	0.5 knots between Balintore and North Sutor. 1.5 knots in the entrance to the Cromarty Firth.
Coastguard	Aberdeen, tel. 01224 592334, VHF weather every 3 hours from 0730.

Introduction

This is a real hidden gem of a trip along a bit of coastline which would be so easy to overlook … yet it offers so much. There is plenty of human history interest at the start and finish, colourful cliffs

107

Balintore Harbour

of red rocks with yellow lichens and gorses to brighten the landscape, the nesting birdlife and the idyllic waterfall beach landing spot. For a short day out it is hard to fault this paddle, and of course there is the pub lunch to finish.

Description

Set off from either the sandy beach of Shandwick or the sheltered harbour at Balintore, at low water the beach can be easier. Leaving the idyllic sands of Shandwick Bay you will quickly get a flavour of the first part of the paddle, with its steep gorse-covered hillside and rocky shoreline. Paddling this trip in early summer is recommended, as this will give the bright yellow colours from the gorse as well as plenty of bird life. Soon you will come across the maze of low lying rocks which is marked as Port an Righ on the map, translating into the 'King's Port'. This was used in the fishing boom when vast amounts of fish were handled. At low tide if you look carefully you may see the old iron ring that the boats used to tie up on. Three reefs are marked on the chart just off Port Righ and they are called the Three Kings. Care should be taken as these reefs could still cause a surprise for the unwary sea kayaker.

Continuing down the coastline there is an easy landing spot by a stream just before the King's Cave as marked on the map. This is a dry cave and landing is difficult. The view is dominated by the impressive headland that guards the entrance to the Cromarty Firth on the north side and then beyond this into the head of the Moray Firth at Inverness. When approaching the entrance to the Cromarty Firth the cliffs get bigger and the rock architecture becomes more notable. A lot of the rock is a deep red colour that is then covered with yellow lichen, and in the summer months the gorse with its bright yellow flowers provides a colourful spectacle. While the colours will bombard your visual senses, your ears and nose will now also approach sensory overload as the sea birds see you approaching. These relatively sheltered south-facing cliffs and rocks are covered with guillemots, razorbills and shags, all enjoying a perfect place to nest. Don't miss the waterfall beach landing spot at Castlecraig as marked on the map. This suntrap with its own waterfall which cascades down a vibrant green watercourse makes for a lovely spot to rest and enjoy for a while.

The final part to this trip takes you on past more red cliffs and nesting birds, and also provides some wartime history at North Sutor. The journey finishes along the sandy beach at Nigg. Here the view will be dominated by another unusual human landscape, a bit more modern this time in the form of oilrigs. It is at Nigg and in the Cromarty Firth where the North Sea's oilrigs are constructed and decommissioned, these metal giants provide a truly unique foreground to the mountains that surround the Firth. If energy and time permit you may want to extend the paddle to get a closer look at one of the oilrigs, if not then the finish is at the ferry slip at Nigg. There is not much here, but looking back along the beach and the headland of North Sutor will more than make up for it.

Tides and weather

The tidal streams are generally fairly weak along this coastline until the narrows at the entrance to the Cromarty Firth where they can run up to 1.5 knots. It is preferable, but not essential, to have the tide with you as it is easy enough to paddle against it close in to shore. Making use of any tailwind assistance will usually be of greater benefit, and this trip can be paddled in either direction to allow this.

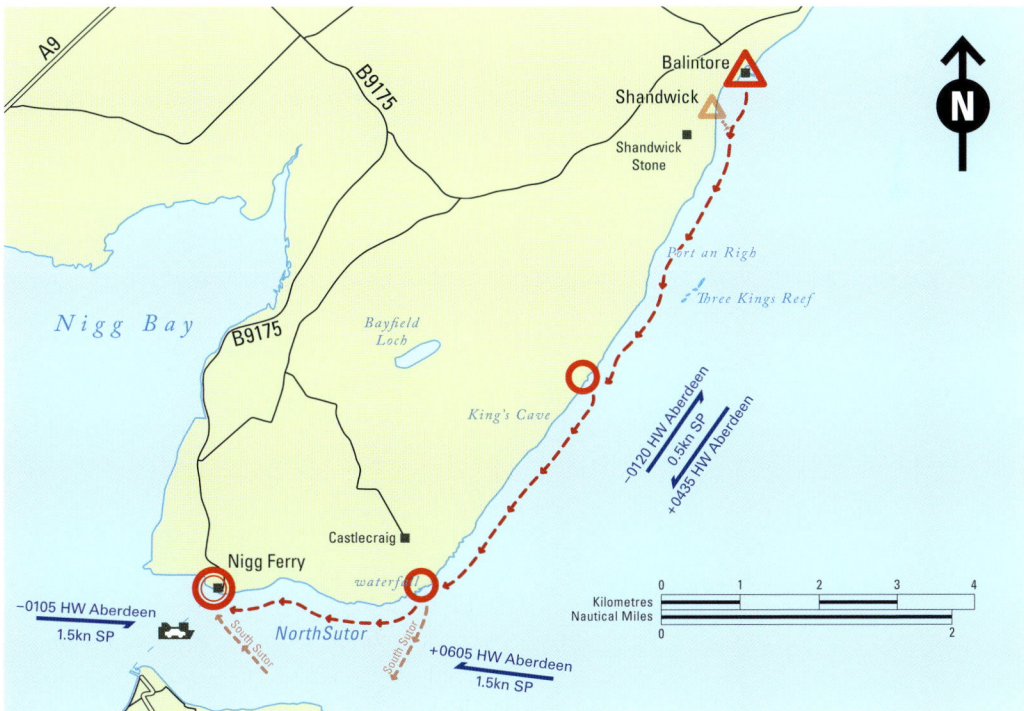

Razorbill

Additional information

There is plenty of car parking at Balintore, Shandwick and Nigg but there are no facilities at Nigg. However there are facilities at Balintore, as well as a handy pub.

Variations

If you want to explore the coastal batteries of North and South Sutor, and enjoy the best of the cliffs and wildlife, you can start and finish at Nigg. Paddling across to South Sutor, then back to the waterfall beach at Castlecraig and along the coastline of North Sutor back to the start, makes for a good day out. More attention will be required with the tidal streams and any shipping entering the Firth with this trip.

North Sutor wartime history

Here you can see the remains of the gun emplacements and coastal batteries built in the early 20th century. These were built to protect the naval anchorage in the Cromarty Firth and saw service in World War I and to a lesser degree World War II, and were then abandoned in the 1950s. In addition to these there were minefields, a boom defence for submarines, lookout posts and searchlight batteries, all to protect the Firth from the U-boats. If landing to take a closer look take a lot of care as these are potentially dangerous buildings.

Balintore and Shandwick

Balintore gets its name from the Gaelic meaning 'bleaching town', a reminder of the days when flax was grown in the north of Scotland, and it's well worth spending the time to enjoy these small fishing villages. The glass encased 'Shandwick Stone', which can be easily seen from the sea as you start paddling, is worth walking up to for a look. This stone is one of three ornately engraved Pictish stones found in this area, the other two being at Hilton of Cadboll (now in the Museum of Antiquities in Edinburgh) and at the Nigg old churchyard (now in the church). The Shandwick Stone is known as 'Clach a Charraidh' meaning 'stone of the burial place'. Legend has it that the three stones were erected to mark the burial places of three Norse princes who were wrecked on a reef just off the bay. It may also be worth searching out the 'Well of Health' at Shandwick, as legend suggests that water from it could cure the ill if drunk from a wooden ladle having had a silver coin dropped in it.

Dolphins at the Sutors

The tidal channel leading into the Cromarty Firth that flows past North Sutor is a regularly used feeding area for the resident bottlenose dolphins. The dolphins will generally feed here on an in going tide and as the channel is wide the dolphins will generally be well spread out. It is very important not to disturb the dolphins, particularly when they are feeding. To minimise any disturbance please abide by the agreed Code of Conduct highlighted on page 11.

111

© *Looking towards North Sutor from Nigg beach*

Sutors Stacks 🚐🚗🚂

No. 20 | Grade A | 18km | OS Sheet 27

Tidal Port	Aberdeen
Start	△ Rosemarkie (NH 738 575)
Finish	○ Cromarty (NH 793 673)
HW/LW	HW/LW at Cromarty is around 1 hour and 30 minutes before Aberdeen.
Tidal Times	Between Rosemarkie and Cromarty: The NE going stream starts at about 1 hour and 5 minutes before HW Aberdeen. The SW going stream starts at about 6 hours and 5 minutes after HW Aberdeen.
	In the entrance of the Cromarty Firth: The ingoing stream starts at about 6 hours and 5 minutes after HW Aberdeen. The outgoing stream starts at about 1 hour and 5 minutes before HW Aberdeen.
Max Rate Sp	0.5 knots between Rosemarkie and Sutor Stacks.
	1.5 knots in the entrance of the Cromarty Firth.
Coastguard	Aberdeen, tel. 01224 592334, VHF weather every 3 hours from 0730.

20

Sutors Stacks

Introduction

This trip provides some surprisingly remote paddling, an old salmon station bothy for lunch and the constant chance to enjoy seeing the resident bottlenose dolphins. Finishing with the Sutors Stacks and the lovely village of Cromarty amidst the unusual backdrop of mountains and oilrigs gives a great day out.

Description

On the south side of Rosemarkie bay there is easy parking and an ideal launch site to start the trip. Once on the water the red sandstone houses of Rosemarkie sea front stand out, whilst across the water Fort George protects this narrow entrance to Inverness at the head of the Moray Firth.

Heading north you get a great view of this long and remote section of coastline, the Moray Firth and beyond to the North Sea. The coastline is constantly steep sided vegetation and trees, and the foreshore is generally rocky. The lack of escape routes is apparent and although there are not the steep cliffs of other coastlines, there is a feeling of remote exposure. The caves marked on the map do not amount to much and out to sea there may well be some large ships anchored off waiting for the tide to enter Inverness. There are a few possible landing spots along the coastline but it is worth heading for the buildings marked at the water's edge at Eathie for a lunch stop.

The steep headland of Gallow Hill lies ahead, and on route there is another landing spot at the now overgrown St Bennet's Well, this is a bouldery landing that requires calm conditions. As the red coloured cliffs are approached McFarquar's Cave is easily seen, an obvious cave though not really large enough to accommodate sea paddlers. As the steep headland of Gallow Hill and it's cliffs come to an end the striking Sutors Stacks can be seen guarding the entrance to the Cromarty Firth. As with the North Sutors on the other side of the Cromarty Firth entrance the remains of gun emplacements and coastal batteries can be seen on top of the rock stacks. It is possible to land on a small pebble beach next to the stacks, although I wouldn't recommend exploring these old and potentially dangerous buildings.

Eathie Salmon Station

Eathie Salmon Station and the bothy where four workers used to live makes an ideal lunch spot. These days it provides shelter from the weather and information boards about the salmon station. The workers lived at the bothy from February until September each year and would catch the salmon by laying cone nets out in the sea parallel to the coast. An average seasonal catch of fish for Eathie was 800–1000 fish. This style of salmon fishing was prevalent on the east coast until the 1980s when most of the stations netting rights were bought by the Atlantic Salmon Trust to try and reverse the decline of salmon in the rivers.

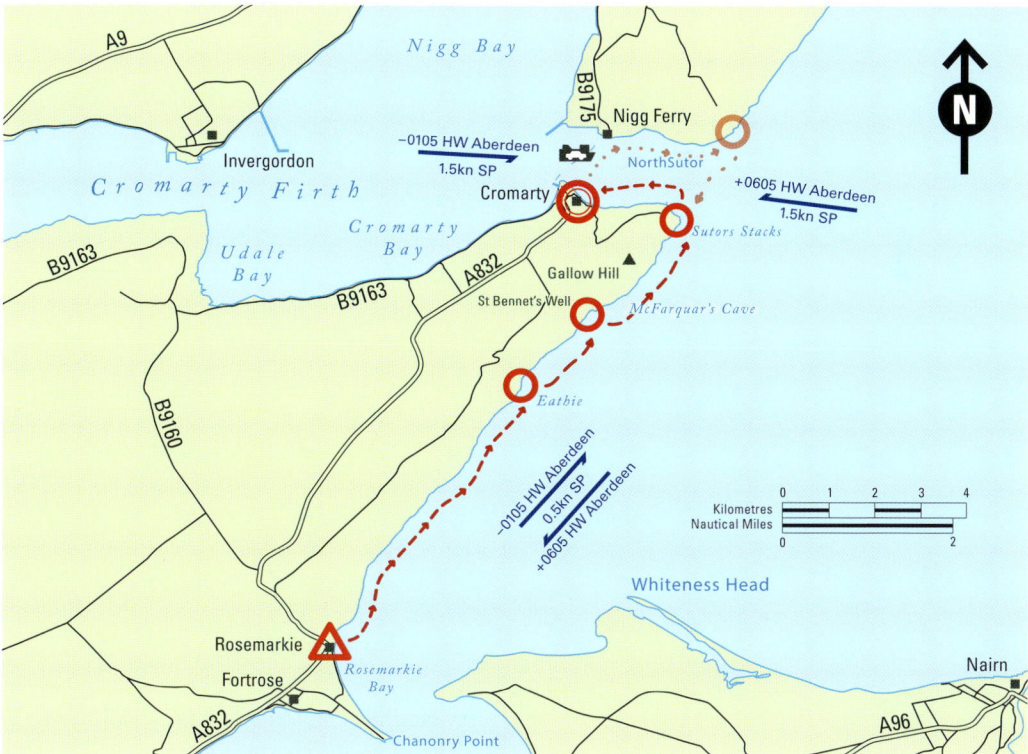

The final part of the journey takes you along the south coast of the entrance channel to the Cromarty Firth. The most striking thing here will be the view into the Firth and the lined up oilrigs being worked on. The trip finishes with an easy landing on the east beach at the beautiful little village of Cromarty. It is fitting that this sea kayak trip finishes here as Cromarty gives its name to the Shipping Forecast Area that the paddle has taken place in. Enjoy the unique architecture of historic Cromarty, and of course enjoy the abundant local pubs and cafés all serving local food.

Tides and weather

Tidal streams are weak and it is only in the narrow entrance of the Cromarty Firth that the tide can flow up to 1.5 knots. Ideally the trip should make use of this; however it is easy enough to paddle against the flow close in to the shore. The coastline is exposed to any wind from the south or east, and with no escape routes this should be the biggest consideration.

Additional information

There is plenty of parking at Rosemarkie and Cromarty, and both have a good choice of cafés and pubs close to the sea front. If heading further north after this trip the four-car Cromarty ferry is a great experience and runs in the summer.

Variations

Starting and finishing at Cromarty makes a great little paddle; heading across to North Sutor, paddling up to a landing spot at Castlecraig stream and then returning via the Sutors Stacks. A little more awareness of the tide will be required to avoid too much hard work, but it is possible at all stages of the tide.

Dolphins at the Sutors

The tidal channel leading into the Cromarty Firth that flows past Sutors Stacks is a regularly used feeding area for the resident bottlenose dolphins. The dolphins will generally feed here on an in going tide and as the channel is wide the dolphins will generally be well spread out. It is very important not to disturb the dolphins, particularly when they are feeding. To minimise any disturbance please abide by the agreed Code of Conduct highlighted on page 11.

Chanonry Point 📷 🚣

No. 21 | Grade A | 12km | OS Sheet 27

Tidal Port	Aberdeen
Start	△ Rosemarkie (NH 738 573)
Finish	⭕ Rosemarkie (NH 738 573)
HW/LW	HW/LW at Rosemarkie is around 1 hour and 25 minutes before Aberdeen.
Tidal Times	Between Chanonry Point and Fort George: The ingoing stream starts at about 6 hours and 5 minutes after HW Aberdeen. The outgoing stream starts at about 1 hour and 5 minutes before HW Aberdeen.
Max Rate Sp	3.5 knots on the outgoing stream and 2.5 knots on the ingoing stream.
Coastguard	Aberdeen, tel. 01224 592334, VHF weather every 3 hours from 0730.

Introduction

The Moray Firth is famous for its resident bottlenose dolphins, and this trip takes us to where they are most regularly seen. So the chance of seeing some dolphins from the sea kayak, along with the grandeur of Fort George and the lighthouse at Chanonry Point make this a great half day or evening out.

Description

21

Chanonry Point

The trip begins at the picturesque village of Rosemarkie. Its sea front is lined with some grand red sandstone buildings, as well as convenient eating and drinking places. There is a great view of the equally grand, if a little more intimidating, Fort George. The south end of Rosemarkie Bay provides easy parking and an ideal launch spot off the pebbly beach. Once on the water head along the beach towards Chanonry Point and its lighthouse.

Chanonry Point is a long, thin, low-lying promontory that protrudes out into the Moray Firth, forming a narrow passage that all vessels must pass through on route to Inverness. The in and out going tide must also squeeze through this narrow passage, forming some fairly fast flows, eddies and interesting currents. As well as funnelling the water as it heads in towards Inverness, it also funnels the salmon as they make their way up towards the River Ness on the incoming tide. This unique combination of factors is probably why the bottlenose dolphins have made the Moray Firth their home; it provides them with a guaranteed dinner table of salmon twice a day. This is one of the few places in the UK you can watch dolphins feeding and playing close up from the land. The whole area is protected and as sea kayakers we need to do our bit in not disturbing the dolphins feeding in the area, so this is why the flood tide is the time we avoid going in close to Chanonry Point. If you want to see the dolphins on a flood tide, please do so from the land, perhaps landing and walking up to the point as opposed to paddling within the tidal feeding area.

Chanonry Point lighthouse was first lit in 1846 and was designed by Alan Stevenson, son of Robert Stevenson, this family being responsible for many of Scotland's lighthouses. The lighthouse has been fully automated since 1984 and is now privately owned. As you pass the light you will start getting the view up to the head of the Moray Firth and the Kessock Bridge that crosses it at Inverness. This bridge was built between 1976 and 1982 and forms the main arterial link to the far North; prior to its completion there was a ferry at Kessock. Heading across the narrowest part of the Moray Firth will soon bring you to the south shore and the village of Ardersier, which provides an opportunity for a stop and leg stretch if required.

The journey home takes you along to the impressive building of Fort George that stands on the northern end of the large curving beach. The Fort was built during the period 1747 to 1769 after the Jacobite risings in 1745/6, and is still in use today by the military. It is in excellent condition despite its age. Historic Scotland looks after this impressive property these days and the Queen's Own Highlanders museum is contained within the fort. It is open to the public throughout the year, and what better way to visit it than by kayak as part of this great day out.

The Jacobites

Jacobite was the name given to those who chose to support James VII and his son James Francis Edward Stuart, and in turn his son Charles Edward Stewart, better known as 'Bonnie Prince Charlie'. The Jacobites rose with Bonnie Prince Charlie in the 1740s to aid his attempt to become king of Scotland, England and Ireland. Although at one point Bonnie Prince Charlie and the Jacobites had captured Edinburgh and Carlisle; they were to be unsuccessful in their attempt, with one of their most notable defeats and biggest massacres being on Culloden Moor in 1746, this being just 15km south of Fort George.

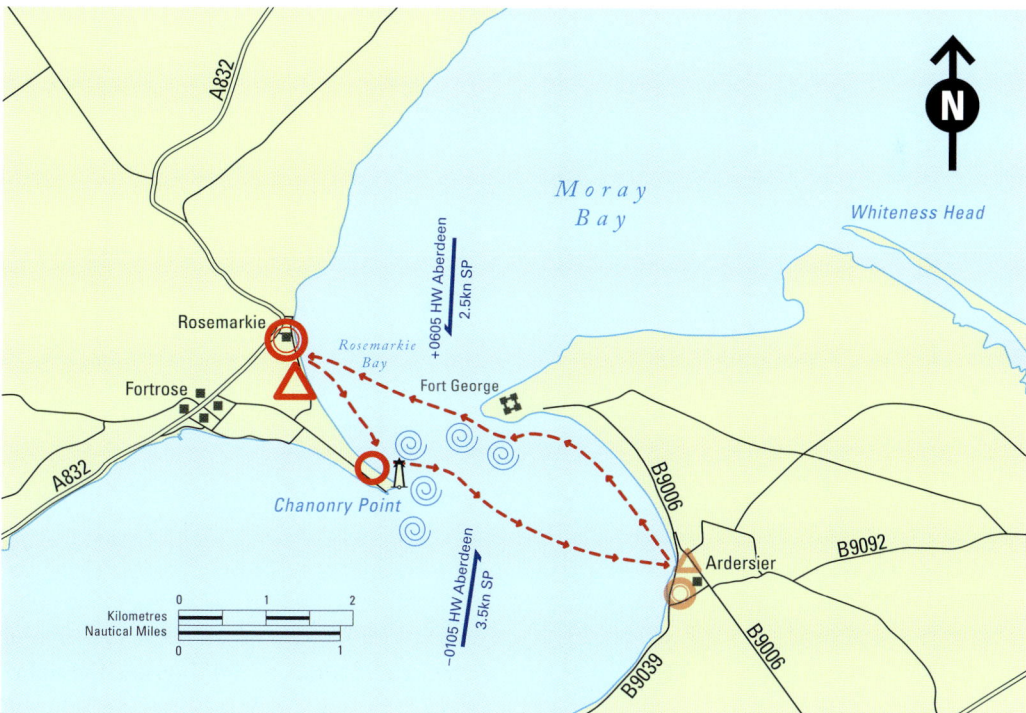

Paddling past the impressive walls and turrets of Fort George is a great experience, imagining the events that took place within those walls gives plenty to fuel the imagination. On leaving the fort behind, you may well have the dolphins around for some company as you head back across to the north side of the Moray Firth. The houses and sea front of Rosemarkie will slowly come closer into view, and before long the beach where you set out from will arrive. After this great little paddle all that will be left to do is to load the boats and walk along to one of the pubs or cafés for some well-earned refreshments.

Tides and weather

So as not to disturb the dolphins feeding the paddle needs to be done on the out-going tide which starts 1 hour and 5 minutes before HW Aberdeen. Arriving at Chanonry Point around slack water before the tidal stream (up to 3.5 knots at springs off the point) really gets going works well. Neap tides are advisable as the tidal streams will be a lot weaker. The area is relatively sheltered from wind and swells from most directions other than the east.

Additional information

There is a great bistro to eat and drink in on the sea front at Rosemarkie as well as good pubs in the village. It is well worth driving out to the Chanonry Point lighthouse on the in going tide to get photographs of the dolphins.

Fort George

Dolphins at Chanonry Point

Immediately off Chanonry Point is the most important feeding area for the resident bottlenose dolphins in the Moray Firth. If the dolphins are disturbed when feeding then this will prevent them getting enough nutrition which will have a detrimental effect to their health and in particular to the well-being of their young. The dolphins are most likely to be feeding in this area between May to September and generally about 2–3 hours after low water. Please try and avoid paddling in this area any time after low water (when the tide is flowing in towards Inverness) during these months, so as to minimise any disturbance of their feeding. If you need to paddle past the point during this time please stay at least 150 metres off the point so as to give any dolphins a very wide berth, and paddle straight through as opposed to lingering. Seeing the dolphins from the water is highly likely anywhere in this area; please refer to the agreed Code of Conduct on page 11 to avoid any accidental disturbance.

The Moray Firth's bottlenose dolphins (Charlie Phillips)

Dolphins

Scotland is lucky to have six different types of dolphin swimming around its coast. Along the east coast it is the bottlenose dolphin that is best known, with the most northern resident population in the world found here and often seen. The other dolphins that can be seen when out sea kayaking in Scotland are the common, white-sided, white beaked, striped and risso's dolphin.

The bottlenose dolphins regularly seen along the east coast are amazing to watch, and are never too shy to put on a show. These fantastic mammals can grow up to four metres long (a lot larger than bottlenose dolphins found in warmer climates) and are very sociable, being known to communicate to each other as well as to hunt for fish. They can swim up to 32 km/h and although generally stay fairly close to the surface they can dive up to 260 metres down and stay up to 15 minutes under water. The dolphins live in very close knit family units (known as pods), and they live from 20–50 years of age. The females produce a single calf every two years, and to support this calf they need to eat up to 15kg of fish a day. If unable to eat enough then the females will start getting their nutrition from stored fat and this can turn the milk toxic. This can clearly have a disastrous impact on the young calf and is a key reason why it is so important that as sea kayakers we do not disturb the dolphins by entering the prime feeding areas along the east coast.

Moray Firth – South

Introduction

The south coast of the Moray Firth is the 'Riviera' of the Scottish Highlands from a weather point of view. In the rain shadow of the mighty Cairngorm Mountains it will often provide a sunny dry day out on the water when it is raining elsewhere. The coastline has numerous welcoming fishing villages and harbours along the way with the likes of Hopeman, Findochty, Portsoy, Gardenstown and Rosehearty to name a few. All of these are ideal places to stop and enjoy some food or drink, and learn about the history and culture of these fantastic fishing villages. The famous 'Cullen Skink' fish soup being just one local delicacy not to be missed.

It is not all about ice-creams and sunshine though as there is no shortage of beaches, cliffs, caves and wildlife. The dramatic rock arch of Bow Fiddle Rock is perhaps the best known, and off Redhythe Point, Troup Head and Pennan Head there will be endless cliffs, caves and sea stacks to explore. The largest mainland colony of gannets is found in this area as well, at Troup Head. It is also home to thousands of guillemots, razorbills and the occasional puffin. The area has plenty of human history to enjoy as well with Sculptures Cave near Hopeman to the west, Findlater Castle near Cullen or at the eastern end of the area Kinnaird Castle and Lighthouse.

Tides and weather

There is not much in the way of tidal streams to consider when enjoying this area, Troup Head and Kinnaird Head being the only places where there is noticeable flow. Weather wise the south side of the Moray Firth often forms its own microclimate, providing drier and warmer conditions. The main consideration when planning to paddle this area is the swell. The coastline is often affected by northerly swells and these can make paddling very challenging, so much so that even getting out of the harbours can become difficult, let alone landing on a rocky beach. When paddling this section of coastline always check the swell forecast to aid planning, as even on a sunny windless day the swell may make a planned paddle inappropriate.

© Troup Head

Burghead to Lossiemouth 🌊🏠🌀 22

No. 22 | **Grade A** | **15km** | **OS Sheet 28**

Tidal Port	Aberdeen
Start	△ Burghead (NJ 109 689)
Finish	⊙ Lossiemouth (NJ 227 709)
HW/LW	HW/LW at Burghead is around 1 hour and 30 minutes before Aberdeen.
Tidal Times	Off Hopeman: The E going stream starts about 20 minutes before HW Aberdeen. The W going stream starts at about 5 hours and 45 minutes after HW Aberdeen.
Max Rate Sp	0.5 knot along this section of coast.
Coastguard	Aberdeen, tel. 01224 592334, VHF weather every 3 hours from 0730.

Introduction

This is a great little trip that gives plenty of variety, for instance the small sandstone cliffs and caves, picturesque harbours, sandy beaches, lighthouses, skerries, history and wildlife. Save this trip for a late summer afternoon when you will have the sun at your back and the red of the sandstone glowing in all its glory.

Description

The journey starts from the impressive harbour of Burghead, locally known as 'The Broch'. To the west of the harbour lie the low-lying beaches leading towards the Inner Moray Firth and Inverness. To the east lies the start of cliffs and caves that line much of the south side of the Moray Firth, which is where this journey takes you. As you leave Burghead you will see the remains of the Pictish vitrified fort that sits high on the headland overlooking the Moray Firth. This fort is thought to be one of the oldest Pictish forts discovered and is why the town is known as the 'Pictish Capital'.

As you paddle towards Hopeman the red sandstone cliffs become more apparent with their ornate shapes, caves, stacks and arches. Unfortunately these are all generally above the high tide mark so not possible to paddle around them, but you may well see rock climbers enjoying them as you go past the popular climbing destination of Cummingston. Although early in the trip, it is worth stopping at Hopeman harbour as it offers a perfect sandy landing spot. The harbour was built in 1838 for the export of stone from the quarry you will see just east of the village. The quarry is still in use and provided high quality stone to clad the extension to the National Museum of Scotland in Edinburgh. On leaving the harbour look out for the brightly coloured beach huts behind the east beach, soon followed by cliffs leading into Clashach Cove that provide homes for nesting kittiwakes. Clashach Cove has a landing spot which is easier at low water but if there is any swell it could prove awkward. Dinosaur footprints have been found at the quarry behind the cove and at other quarries along this coast.

Looking along the coastline Covesea lookout tower is visible up on the cliffs, with Covesea Skerries out to sea beyond. Just before the lookout tower there is a rising line of dry caves above the rocky beach. One of them is known a 'Sculptures Cave' and has Pictish drawings on its walls. Just along from here there is a two-legged sea stack known as Gow's Castle and it is possible to land just in front of it. If you go around the back of the stack you will see where the egg hunters of years gone by have cut out hand and footholds to get up the initial steep part of the stack.

On the final part of the journey the bright white tower of Covesea lighthouse dominates the view, with the finish point of Lossiemouth behind. The lighthouse was finished in 1846, one year after the gridiron tower was erected on nearby Halliman Skerries. The lighthouse is another testament to the Stevenson lighthouse-engineering dynasty, this time being built by Alan who also built Tarbat Ness lighthouse that you may be able to see in the distance to the north-east. It is well worth finishing the trip by heading out around Covesea and Halliman Skerries as there will be some good wildlife to see as well as getting a closer look at the gridiron tower. There is easy landing with plenty of parking on the west beach of Lossiemouth as marked on the map.

Tides and weather

There is very little in the way of noticeable tidal streams, so plan the trip to make best use of the wind as it can be paddled in either direction. As with much of this coastline it will be the swell that could offer the biggest challenge. It can be tricky to land at Lossiemouth and even getting into Hopeman harbour can be difficult in bigger swells.

Additional information

There is a visitor centre in Burghead for more information on the Pictish history of this area and at the entrance to Clashach Quarry there are interpretive notice boards providing information about the dinosaur footprints found along this section of coast. All of the villages on route have good local amenities and at Hopeman there are handy toilets and an ice cream shop!

Lossiemouth beach with Covesea lighthouse behind

Variations

To avoid the need for a shuttle, start and finish at Hopeman. The main points of interest along the trip can still be visited by padding down to Cummingston cliffs, then returning past Hopeman and continuing out to Covesea and back. This trip can be made as long or as short as time and group ability allows.

Looking east from Findochty

Bow Fiddle Rock 🚶 🚐 🚌 〰️

No. 23 | Grade A | 15km | OS Sheet 28 & 29

Tidal Port	Aberdeen
Start	△ Portessie (NJ 446 668)
Finish	⬭ Sandend (NJ 555 666)
HW/LW	HW/LW at Portessie is around 1 hour and 35 minutes before Aberdeen.
Tidal Times	Between Portessie and Bow Fiddle Rock: The E going tidal stream starts about 20 minutes before HW Aberdeen. The W going tidal stream starts about 5 hours and 45 minutes after HW Aberdeen.
	Between Bow Fiddle Rock and Sandend: The E going stream starts about 4 hours and 10 minutes before HW Aberdeen. The W going stream starts about 2 hours and 10 minutes after HW Aberdeen.
Max Rate Sp	1 knot between Bow Fiddle Rock and Findochty.
Coastguard	Aberdeen, tel. 01224 592334, VHF weather every 3 hours from 0730.

129

23

Introduction

This is a real east coast hidden gem. The rock architecture, caves and arches around Bow Fiddle Rock rival anywhere. The beaches, friendly harbour communities, wildlife and finally a remarkable castle make this journey a truly exceptional one.

Description

There is a handy launching spot to the east of Buckie at Portessie, where there is plenty of parking and toilet facilities. Portessie was a separate community created when five houses were built in 1727 to form a fishing station. Staying in close to the shoreline offers plenty of interest as Craig Head is passed on route to the beautiful fishing village and harbour of Findochty, pronounced 'Finexti' by the locals. If you call in at this harbour look out for the statue of the seated fisherman looking out for you as you come in to land. If a stop can be timed with lunch at the pub right next to the sandy landing spot at the back of the harbour all the better. The harbour is now mostly used by pleasure craft; however in the mid 1800s it was home to a fleet of 140 fishing boats, but by 1890 this fleet had left the harbour with the expansion of the better Buckie harbour to the east.

After Findochty the cliffs rise toward Tronach head, honeycombed with caves and inlets. Do not rush this section, take the time to explore. High tide is best as it gives some great options for weaving in and out of the colourful rock formations. Many of them have local names such as: 'the Priest Craigs' or 'the Horses Head'. The numerous seabirds will be watching you carefully as you paddle by, perhaps the eider ducks will call out to you or the rock you are weaving by might be the drying platform for the shag with its outstretched wings. There is rarely a day when there will not be a bit of excitement to be had in amongst the rocks from swell coming in from the North Sea, adding to the experience and the remote feeling this bit of coastline offers. With its cliff top village overlooking it, Portknockie harbour soon provides another rest spot if required, its name translates very aptly into 'the hilly port'.

As you rock hop along the coast there are plenty of surprises in store. The biggest surprise of all will undoubtedly be your first view of the amazing Bow Fiddle Rock, a wave cut, dramatic natural arch that will rival anything you have seen before. Paddling through the arch with its resident gulls, kittiwakes and shags looking on is a fantastic experience. There is a rocky beach where you can land for a rest and get some great photos of the arch with someone paddling through. Again spend the time to fully explore this area; at low tide can you find the hidden mini arch at the head of a small rock geo? Or can you find the long narrow cave that almost forms a through route? Heading on towards Cullen beach the biggest cave of all is found, and if timed with a high tide it also provides a dramatic through route into a hidden bay.

When arriving at the start of the beach it is best to cut across the bay and head towards the coastline beyond Cullen harbour, the harbour and beach provide resting or stopping points if required. Passing Logie Head look out for climbers who may be enjoying the challenge of climbing on this steep bit of rock that protrudes out into the sea. Just beyond this there is a fantastic beach to take a stop on before paddling under the dramatic Findlater Castle. This castle is best seen from the sea to get a true sense of its dramatic position. The first historic reference to the castle is in 1246 and in 1260 the castle was repaired in preparation for the invasion of King Haakon IV of Norway. What is seen now are the remains from the 14th century rebuilding after the castle had been taken over by the Vikings for some time prior to this. Leaving the castle you are on the final leg of this fantastic journey, keep exploring all the nooks and crannies though and make sure you do not miss the hidden arch guarded by nesting Fulmars just before Crathie point. Soon the small harbour at Sandend will be in sight and this marks the end of the journey. This is the easiest place to land; however Sandend is a favourite local spot for surfing so if you fancy a final bit of action you may prefer a surf session on route to the beach.

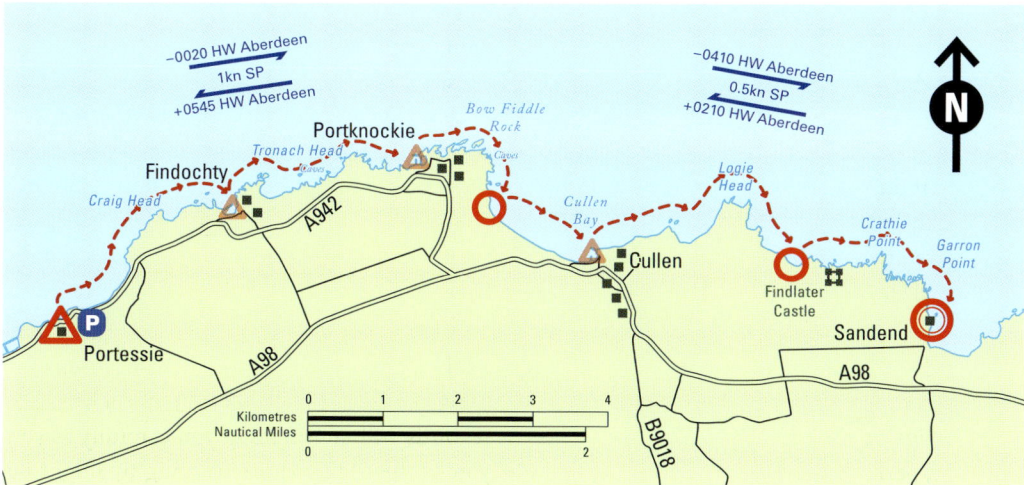

Tides and weather

You will notice a small amount of tide along this coastline, however if there is any wind around it is best to plan considering this, as it will have greater effect. With the large number of rock inlets and caves to be explored, along with Cullen and Sandend beach that can produce big surf, swell should be a key consideration to ensure the best conditions are chosen to enjoy this trip. I would suggest saving it for a day with minimal swell.

Additional information

At Portessie use the Great Eastern Road parking area, alongside a handy café/restaurant. The pub marked on the map at Findochty harbour provides a great place for refreshments mid route and is well worth making the most off. In Cullen be sure to try the world famous Cullen Skink, there is no better way to refuel after a good day's paddle then with a bowl of this fantastic local soup.

Variations

To avoid having to do a shuttle, starting at Portknockie provides a fantastic alternative. There is plenty of parking as well as toilets and an easy launch spot. Paddling out of the harbour and heading east to explore Bow Fiddle Rock and then on to a rest spot at the west end of Cullen beach works well. Heading back past Portknockie and on to Findochty will ensure you get to see the best this coastline has to offer. A refreshment stop at Findochty and then a short paddle back

Findlater Castle

to your vehicle provides a perfect day out and plenty of time to explore as much as you wish on route. Other alternatives could be finishing at Cullen as opposed to continuing to Sandend, or paddling Cullen to Sandend as a separate short trip.

Cullen Skink

Cullen Skink is a thick soup made of smoked haddock, potatoes and onions that originates and is therefore a speciality of the village of Cullen. The rather odd name is said to come from the Gaelic word "Essence" and this essence of Cullen has certainly become a worldwide favourite. Initially Cullen Skink referred to a type of broth made from the scrapings of beef from the front legs of cattle, however hard times in the 1890s left those in the NE of Scotland unable to buy this product. With the village of Cullen specialising in the production of smoked haddock amidst the herring boom during this time the village turned to making their soup out of this more readily available product. Hence the distinctive and delicious Cullen Skink was born and these days can be found served all over Scotland. In July 2012 the inaugural Cullen Skink World Championships were held and of course the winner was born in Cullen and used the traditional family recipe.

Bow Fiddle Rock

© Bow Fiddle Rock

Portsoy harbour

Redhythe Point

No. 24 | Grade A | 16km | OS Sheet 29

Tidal Port	Aberdeen
Start	△ Sandend (NJ 555 666)
Finish	◎ Whitehills (NJ 661 659)
HW/LW	HW/LW at Whitehills is around 1 hour and 30 minutes before Aberdeen.
Tidal Times	Off Knock Head: The E going stream starts at about 3 hours and 50 minutes before HW Aberdeen. The W going stream starts about 2 hours and 10 minutes after HW Aberdeen.
Max Rate Sp	0.5 knots along this section of coast.
Coastguard	Aberdeen, tel. 01224 592334, VHF weather every 3 hours from 0730.

Introduction

This short section of coastline provides plenty of interest with some great rock architecture and remote sandy beaches. There is also the picture-perfect Portsoy harbour to visit and grey seals to keep you company.

Heading towards Redhythe Point from Portsoy

Description

It is easy to launch at either the harbour or the beach at Sandend. There is limited parking if using the harbour so please consider parking at the beach car park once you have dropped the kayaks off. If launching from the beach you may well be doing so with surfers who travel to Sandend for its good surf. Look out for the remains of anti-tank positions and pillbox defences on the beach which were build during World War II to protect against German invasion.

Around the point there are some small caves and this section of coastline offers some great opportunities to weave through some great rock gardens. A few hundred metres past the point be sure to find the tall and narrow arch that hides in amongst the surrounding rock scenery.

Portsoy harbour is one of the most attractive along the Moray Coast and it is rich with history. The village was established as a burgh in a charter signed by Mary, Queen of Scots in 1550. The harbour you will paddle into today was built in 1692 by the 8th Laird of Boyne by placing large stones vertically to form the walls. This was done because they believed the stones would stand less chance of being washed away; the theory seems to have worked as the old harbour you see today is pretty much as it was built originally. There is a sandy beach to land on in the old harbour and it is a great place to take a break from the paddling. There are handy cafés and pubs for well-earned refreshments and it will also allow time to soak in the history of this special place. The old trade buildings of the harbour surround you as you walk around; coal was imported here and locally-produced thread and linen were exported. A particular speciality is the locally-quarried green Portsoy marble or serpentine which was a key export in years gone by and is still used and sold today. The new outer harbour was built in 1825 to meet the demands of the herring boom,

Redhythe Point

although the fishing trade has declined the history and beauty of Portsoy has lead to a very sustainable tourist trade.

On leaving Portsoy you will head across to the lower lying headland of East Head. Once around the headland the grassy slopes that lead down to the sea become steeper and the coastline will feel a little more remote. There are a couple of lovely beaches to land on at Strathmarchin Bay and in Boyne Bay that are not really marked on the map.

Whitehills has a long fishing history as many of the Moray Firth harbours do. However with Whitehills the fishing continued until the late 1990s when eventually it was decide to build a marina as the fishing was no longer sustainable. Before this happened Whitehills made its name as the smallest port in Scotland that operated its own vessels and had its own fish market. It is also the home to a lifeboat station that opened in 1860, which is still operational and can be seen as you enter the harbour. As the harbour and marina are busy places, it is worth continuing on to Knock Head. As you go around this low-lying headland you will be rewarded with a view across to Banff and Macduff, and then on to the spectacular headland of Troup Head. The finish to this trip is a few hundred metres past Knock Head near the old harbour that was used by the Blackpots Brick and Tile Works; there is a caravan site and café in the former brick works location now. As you land you may well notice some of the red-coloured clay along the foreshore that was used for the bricks and tiles. The clay was quarried from Knock Head and supplied essential material for the manufacture of pipes, tiles and bricks at the factory from about 1788 until it finally closed in 1974.

Tides and weather

There is very little tidal movement along this section of coastline, so it is best to plan the trip to take advantage of the wind rather than the tide. This section of coastline is exposed to any north

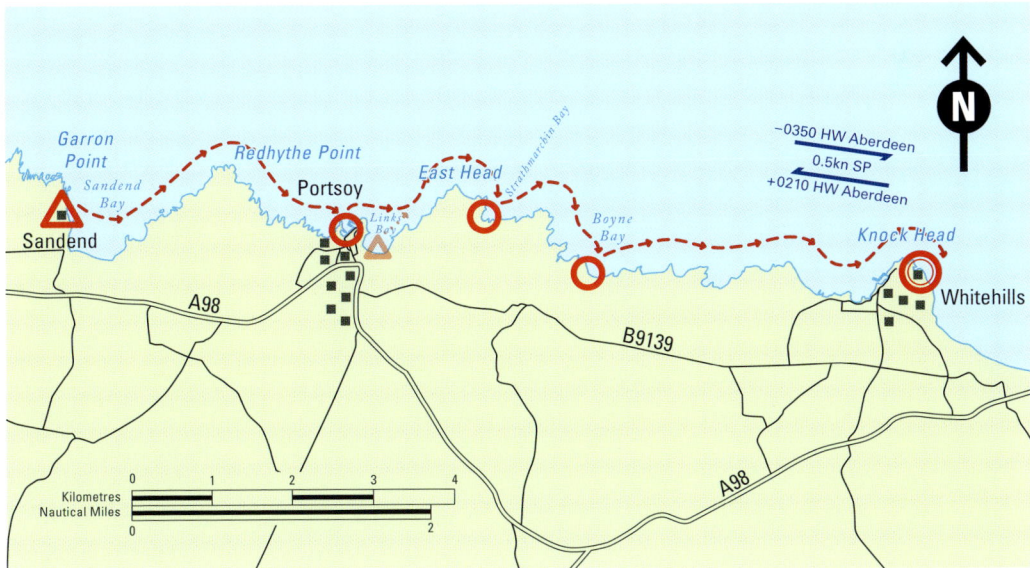

Whitehills harbour

or east swell and this should be taken into account when planning the trip, as launching and landing could become a challenge.

Additional information

There are no amenities at Sandend, however at Portsoy there are plenty of cafés and pubs to choose from. Whitehills also provides local amenities. If choosing to launch or land at Portsoy the harbour has limited parking so please consider launching at Links Bay to the east where there are toilets and parking available.

Variations

To avoid a shuttle the trip could be started and finished at Links Bay/Portsoy, heading along to Knock head and then coming back past Portsoy, stopping for a refreshment break in the harbour, and continuing out to Redhythe Point and back. This would ensure the best part of this coastline is explored and could be tailored to meet time and ability considerations. To lengthen the trip, starting at Cullen would make for a great day out.

Banff to Gardenstown

No. 25 | Grade A | 14km | OS Sheet 29

Tidal Port	Aberdeen
Start	△ Banff (NJ 694 642)
Finish	○ Gardenstown (NJ 799 648)
HW/LW	HW/LW at Banff is around 1 hour and 30 minutes before Aberdeen.
Tidal Times	Off Banff Bay: The E going stream starts about 3 hours and 50 minutes before HW Aberdeen. The W going stream starts about 2 hours and 10 minutes after HW Aberdeen.
Max Rate Sp	0.5 knots along this section of coast.
Coastguard	Aberdeen, tel. 01224 592334, VHF weather every 3 hours from 0730.

Introduction

The contrast of a busy working harbour at the start and a sleepy picturesque harbour at the finish, along with a steep grassy coastline provide the key ingredients for this short trip. An impressive headland at the end of the trip with the possibilities of dolphins on route make for a good short day out.

Macduff coastline

Description

Launching into Banff Bay from the beach on the east side of the River Deveron offers plenty of parking and not too long a carry. If there is any surf around it will also provide for a start of the trip wake-up call, with a wave in the face while leaving the beach. Along this section of coastline the fishing town of Macduff dominates the view. The large harbour is separated into a few parts, the entrance being marked by an impressive white tower. Be aware that this is still a very active harbour and there will be large boats operating in the area. Note the large fishing boats up on the shore being built and worked on. This is now the only place in the UK where deep-water wooden fishing boats are still built. Before the houses of Macduff are left behind the first cave of the trip is found, unnervingly it leads into the cliff right below a housing estate, I wonder if the owners of the houses realise this? Just beyond this there are some small stacks and rocks that lead into a bay that has a large seawater swimming pool built on its shore. Although run down and a bit dilapidated now, it used to be a key local and tourist attraction in the Victorian era. Look out for the rock arch on the shore alongside it.

On leaving Macduff the coastline takes on a far remoter feel, and staying in close provides plenty of opportunity to paddle amongst small skerries and stacks as well as the occasional cave. At the Head of Garness the steep headland of More Head will come into view, which provides a fitting climax to this section of coastline. The cliffs leading towards the headland are steep and grassy. There are a couple of possible landing spots along this section of coastline, both rocky beaches with one just beyond the Head of Garness and the other around the corner from

Stocked Head. The coastline provides ideal nesting conditions for peregrine falcons, which can be seen, or more likely heard, whilst paddling along. At More Head the cliffs rise out of the Moray Firth and start to tower above. In the distance Troup Head will be visible, the most dramatic of all the Moray Firth headlands on its south coast. The striking white colour is caused by the thousands of gannets that make it their home.

As you paddle across the bay to the finish at Gardenstown you will see the historic church of St John's above which was built in 1513 and offers fantastic views of the town and Troup Head beyond. The original part of the town is nestled at the foot of the hillside by the harbour and the new part of town is up on the hill. It is impossible not to fall in love with the bright coloured boats and houses that surround the harbour, along with the way they are all packed in so tightly at the foot of the hill just metres back from the sea front. The harbour is still used on a small scale, with tourism playing a key part. It is well worth paddling in to enjoy the harbour, but if it is around high tide finishing the trip on the stony beach to the east of the harbour provides better parking and is more out of the way.

Tides and weather

There is little tidal movement along this section of coast so plan the trip to take into account the effect of the wind. Any swell from the north or east will affect this trip and make launching at the start challenging, and any further landings until Gardenstown will also be very awkward.

Additional information

Banff and Macduff have plenty of local amenities, with Macduff also having a good aquarium, www.macduff-aquarium.org.uk If the conditions are not suitable to land on the stony beach at Gardenstown then the harbour can be used, but if you choose to launch here please pay the launching fee that goes towards the upkeep of the harbour that the villagers maintain. There is a restaurant in the harbour area at Gardenstown that is open a few evenings a week.

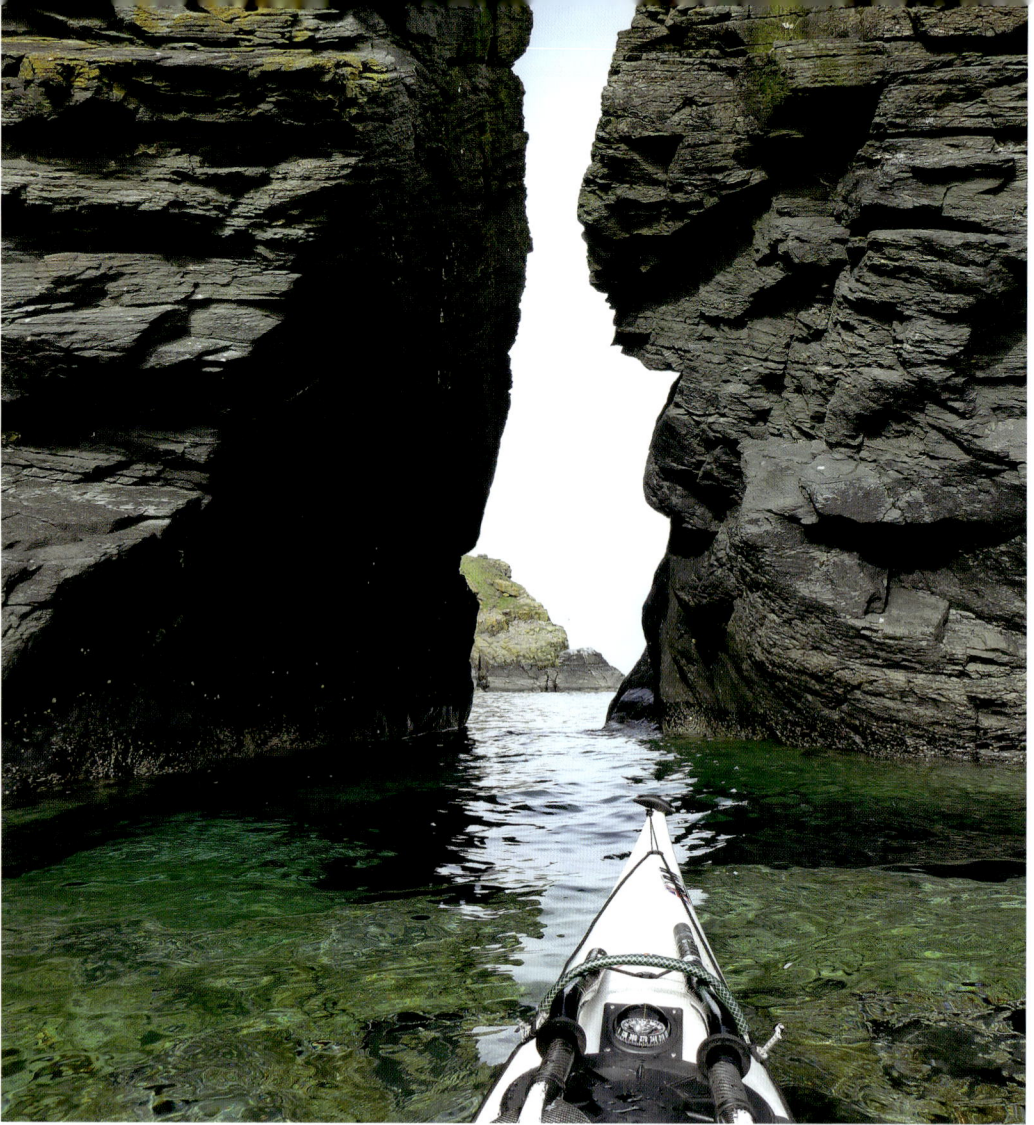

Rock gap under More Head

Variations

This trip can be extended by continuing on around Troup Head and finishing at the get out at Cullykhan Bay (NJ 839 657) or Aberdour Bay (NJ 886 646) as described in the next chapter. This is recommended if time and conditions allow, however this section of coastline is more exposed than the sections previously paddled. If launching in Banff Bay is challenging with the surf an alternative put in at the old sea swimming pool (NJ 719 646) may be easier.

© *Heading towards Crovie village and Troup Head*

Troup Head ⬛⬛⬛⬛⬛⬛

No. 26 | Grade B | 19km | OS Sheet 30

|---|---|
Tidal Port	Aberdeen
Start	△ Gardenstown (NJ 799 648)
Finish	○ Rosehearty (NJ 935 677)
HW/LW	HW/LW at Gardenstown is around 1 hour and 10 minutes before Aberdeen.
Tidal Times	Off Troup Head: The E going stream starts about 3 hours and 50 minutes before HW Aberdeen. The W going stream starts about 2 hours and 10 minutes after HW Aberdeen.
Max Rate Sp	2 knots off Troup Head, 0.5 knots along the rest of the coast.
Coastguard	Aberdeen, tel. 01224 592334, VHF weather every 3 hours from 0730.

Introduction

This is a fantastic trip and arguably the best that the Moray Firth has to offer. The cliffs rise up to 100 metres with caves, arches and hauled out seals at their feet. Troup Head itself offers the only mainland gannet colony in Scotland, and the villages en route are picturesque with small harbours and colourful houses. This is a trip that you will not forget.

Description

Gardenstown harbour, with the old fishing houses crammed in side by side is the perfect starting point for this trip. You can launch at the rocky beach just to the east of the harbour from mid tide to high water. If you choose to launch at the harbour please pay the launching fee that goes towards the upkeep of the harbour that the villagers maintain. Leaving Gardenstown, or 'Gamrie' as the locals would call it, you head along the coast towards the tiny village of Crovie, a single row of houses that nestle into the hillside tight under the cliffs, so much so that there is no road access and cars have to be left to the south of the village. The village was established in the late 18th century when families were cleared from the inland farms and estates to make way for sheep. The displaced families soon learnt the trade of fishing, as it was the only way to make a living. This was the sole source of income until it came to a sharp end in January 1953 when a storm washed away a number of structures and forced the residents to flee. Nowadays most of the buildings have been turned into holiday lets.

Towards Troup Head sea stacks start to appear as the cliffs rise dramatically above. Beneath these cliffs you may well see puffins casually paddling in the water and above you the unmistakable shape and bright white of gannets circling. Troup Head is home to the only mainland colony of gannets in Scotland and there are over 500 pairs breeding here. The cliffs that soar high above are covered with gannets, their nests clinging to the rock face. Looking up it may well be difficult to make out the sky through the mass of gannets. As you paddle on to Lions Head there are numerous seabirds including over 44,000 pairs of guillemot and 30,000 pairs of kittiwake alongside fulmars, razorbills and puffins. Look out for the subterranean tunnel that leads from the sea to the blowhole known as 'Hell's Lum' (a Lum being a chimney in Scots); the tunnel is marked with two dashed lines on the map. If you go in close you can look into this narrow slot and see the shaft of light that comes down through the blowhole illuminating the deep insides.

The village of Pennan provides a picturesque resting point and a handy pub if refreshments are required. Here is another example of a purpose built fishing village that is squeezed in between the steep hillside and the unforgiving sea, the houses being tightly packed together. It became famous in 1983 when it was used as one of the main locations for the film 'Local Hero'; film enthusiasts travel from all over the world to visit Pennan and see the red telephone box that was a key focal point in the film. The phone box in the film was in fact just a prop, but as a result of popular demand a genuine telephone box was installed after the film and has been a listed building since 1989. Leaving Pennan you will also leave the grey metamorphic rock that has made up the cliffs so far, soon coming across the interesting shapes and colours of the conglomerate rock that rises up to over 100 metres along the next bit of coastline. This fascinating section of coastline has numerous caves, arches and through routes. The cliffs are steep with rock and grass towering above, and there may well be seals hauled out resting on the numerous skerries. As you approach Aberdour Bay make sure you don't miss the final dramatic arch that is a fitting finale to this stunning section of coastline.

Aberdour Bay provides another good stopping point, or alternative finish if required. The final section of coastline to Rosehearty should provide a relaxing finish to this dramatic journey, although not as spectacular there will still be some sea birds and seals for company and it should allow time to reflect on a great day out. Rosehearty is one of the oldest seaports in Scotland, having been associated with fishing for at least 600 years.

Whilst coming into land at the sandy beach next to the harbour spare a thought for the less lucky shipmates of the SS *Fram*. In the early hours of a stormy February morning in 1940 a German U-boat attacked the SS *Fram* just out from Rosehearty; she went down quickly and the local fishing boats did all they could to save the lives of the crew, but sadly ten did not make it. The wreck of the SS *Fram* is still on the seabed and divers can explore this reminder of a sad event in the Moray Firth's history.

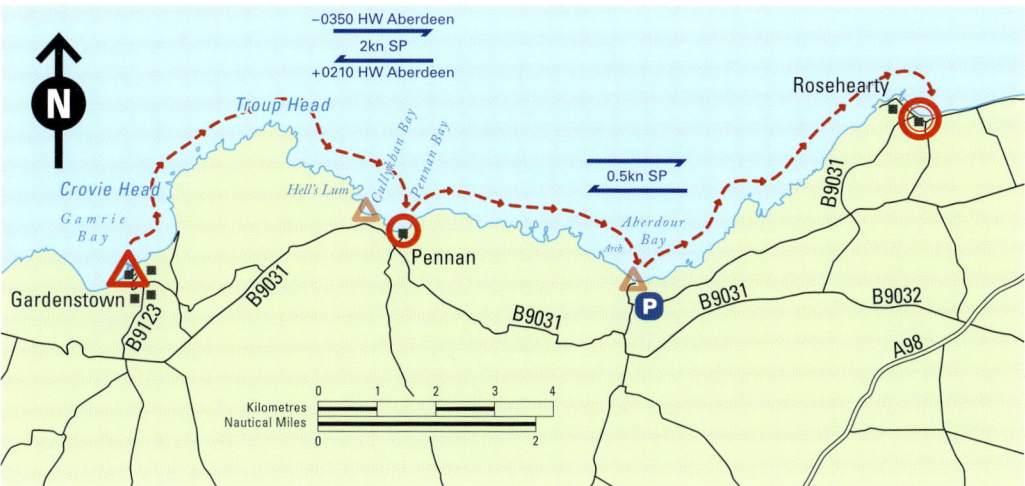

Tides and weather

The tides run up to 2kn off Troup Head so it is best to time this trip starting when the east going tidal stream starts. This will give tidal assistance throughout the journey. The high cliffs can produce down draughts and funnelling in strong winds and care should be taken. The trip can be paddled in the opposite direction if the wind is from the east, planning the tides accordingly by starting when the west going stream starts.

Additional information

There is a restaurant in the harbour area at Gardenstown that is open a few evenings a week, along with a pub in Pennan and plenty of local services at Rosehearty. There are no services at Aberdour Bay. There can be quite dumpy surf at Aberdour Bay, and if this is the case, by landing or launching beyond the little burn to the west of the car park you can make use of the channels between the skerries that stretch out to sea and dampen the down the waves.

Variations

If a shorter journey is preferred, finishing at Cullykhan Bay (NJ 839 657) or Aberdour Bay (NJ 886 646) works well. To avoid the need for a shuttle by starting and finishing at either of these bays you can paddle to Troup Head and back, making the most of Pennan as a stopping place if you wish. This will allow you to enjoy the most spectacular part of this journey, and paddle it twice!

Shipwrecks

It was in 1884 that Jane Whyte, a local lady, saved the lives of fifteen men whose ship had lost power whilst passing Troup Head in a storm. Having drifted at the mercy of the sea and storm the crew were clinging onto their sinking ship when they saw Jane on the beach. They threw her a rope and she swam out into the stormy sea to reach the rope that she then took ashore. All of the crew were saved thanks to her heroic efforts. In due course Jane's bravery was to be recognised and she received the RNLI's Silver Medal.

Fraserburgh Bay

Kinnaird Head 🦪🌊

No. 27 | Grade A | 8km | OS Sheet 30

Tidal Port	Aberdeen
Start	△ Sandhaven (NJ 967 675)
Finish	◯ Cairnbulg (NK 034 656)
HW/LW	HW/LW at Fraserburgh is around 1 hour and 10 minutes before Aberdeen.
Tidal Times	Off Kinnaird Head: The SE going stream starts about 4 hours and 40 minutes before HW Aberdeen. The NW going stream starts about 1 hour and 40 minutes after HW Aberdeen.
Max Rate Sp	1.5 knots off Kinnaird Head.
Coastguard	Aberdeen, tel. 01224 592334, VHF weather every 3 hours from 0730.

Introduction

This short trip involves a paddle around the headland where the waters of the Moray Firth meet the North Sea. For the lighthouse spotters out there it also provides a great view of the first lighthouse to be constructed by the Northern Lighthouse Board. This along with the immaculate sands of Fraserburgh Bay and seals basking at Cairnbulg Point makes for a more than worthwhile trip.

The Wine Tower and 'blood coloured rocks'

27 Kinnaird Head

Description

The dilapidated harbour walls of Sandhaven provide plenty of evidence of the North Sea storms that batter this coastline. With the fishing industry long gone, any form of repair and maintenance of this historic harbour is too much of a financial challenge for the village. Local fisherman petitioned the Herring Fishing Commissioners in Edinburgh for a harbour in 1835. Permission was granted and the local laird paid the fishermen's twenty-five percent portion of the harbour costs. They repaid this in kind by fish landings over a period of four years. Paddling out of this now almost forgotten harbour it is hard to believe that at its busiest there were over 100 fishing boats employing more than 700 men, along with an additional 300 fish workers processing the catch in Sandhaven.

A low-lying shore leads to the town of Fraserburgh and very soon Kinnaird Head with its lighthouse will be clearly visible. Although not a significant headland in stature, it is significant in location as it marks the turning point for ships entering the more sheltered waters of the Moray Firth from the North Sea.

On the North Sea side of the head stands a square building called the Wine Tower which is thought to have been either a customs house for the port or a private chapel for the Lord's wife. Legend has it that the angry Lord locked his daughter in the tower while her lover, a piper who the Lord disapproved of, was imprisoned in a cave below. At high tide the imprisoned piper drowned and the heartbroken daughter threw herself from the top window of the tower. It is said that the haunting tunes of the piper can still be heard today as his ghost searches for his lover yet finds only the blood soaked stones beneath the tower. These blood coloured rocks can still be seen, due to the lighthouse keeper throwing paint every year on the spot where the tragedy happened.

Just around the corner you will pass the tower that marks the entrance to the busy Fraserburgh harbour. Take extreme care in this area as big ships use this port and most definitely have right of way. This is one of the main commercial ports on the east coast, the biggest shellfish port in Europe and a major whitefish and cargo port. Fraserburgh was also the first place in Scotland for an official RNLI station to open, in 1858, and since then it has provided assistance to numerous seafarers and saved many lives. Sadly it has also been faced with tragedy with three lifeboat disasters, in 1918, 1953 and 1970. A monument was unveiled in 2010 to honour the fourteen men who lost their lives in these disasters.

Lights and legends

Kinnaird Head is such an important location from a navigation point of view it is no wonder that the Northern Lighthouse Board chose it as the first place to construct a light. The original lighthouse does not conform to the classic design we have since become used to. Fraserburgh Castle dates back to 1570 and in 1787 a light was simply fitted to the top of it. The master lighthouse engineer himself, Robert Stevenson, then updated the light in 1824, with the original castle structure still being used as part of the new light. The modern light, which the ships look for these days, is a far less grand affair alongside.

The stunning beach that forms Fraserburgh Bay will provide an ideal resting spot, providing there isn't too much swell. The beach is over three kilometres long and provides a fantastic backdrop while paddling to the finish at Cairnbulg harbour. Take the time to paddle out for a closer look at the beacon off Cairnbulg Point. The beacon marks the skerries with the wreck of a boat sitting upon them. These skerries are home to numerous grey seals. Be sure to avoid disturbing them, particularly if it is in the September pupping season. The harbour at Cairnbulg has plenty of parking as well as shelter from any swell.

Tides and weather

A small amount of tidal movement affects Kinnaird Head so timing the trip to take advantage of this is useful, but not essential. The headland is exposed to wind and swell and this should be a greater consideration when planning this trip. The swell will make a landing on the beach challenging and will also provide waves and rough water around the low-lying rocks off much of the coastline.

Additional information

There are no facilities in Sandhaven or Cairnbulg, however there is a small shop in Inverallochy. Fraserburgh offers a full range of amenities including the Scottish Lighthouse Museum at Kinnaird Head. This is well worth a visit and also has a great café. www.lighthousemuseum.org.uk

Variations

To avoid the need for a shuttle, launching at Fraserburgh beach (NK 001 663) provides a useful alternative. Paddle out to Kinnaird Head then across the bay to Cairnbulg Point and along the beach back to the start.

Aberdeen Coast

Introduction

Aberdeen is known as the 'Granite City', and perhaps this area should be known as the granite coast. It has the most spectacular granite coastal scenery that Scotland has to offer and the cliffs are constantly eroded and sculpted by the North Sea swell. The area starts and finishes with two of Scotland's most famous lighthouses, namely the historic Kinnaird Head to the north and Bell Rock to the south, the latter often referred to as one of the wonders of the industrial world. In between there is a host of other dramatic lighthouses, all built by the Stevenson dynasty of lighthouse engineers. This coastline also offers some of Scotland's most dramatically famous castles. The haunting Slains Castle near Cruden Bay being one example and the historically significant Dunnottar Castle near Stonehaven another.

Another aspect of man's impact on the area is the exploitation of the North Sea oil reserves. The oil industry is all too apparent along this coastline, whether it be the large ships seen off the coast, the helicopters overhead ferrying out the workers, or the huge oil refinery plants along the shores.

Despite so much evidence of human activity you will have plenty of wildlife for company when paddling along this coastline. The birdlife in this area is incredible and in the summer months a day's paddle will be shared with thousands of birds, including guillemots, razorbills, kittiwakes and plenty of puffins. The bird reserve of Fowlsheugh near Stonehaven is particularly noteworthy for its birdlife, as are the cliffs south of Boddam and south of Crudden Bay. There will often be numerous grey seals hauled out on the rocks, in particular off Cairnbulg Point and just south of Cruden Bay at the 'Skares'. Near Aberdeen keep an eye out for the dolphins that have taken up residence close to the harbour entrance.

As well as the big towns and key commercial fishing ports of Fraserburgh, Peterhead, Aberdeen and Montrose there is a wealth of picturesque small fishing villages to enjoy. Stonehaven, with its harbourside pubs, restaurants and cafés, is a great place to relax after a day on the water, as are Port Errol, Collieston and Inverbervie, and many other small harbours and villages. Fishing harbours, beaches, cliffs, caves, stacks and arches litter this coastline. In the north of the area the Bullars of Buchan section has to be seen to be believed; it is a magical place to paddle. South from here, the trips from Cove and Stonehaven provide some fantastic cliffs as well as the hidden gem of the sandstone cliffs just north of Arbroath.

Arbroath and Bell Rock provide a fitting finish to this area with amazing paddles of great contrast. Whichever is chosen the fish shops of Arbroath are second to none and enjoying a traditional 'Arbroath Smokie' is not to be missed.

Tides and weather

The strongest tidal streams in this area are at Rattray Head, this combined with the shallow water and sand bars can make for some interesting water. There are some slightly faster flows off the

© Natural arch near Bullers of Buchan

headlands just south of Stonehaven, but in general the tidal movement is fairly insignificant. The exposure to any swell coming from the North Sea is the biggest consideration when paddling in this area. Getting a swell forecast is essential when planning any of the trips as any swell from the north or east could well make a day's paddle unpleasant at best and impossible at worst. Due to the linear nature of this coastline there is no hiding from any swell or wind, thus many of the trips have the potential to be quite a committing undertaking and this should be considered before starting out.

Rattray Head ▦▦〰

No. 28 | Grade B | 19km | OS Sheet 30

Tidal Port	Aberdeen
Start	△ Cairnbulg (NK 034 656)
Finish	○ Scotstown (NK 113 523)
HW/LW	HW/LW at Scotstown is around 40 minutes before Aberdeen.
Tidal Times	Off Rattray Head: The SE going stream starts about 4 hours and 40 minutes before HW Aberdeen. The NW going stream starts about 1 hour and 40 minutes after HW Aberdeen.
Max Rate Sp	2–3 knots off Rattray Head.
Coastguard	Aberdeen, tel. 01224 592334, VHF weather every 3 hours from 0730.

Introduction

For those familiar with the inshore waters forecast Rattray Head will be a household name. As it happens it is not a headland at all, but more an area of sand dunes that project into the North Sea. Its lighthouse rises up from the shallow waters with a backdrop of sand, and this provides an unusual focus for the journey.

Description

28

The harbour at Cairnbulg provides ample parking and an easy launching spot to head off from. Once a busy harbour home to many fishing boats it is a quiet and almost deserted place now. Leaving the harbour the view will be across to the large harbour and town of Fraserburgh and Kinnaird Head that marks the south eastern entrance into the Moray Firth. The beacon at Cairnbulg Point marks some treacherous skerries that guard the approach to the harbour. The wreck of the Banff registered *Sovereign* that foundered here in 2005 is evidence of the hazard these skerries pose. Along with the wreck you may see some Atlantic grey seals hauled out on the rocks as you paddle past.

The coastline consists of low-lying rocks and sandy bays that are backed by the Inverallochy golf course. This leads down to the village of St Combs. This tightly packed village provides the final section of rocky foreshore before the extensive beaches and sand dunes that lead down to Rattray Head and beyond. These sand dunes can reach up to seventy-five feet high and stretch approximately seventeen miles along this section of coastline. There will often be surf along this entire section of coastline, so if you wish to save the surf landing until the finish, take a break at St Combs.

At Rattray Head the sea can often be quite confused as the waves collide from two different angles and the tide pushes around the sandy low lying headland. At low tide the skerries will be exposed as well as the causeway that was built to allow access to the lighthouse. The light's white tower is built on carefully crafted granite blocks and stands thirty four metres high, again it was the Stevenson family who was involved in the construction, this time David in 1895. The

Cairnbulg Point

△

Cairnbulg
Inverallochy

B9107

B9033

St Combs

B9033

Loch of
Strathbeg

A90

Crimond

N

−0440 HW Aberdeen
2kn SP
+0140 HW Aberdeen

Rattray Head

Kilometres
Nautical Miles

0   1   2

0   1

St Fergus
Gas terminal

A90

Scotstown

P

Scotstown
Head

lighthouse, with the beautiful sand dunes as the backdrop and surrounded by shallow seas is simply beautiful. If the surf allows, there are plenty of landing opportunities here.

The sands continue, yet the backdrop changes quite dramatically along this final section of coastline. Keep an eye out on the beach for the remains of four wrecks mostly buried by the sand (easiest seen at low water). These wrecks are from the 1800s and go to show why the local seafarers pressed hard to get a light built at Rattray Head (they had to agree to pay for the upkeep of the light).

The huge St Fergus gas plant dominates the scenery, with three main pipelines that come ashore here and it is a stark reminder that this paddle is taking you into the heart of the UK's oil and gas industry that supports the North Sea rigs. This gas plant receives about twenty percent of the UK's gas.

Scotstown is a useful place to finish this trip. The sand dunes continue on to Peterhead, so the carry out to the convenient parking area will save the additional paddle along this unchanging coastline. There may well be some surf to contend when landing and it will require a keen eye and careful navigation to land at the sandy track through the dunes that leads to the parking area. Arriving near high water will avoid too much of a carry, and a kayak trolley would be useful.

Tides and weather

Wind and surf will have a large impact on how pleasant this trip is. Save it for a day when there is little wind and no surf so that the beaches and lighthouse can be enjoyed rather than avoided. Any swell from the north through east will affect this coastline.

There is tidal movement off Rattray Head, and this can flow fast close in around the light with a small tidal race forming off the light in certain conditions. Aim to make use of the south going tidal stream that starts at 4 hours and 40 minutes before HW Aberdeen when planning this trip.

Additional information

There are no amenities at Cairnbulg or Scotstown, however nearby Fraserburgh and Peterhead are large towns with plenty to offer.

The Fable of Rattray Head

for some reason they made Rattray Head big
so big it reached up into the clouds
flat iron big: empire state big

ships had no trouble seeing its light
trouble was
all over Scotland and even in England
they could see it

this was no good for navigation
"it's not local enough": said the captains
of the herring boats and the whalers
the committee responsible had to agree

the engineer said, "no problem
this light was built on the Matryoshka Principle
like the Russian nesting dolls
I'll organise a crane"

and when they lifted the tower up
underneath was an identical but smaller lighthouse
much more suited to local navigation
this is what we see today…

(Scottish Lighthouse Poems, Knotbrook Taylor, www.knotbrook.co.uk and Blue Salt Publishing, www.bluesalt.co.uk Working with the Scottish Lighthouse Museum, www.lighthousemuseum.org.uk)

Rattray Head

Rattray Head lighthouse

Arch just south of Bullers of Buchan

Bullers of Buchan ▣▣▣

No. 29 | Grade B | 10km | OS Sheet 30

Tidal Port	Aberdeen
Start	△ Boddam Harbour (NK 134 426)
Finish	⬭ Port Erroll (NK 094 356)
HW/LW	HW/LW at Boddam is around the same time as Aberdeen.
Tidal Times	Along this section of coastline: The SSW going stream starts about 4 hours before HW Aberdeen. The NNE going stream starts about 2 hours after HW Aberdeen. On spring tides the above times may be up to one hour earlier.
Max Rate Sp	1 knot along this section of coastline.
Coastguard	Aberdeen, tel. 01224 592334, VHF weather every 3 hours from 0730.

Introduction

This is a gem of a trip along an impressive coastline dominated by granite cliffs. For many years rock climbers have used the cliffs for sport, but for an even longer time thousands of seabirds have made these cliffs their home during the breeding season. Despite the hardness of the rock, the relentless work of the waves has produced some fine caves and incredible natural arches.

Description

Boddam provides plenty of parking and an easy launch site to start this fantastic trip from. As you leave the harbour the impressive Buchan Ness lighthouse will overlook you. Built by Robert Stevenson in 1827, it stands on an island connected to the mainland by a bridge. The distinctive red bands on the tower were added in 1907 as an aid to identifying it more easily during the day.

Monkey business

A ship was wrecked just off Boddam and the villagers could not claim salvage rights due to a monkey being the sole survivor, as those rights could only be applied if all had perished or abandoned ship. A verse of a traditional local song will provide the answer as to how the locals overcame the problem.

A ship went out along the coast,

And all the men on board were lost,

Except the monkey, who climbed the mast,

And the Boddamers hinged the monkey O!

If the local dialect is a challenge then a pub in Aberdeen that was named "Noose and Monkey" will also provide a clue!

The coastline to Long Haven provides plenty of nooks and crannies to explore, and you may well see some rock climbers enjoying the granite cliffs as well. Hare Craig and the other islands in this area are favoured nesting sites for birds, being inaccessible for land-based predators. Be sure to give the nesting birds a wide birth to avoid too much disturbance. Just past Murdoch Head is the Round Tower, sitting high up on the left. It is an impressive tower with one of the finest concentrations of hard rock climbs on the coast. Beyond this the granite walls of rock continue to provide plenty to explore and discover, with caves and inlets all the way to a landing spot at North Haven. As with other landing options on the trip, this is likely to be a bouldery experience so care should be taken. The little subsidiary bay on the left has an interesting small natural arch, which you can pass through just before landing.

Soon the impressive 'Bullers of Buchan' are reached. Enter into the 'Boiler of Buchan' through the large entrance arch and you should arrive in an amazing place of calm and verticality. With a big sea from the east it really would be a 'boiler' and you can only imagine what a ferocious place it must be. Although this incredible rock feature is justifiably well known, as you continue along the coast as there are plenty of amazing rock features of a similar grandeur. Along with these the cliffs will also become smothered with seabirds. The island of Dunbuy with its arch in the sky

will have guillemots constantly streaming off the cliffs and heading out to sea, and the mainland cliffs will be awash with kittiwakes noisily calling out to each other warning of your approach.

After the double inlet called Twa Haven comes the last arch of the day, called the Bow. This double arch sits high above the sea. The ruin of Slains Castle now dominates the skyline. Some say that it was this castle that provided Bram Stoker with inspiration to write his famous novel 'Dracula', as he regularly holidayed in this area. The castle is an imposing sight from the sea, perched on the very edge of the cliffs with huge gaping holes in the walls where the large windows once faced the full rage of storms coming in from the North Sea. It is possible to paddle up a long narrow inlet behind the castle, accessed from the north, and make a landing.

Weaving in and out of small skerries will take you to the finish at Port Erroll, which is situated on the north end of the Bay of Cruden. The harbour here has a fine sandy beach along with parking close to the slipway.

Tides and weather

This section of coastline is exposed to any swell from the north and east and this should be avoided so as the caves and arches can be explored. Making use of the south going tidal stream is ideal, however this is relatively weak and if the wind or timing dictate otherwise then it is not too much of a problem.

Additional information

There are plenty of local amenities at both Boddam and at Port Erroll.

Variations

It is well worth extending the start of the trip by paddling out around 'The Skerry' just north east of Boddam. This little rock usually has many Atlantic grey seals relaxing on it as well as plenty in the sea swimming around. The trip can be paddled in either direction and to avoid a shuttle the distance is not too excessive to paddle to Port Errol and back, thus enjoying the amazing rock scenery twice!

Colllieston harbour

Port Erroll to Collieston

No. 30 | Grade A | 10km | OS Sheet 30 & 38

Tidal Port	Aberdeen
Start	△ Port Erroll (NK 094 356)
Finish	○ Collieston (NK 043 286)
HW/LW	HW/LW Collieston is around the same time as Aberdeen.
Tidal Times	Along this section of coastline: The SSW going stream starts about 4 hours before HW Aberdeen. The NNE going stream starts about 2 hours after HW Aberdeen. On spring tides the above times may be up to one hour earlier.
Max Rate Sp	1 knot along this section of coastline.
Coastguard	Aberdeen, tel. 01224 592334, VHF weather every 3 hours from 0730.

Introduction

Paddling this trip feels like exploring a forgotten coastline and although only short it offers a great deal. An amazing beach, good cliff scenery, picturesque harbours and an incredible array of birdlife will more than make up for its short distance. A perfect short day out or evening paddle.

Description

Port Erroll overlooks the sweeping sands of Cruden Bay. At high tide, the sandy beach in the heart of the small harbour is a perfect launching site. The harbour was constructed in 1875 with as many as 180 fishermen and 68 boats operating from it at its peak; nowadays the main business for this small community is tourism. Many years ago, the Great North of Scotland Railway company promoted Cruden Bay as the Brighton of the north, only twelve hours from London with the opening of the new railway. Luckily this level of tourism never quite took off and as you leave this picturesque community and paddle along the amazing sands of the Bay of Cruden it certainly will not be crowded.

Head out to explore the mass of skerries known as the 'Skares'. These are a haven for seals and as you pass by there will be plenty hauled out on the rocks sleeping or warily watching you pass; try not to disturb them if at all possible. The next section of coastline starts with a cacophony of sound as the kittiwakes and guillemots will be calling out from their nests on the cliffs ledges above. Having picked a way through a few close-in skerries, an obvious sea stack that forms an eye of a needle high above will soon come into view. It is guarded on all sides by nesting birds and as you paddle past it and turn the corner it will be to see cliffs lined with hundreds of birds, perhaps this is the Brighton of the north for the birds!

As you paddle towards the sandy beach at Broad Haven there will be a few more caves to explore as well as a wide tower like sea stack that can be paddled around at high water. The sandy beach at Broad Haven is an ideal stopping place and it is overlooked by Old Slains Castle. There is not much left of this 13th century castle today as it was destroyed in the late 1500s by cannons during a battle between the Earl of Errol and James VI. You may well have noticed puffins out on the water if it is early summer. Watch out for the detached grass and earth-topped wide stack of rock as you paddle around the headland below the castle. Looking closely you will see it is covered in the burrows that the puffins make their nests in. There will be plenty stood around on the stack watching for their breeding partners to return with a load of fish to feed the young 'pufflings' in the burrows.

Low-lying cliffs and skerries lead all the way to the small beach at St Catherine's Dub, Collieston. There is ample parking here compared to the small harbour that can get busy in the summer months. Before getting off the water, it is worth paddling into the harbour to see the fantastic beach that it encloses. It is surrounded by a colourful amphitheatre of fishing houses, hauled up boats and a hillside of summer flowers.

Tides and weather

There is little tidal movement along this section of coastline so planning the trip to take into account the wind is recommended. At low water the harbour at Port Erroll can dry out and be quite muddy, so planning to launch or land there towards high water is worth considering. As with all trips along this coastline any swell from the north or east will make this trip considerably more committing, however it will be possible to launch and land at the harbours.

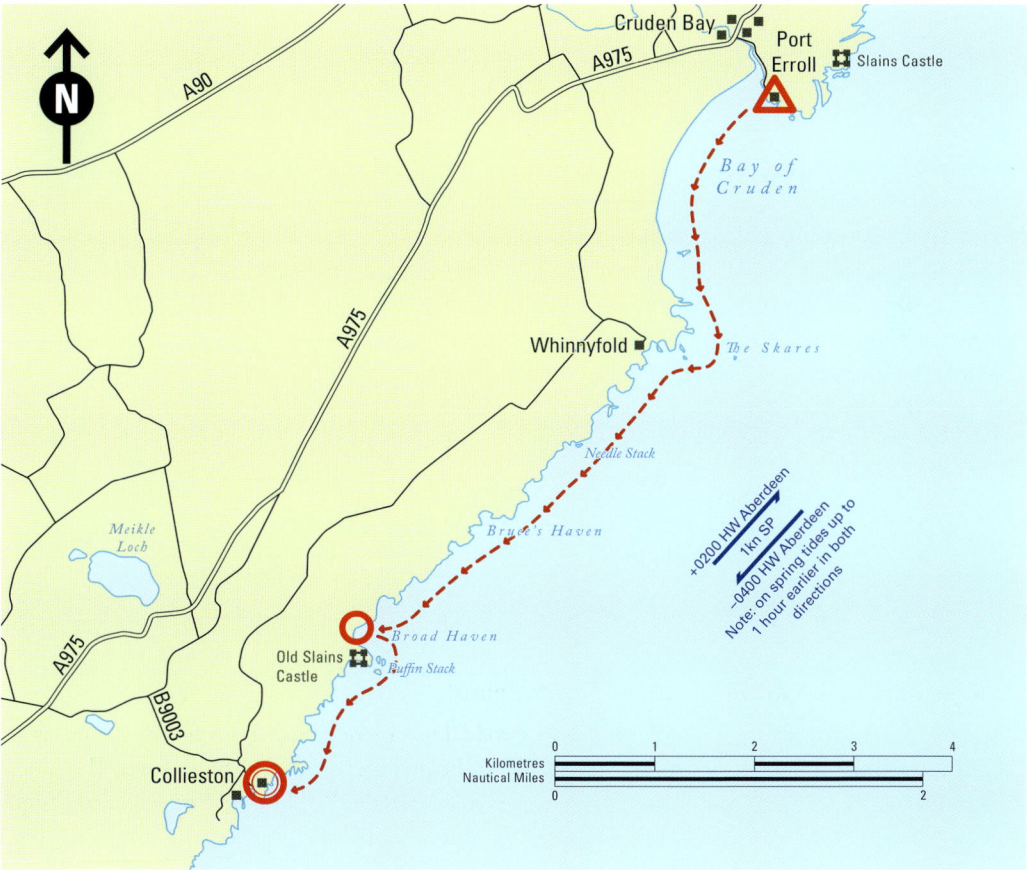

Additional information

There are local amenities at the start and finish of the trip. If there is any surf coming in to the coastline then landing/launching within Collieston harbour will be easier than at the recommended St Catherine's Dub. If launching here please park considerately, perhaps dropping off boats and parking at the large car park already described. Please contribute to the harbour's upkeep using the honesty box that is at the top of the slipway.

Variations

If a longer trip is desired, starting or finishing this trip at Boddam works well, see previous trip for further information.

Smugglers

No doubt you will have enjoyed exploring the caves, nooks and crannies along the way, as did the smugglers of Collieston in days gone by. A great deal of illegally landed foreign spirits were hidden along this coastline and in 1798 Phillip Kennedy, a notorious village smuggler, was killed by an excise man's cutlass. You may want to try and discover his grave and tombstone that still stands in the village graveyard.

Heading south from Cove

Cove to Stonehaven 🌊🌊🌊

No. 31 | Grade B | 19km | OS Sheet 38 & 45

Tidal Port	Aberdeen
Start	△ Cove (NJ 955 005)
Finish	◯ Stonehaven (NO 877 854)
HW/LW	HW/LW at Cove is around the same as Aberdeen.
Tidal Times	Along this section of coastline: The SSW going stream starts about 4 hours before HW Aberdeen. The NNE going stream starts about 2 hours after HW Aberdeen. On spring tides the above times may be up to one hour earlier.
Max Rate Sp	0.5–1 knot along this section of coastline.
Coastguard	Aberdeen, tel. 01224 592334, VHF weather every 3 hours from 0730.

Introduction

This is a great trip that starts close to the city of Aberdeen and yet provides everything a sea kayaker could ask for. There are caves, cliffs, stacks and wildlife aplenty, along with a selection of unique and historic fishing stations and harbours. Add to that the occasional sandy beach and a pub at the finish, what more could be asked for?

Description

The harbour at Cove bay is a perfect launch site with easy access and plenty of parking; all this in a beautiful setting with bright-coloured boats pulled up on the shore. The harbour walls were built in 1878, yet it was used long before that as it provides plenty of natural shelter from the east-coast weather. Leaving the harbour it is hard to believe the city of Aberdeen is so close that you are immediately immersed in red granite cliffs, caves and an abundance of sea birds. The intriguing inlet of Colsea Yawn has cliffs with plenty of impressive caves either side. This sets the scene for the journey on to Portlethen, the red granite rock provides plenty of hidden surprises, and is home to numerous sea birds. Look out for a hidden waterfall not far beyond the amusingly named 'Blowup Nose' headland. Just before Portlethen there is a disused fishing station positioned at the back of an improbable inlet, a reminder how important and lucrative the fishing once was on the east coast. Portlethen also provides a stopping opportunity where the brightly-coloured boats decorate the old harbour, known locally as Portlethen Shore. Nowadays the boats are just used for pleasure, although at its busiest in 1881 there were thirty-seven fishing boats crammed into this small inlet and up until 1980 there was a commercial salmon fishing station operating out of the harbour.

Another disused fishing station is passed at Downies and approaching Newtonhill the cliffs rise in stature a little and provide a home to numerous kittiwakes and guillemots. Newtonhill is another old fishing station and provides an ideal halfway rest spot for this trip with its row of colourful huts overlooking the shore. Although now known as Newtonhill, prior to 1910 when this was a busy fishing community the village and harbour were known as Skateraw.

On the second half of the trip the caves are not quite as dramatic as those at the start of the trip, however there are still a few hidden gems. Just before Doonie Point look out for the double dry arch with its colourfully shaped red rock, just before another cave, forming a arch through route on a high tide. Having paddled a route through skerries and small stacks the final mini headland of the day will be reached, Garron Point. Numerous seals sunning themselves on the low-lying skerries often guard this headland and there is a picturesque beach just before it if a landing is required. As you paddle towards the finish at Stonehaven harbour, look out for the historic Cowie Chapel situated on the cliff top just before arriving at the sandy beaches. This ruin is one of the oldest surviving structures in the area and commands a fine view across to the harbour and onto the impressive cliffs of Fowlsheugh, to the south of Stonehaven, and Dunnotter Castle.

The shingle beach by the sailing club next to Stonehaven harbour provides an easy and out of the way landing to finish the trip. Take the time to paddle into the harbour, as it is one of the more scenic historic harbours around with plenty of character. Once you have landed all that is left is to enjoy one of the pubs or cafés that overlook this beautiful spot and reflect on a great day out.

Cove to Stonehaven

Tides and weather

The tidal movement along this section of coastline is minimal and it is best to plan this trip taking into consideration the prevailing wind. As with the rest of this coastline it is very exposed to any swell from the north or east. This will not affect launching and landing as the harbours provide protection, however it would limit the exploration of the fine caves and cliff scenery.

Additional information

Stonehaven provides a full range of amenities with fine pubs and restaurants overlooking the harbour. Please park considerately here as it is a busy place; consider dropping the boats off and parking in the large public car park next to the public toilets. Cove provides plenty of amenities up in the village but there is nothing down by the harbour, again please park considerately.

Variations

The section of coastline north of Cove up to the lighthouse at Girdle Ness is well worth exploring, as it provides plenty of cliffs and caves of interest. This can be done as a short out and back trip in its own right, or as an addition prior to continuing on to Stonehaven. Do not go on beyond the lighthouse and into Aberdeen harbour as this is a busy shipping area and kayaks are appropriately not allowed. There is a good chance of seeing dolphins along this section of coastline or, when finishing the trip, drive to the car park overlooking the harbour entrance (NJ 965 056) and enjoy a ringside view of them performing.

Stonehaven
to Inverbervie ▨▨◠▨

No. 32 | Grade B | 15km | OS Sheet 45

Tidal Port	Aberdeen
Start	△ Stonehaven (NO 877853)
Finish	◯ Inverbervie (NO 834723)
HW/LW	HW/LW at Stonehaven is around 10 minutes after Aberdeen.
Tidal Times	Along this section of coastline: The SSW going stream starts about 4 hours before HW Aberdeen. The NNE going stream starts about 2 hours after HW Aberdeen. On spring tides the above times may be up to one hour earlier.
Max Rate Sp	1.75 knots along this section of coastline.
Coastguard	Aberdeen, tel. 01224 592334, VHF weather every 3 hours from 0730.

Introduction

This section of the Scottish east coast is a haven for breeding birds. The conglomerate cliffs are steep and inaccessible to most predators, so the birds can nest in their thousands. Many skerries,

32

inlets, caves and sheer cliffs make this an interesting trip, best seen in the early morning light when the sun enhances the colours of the rock and the colourful lichens that grow on them.

Description

The historical and beautiful Stonehaven harbour is the launch site for this magical east coast paddle; take note of the handy pubs right by the water's edge for the end of the trip! Unexpectedly it was the famous lighthouse engineer Robert Stevenson who oversaw the harbour improvements in the 1820s that were required due to the increasing herring trade.

On leaving the harbour there is plenty of interest to be found by hugging the cliffs while paddling along. Dunnottar Castle is one of the more famous and photographed castles in Scotland and is soon reached.

At Maiden Kame, there is a long slender passage under an arch that can be paddled through into another inlet leading back out to the sea. From here down to Crawton the cliffs are spectacular and they are lined with thousands of birds. The numbers of birds estimated to be here during the breeding season is a staggering 170,000. It is little wonder that this section of coast, known as Fowlsheugh, is a RSPB bird reserve. Keeping a couple of hundred metres off from the cliffs to afford the nesting birds a bit of space doesn't lessen the experience. The air is full of birds, great waves of guillemots pass overhead. The sea is also peppered with birds, many of them puffins. The cliffs are made of conglomerate, which could be described as nature's concrete, but for its more interesting colours and variety of stones between the cement. As the cliffs weather, rounded rocks fall from the cliff leaving a hemispherical space behind. These isolated holes of many sizes make great nesting sites for birds, small ones occupied by single pairs with larger holes being occupied by several breeding pairs, most commonly guillemots.

Just past Crawton look out for the Garran; this is a fantastic hidden bay accessed through a wide arch. It might be possible with a really high tide to get out over the rock bar to the north of the bay, but otherwise you come in and go out the same way. Catterline, a small village with a long association with fishing, is now more associated with art. It provides an ideal place to break up the journey and stretch the legs. There are several well-known artists living in Catterline who get inspiration from the contrasting weather, calm and peaceful in the summer months but a wild place at the height of a January storm coming in from the east. During the World War I a German U-boat was able to capture five fishermen who were line fishing off Catterline. Their boat the *Bella* was blown up and they remained prisoners until the end of the war.

Hopefully you will escape Catterline with no incidents and shortly be paddling beneath Todhead lighthouse. David Stevenson built this typical white towered light in 1897, showing a feeble 42,500 candlepower light. It now shines at 3 million candlepower reaching out for 18 miles into the North Sea. Beyond the light and all the way to the finish at Inverbervie the coastline remains alive with busy birds, whilse skerries and inlets provide plenty to explore. Up above Crooked Haven is the old church of Kinneff; it was here that the Scottish crown jewels were hidden under a clay floor.

Stonehaven to Inverbervie

The trip finishes at Inverbervie, it was a mill town that for almost 200 years spun flax in a number of mills along the River Bervie. It was the first village in Scotland to open a fax-spinning mill in 1790. Inverbervie is also where Hercules Linton, the designer of the famous *Cutty Sark*, was born. The *Cutty Sark* was designed to be fast, a sailing ship that could hopefully be the fastest back from China with the first cargo of the new season's tea. In this she failed but later in life she was several times the fastest ship from Australia to Britain. Landing at the stony beach within Bervie Bay the only thing left to do will be try out another famous claim to fame of Inverbervie; its award winning fish and chip shop!

Tides and weather

The tidal streams close in to shore can run up to 1.5 knots off some of the headlands, so when planning the trip to take this into account is worth considering. This is most noticeable along the cliffs at Crawton and at Todhead lighthouse. On neap tides the wind would have greater effect and should be the focus of any planning. Swell coming in off the North coast would make landing at Inverbervie difficult and not allow the cliffs, caves and arches to be explored, so plan for a day with minimum swell.

Additional information

The best spot to launch from at Stonehaven is the little jetty by the sailing club south end of the harbour. It is worth considering leaving cars parked in the large public car park with toilets the other side of the harbour. To get to the landing spot by road follow the signs off the main street

in Inverbervie down to the caravan park, the car park is just beyond this. Both Inverbervie and Stonehaven have a full range of amenities.

Variations

It is possible to start or finish the trip at Catterline; this may be useful if there is swell coming into the stony beach at Inverbervie making the landing/launching difficult. On a sunny day, paddling the route from Inverbervie works better as the sun will be at your back and make the views and photographs better.

Dunnottar Castle

As with so many of the castles the view of it from the sea is impressive, the castle sitting on an isolated rock 50m high, only connected to the mainland by a narrow ridge. This rock was an ideal place to build a castle, as it is very easy to defend if only attacked by foot soldiers. When cannons came on the scene it was possible to damage the structure as well as starve the occupants by making sure no supplies went into the castle. Oliver Cromwell's siege with artillery lasted eight months in 1651 until the occupants surrendered, but not before the Scottish crown jewels had successfully been smuggled away. They were smuggled out and taken to nearby Kinneff Church where they remained hidden and safe for nine years before being returned to Edinburgh Castle. In 1990 Dunnottar Castle was used as a location to film a version of 'Hamlet' starring Mel Gibson.

Stonehaven to Inverbervie

Looking into The Garran

Scurdie Ness ⬛⬛⬛⬛⬛⬛

No. 33 | **Grade B** | **24km** | **OS Sheet 54**

Tidal Port	Aberdeen
Start	△ Montrose - Ferryden (NO 720 567)
Finish	ⵔ Arbroath (NO 642 403)
HW/LW	HW/LW Montrose is around 55 minutes after Aberdeen.
Tidal Times	Along this part of coastline: The SW going stream starts about 4 hours before HW Aberdeen. The NE going stream starts about 2 hours after HW Aberdeen.
	Montrose Harbour: In going starts about 5 hours and 20 minutes before HW Aberdeen. Out going starts about 55 minutes after HW Aberdeen
Max Rate Sp	1.5 knots along this section of coastline.
Coastguard	Aberdeen, tel. 01224 592334, VHF weather every 3 hours from 0730.

Introduction

Red sandstone sculptured cliffs, geos, caves and arches provide the finish to this trip and a classic lighthouse provides the dramatic start. In between there is a spectacular sandy beach along with

33

Scurdie Ness

imposing cliffs, huge caves and birdlife all around. Add to this an abundance of fish shops selling the famous Arbroath Smokie to finish it all off with and you get a recipe for a perfect day out on the east coast.

Description

The best place to start this trip is at the end of the road at Ferryden on the south side of the river that forms the busy port of Montrose. Ferryden itself used to be a busy fishing village as well as where the ferry operated prior to the bridge being built. The port of Montrose has been an important trading place for many generations and to this day it is still a hive of industry, much of this serving the oil business. In the past it has provided an important fishing port, used for various types of fishing from salmon and herring to whaling. It once had a thriving smuggling trade, with many of the caves that are soon to be paddled by and explored being used to hide and store the stolen goods. The river that leads out to sea to start this trip drains and fills the Montrose Basin, which is a large tidal nature reserve providing a home and nesting place for a significant number of birds.

As you head out to Scurdie Ness lighthouse take care with the boat traffic. Staying in close to the edge is recommended and this will also help avoid the worst of the tidal flow. With the possible mix of tidal flow, swell and shallow rocks on the way out to Scurdie Ness be prepared for some waves, staying on the south side of the channel will avoid the worst. The lighthouse at Scurdie Ness provides a dramatic start to the trip, standing thirty-nine metres tall. During World War II the lighthouse was painted black so as not to attract German boats, and was then only lit when the RAF wanted to lure German planes into the area.

While paddling along the coast the salmon fishing bag nets will be seen at regular intervals. These are unique to this area and when looking at them it can be seen how a net is fixed into shore stopping the salmon swimming along. This then feeds then into a netted trap where the fishermen can collect them. The cluster of houses at Usan approaches and here you will see many of the nets drying and being repaired as this is the fishing station that works this section of coastline. It is one of the few remaining wild salmon fisheries in Scotland and exports salmon all over the world. At Todd's Hole look out for the first of the sea arches on this trip, on a high tide you may just be able to get through. Some sea stacks and nesting kittiwakes are found just before the stunning beach at Lunan Bay. It is worth stopping here, but there may well be a bit of surf to contend with. Look out for the salmon fishing nets fixed on the beach and land well away from them as getting tangled up in them would not be good.

On leaving the beach, head across the bay to the historic fishing village of Ethie Haven, once thriving with salmon netters, now used for holiday homes. Around the corner lies the spectacular Red Head, this provides the highest cliffs of the paddle, towering up to eighty metres high. The deep red sandstone colour dominates the coastline from here and with it starts the abundance of caves and arches. At Prail Castle there is a double arch, weather worn, through the imposing red cliffs, as with much of the cliffs along here the nesting birds noisily

stand guarding the entrance. The dilapidated harbour of Auchmithie provides the next landing opportunity. This was a busy fishing village in the herring days as well as being the birthplace of the now famous Arbroath Smokie.

The final section of coastline to the finish at Arbroath is one to be savoured. The rock architecture is stunning and the opportunities to explore caves, arches and geos are endless, it may take some time to reach Arbroath! Just past Castlesea Bay the first of the large caves will be found, beckoning the sea paddler in to explore them. These will lead quickly on to the Gaylet Pot, possibly the most dramatic of them all and guarded by the usual abundance of sea birds. Here a large cave will eventually open up into a hidden bay a good few hundred metres into the headland. The unique sandstone stack of the 'Deil's Heid' (Devil's Head) will lead you on to the next section of non-stop caves and geos to explore. The kilometre of coastline from this sea stack provides spectacular coastal exploration, all set amongst the beautifully sculptured red sandstone. Along with the birds you may well share these cliffs with some rock climbers, as this is a well known and justifiably popular sports climbing area. Hence the numerous steel bolts you will notice leading up the vertical rock wall, use by the climbers to protect themselves against a fall whilse climbing. Soon 'Needle E'e' will be passed looking down on paddlers below and just beyond this will be the final impressive geo and cave of the day.

From here all that is left is the paddle alongside the town of Arbroath that will lead to the harbour overlooked by the Bell Rock signal tower. As with all harbours take care with boats entering and exiting. The finishing landing spot is on the beach and slip on the left of the outer harbour walls. Allow time to explore the beautifully historic Arbroath, and of course savour a well earned 'Smokie'.

Tides and weather

Care needs to be taken with the potentially strong tidal flow leaving Montrose. Leaving just before low water will allow for an easy paddle out to Scurdie Ness and then tidal assistance with the south going flood tide down to Arbroath. It is possible to paddle the trip without using the tidal assistance, although on a spring tide the 1.5 knot tidal flow will be noticeable. Any swell from the north or east will have a big impact on the ease of landing at Lunan Bay, as well as making the amount of cave exploration limited. Plan for a day with minimum swell.

Additional information

There are plenty amenities in Arbroath and Montrose as well as numerous fish shops in Arbroath. There is plenty of parking at both the start and finish, though Ferryden is a very small community with narrow roads so please drive courteously. It is well worth taking the time to visit the Arbroath Signal Tower Museum, the museum has a lot of interesting information about Bell Rock Lighthouse and its history.

Variations

The trip can be paddled in either direction to make best use of the tide or wind. If a shorter trip is preferred, or time wants to be spent just exploring the Arbroath coastline and associated geos and caves, an alternative start/finish point can be used at Auchmithie. It is possible to drive down to the disused harbour and there is parking available.

Smokies

The Arbroath Smokie is said to have originated from the small fishing village of Auchmithie, three miles from Arbroath. In the 19th century many of the fisherfolk from Auchmithie relocated to Arbroath to make use of the modern harbour, they not only brought their boats but the smokie recipe as well. Since this day it has become the famous Arbroath Smokie that we all can enjoy and many from all over the world search out. Local legend has it that the smokie recipe was discovered by a fish store catching fire one night, destroying many barrels of haddock preserved in salt. The following morning the local people found some of the barrels that were not totally destroyed by the fire had in fact cooked the haddock inside, and these cooked and smoked fish tasted good and became the modern day smokie. To this day the smokie is made in a similar way, the haddock are salted and tied up in pairs to dry before being hung over a triangular length of wood to smoke. The fish are smoked over a hardwood fire in a special barrel that creates a very hot, humid and smoky fire. Typically in less than an hour in this intense heat and thick smoke the fish are ready to eat, and they of course have that strong, smoky taste and smell we expect from Arbroath smokies.

Bell Rock 🛶⛅

No. 34 | Grade C | 36km | OS Sheet 54 & Admiralty Chart 190

Tidal Port	Aberdeen
Start	🔺 Arbroath (NO 642 403)
Finish	🔴 Arbroath (NO 642 403)
HW/LW	HW/LW at Arbroath is around 45 minutes after Aberdeen.
Tidal Times	In the area between Arbroath and Bell Rock: The NE going stream starts at about 3 hours and 30 minutes after HW Aberdeen. The SW going stream starts at about 3 hours and 20 minutes before HW Aberdeen.
Max Rate Sp	1 knot in the general area.
Coastguard	Aberdeen, tel. 01224 592334, VHF weather every 3 hours from 0730.

Introduction

This book would not be complete without including a trip out to Bell Rock, one of the most famous lighthouses in Scotland. Many would hail the construction of Bell Rock as one of the greatest feats in lighthouse engineering ever accomplished, and newspapers at the time called Bell Rock "one of the wonders of the modern world".

34

Bell Rock

Description

When launching at the small beach just outside the main harbour but within the outer harbour walls be aware of other vessels entering and exiting. There is plenty of parking at the launch site as well as amenities in Arbroath.

It is an eighteen kilometre crossing to the rock, and there is no guarantee that you will be able to land when you get there. Time your departure so as to arrive towards low water with a calm sea. This will give you the opportunity to stretch the legs, relieve yourself, and take in the immense structure of the lighthouse. The best landing is a sheltered inlet between the skerries, best accessed from the north.

Whilst paddling the long crossing back to the distant town of Arbroath, spare a thought for the three hardy lighthouse keepers who had the rock as their home, manning the light until it became fully automated in 1988. As it was a 'rock station' they were paid more than other keepers, and passing ships had to pay double the duty of other lighthouses due to the cost of its construction and maintenance. The weather clearly made it a challenging life for the keepers, however during the World Wars they were often in even more jeopardy. In 1915 a 650-man ship was totally destroyed on Bell Rock within 420 feet of the base of the tower, miraculously there was no loss of life. Then in World War Two the lantern glass was smashed when it was shot at by German planes, and a bomb exploded within ten yards of the tower.

Bell Rock lighthouse has stood the test of time, as it is the oldest standing offshore lighthouse anywhere in the world. On landing back at Arbroath you will likely conclude that the memories of the Bell Rock lighthouse will stay with you for a lifetime. The light itself will probably continue shining even longer.

Tides and weather

The trip cuts across the tidal streams in this area, however they are relatively weak. Wind will have a greater effect on drift and use of transits and GPS is recommended to ensure minimum distance is lost due to wind or tide. Arriving at Bell Rock at or near low water is the most important part of planning to ensure the possibility of landing. A spring tide should give an hour or two either side of low water, however a neap tide may make any landing a challenge. Leaving Arbroath three hours before low water should facilitate arriving at low water.

Additional information

The Arbroath Signal Tower Museum, situated right next to the launch site, has a lot of fantastic information about Bell Rock Lighthouse and its history. Bell Rock lies beyond the area covered in the *OS Landranger Sheet 54*, the *OS Road 3 Travel Map of Southern Scotland and Northumberland* offers a big picture view of where it lies, with Admiralty *Chart 190 Montrose to Fife Ness* providing 1:75000 scale detail for navigation.

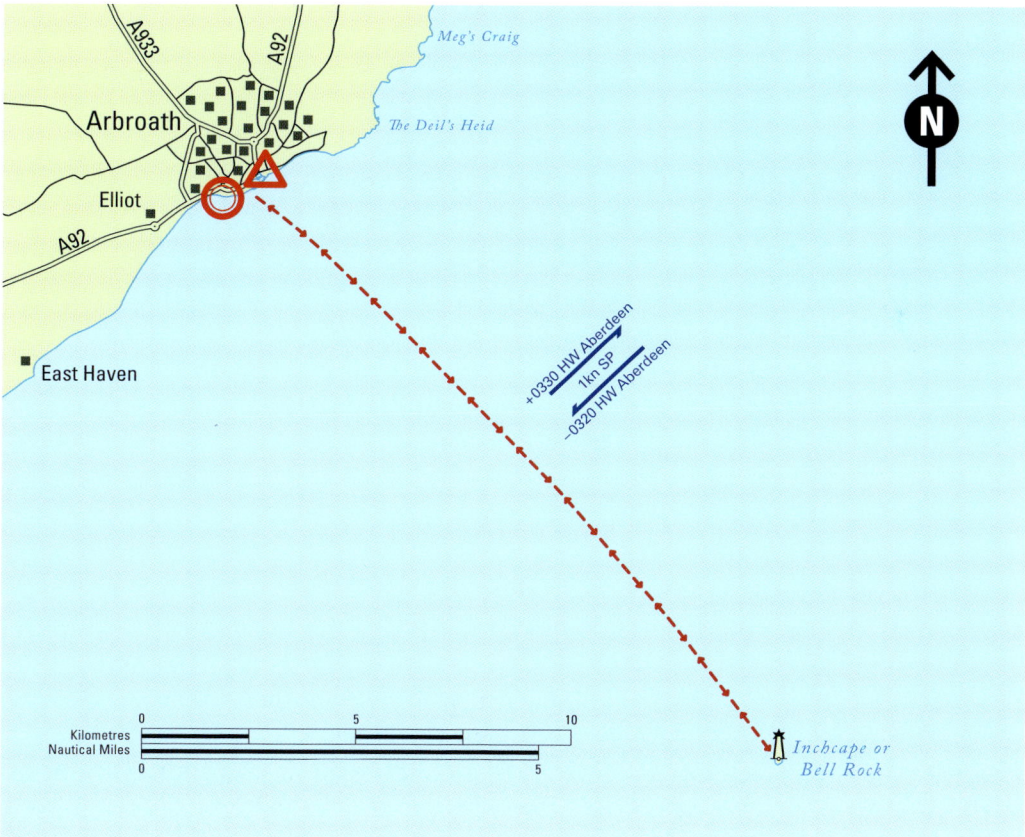

The building of Bell Rock lighthouse

Bell Rock gets its name from the legend that in olden times an abbot attached a bell to a tree on the rock. The bell rang continuously, being moved by the sea when the rock was covered, to signify danger and warn ships. What Stevenson ended up building could not be more removed from this if he'd tried, an immense tower standing 115 foot tall with its bright light on top.

Robert Stevenson became interested in lighthouse engineering at the tender age of 15, when he accompanied his stepfather, Thomas Smith, to work on Kinnaird Head lighthouse in 1787. It took some persuading of Robert's mother that lighthouse engineering was a suitable career, as she had chosen the profession of minister for him. He went away to study before working under Thomas Smith as an apprentice for five years, becoming a fully-fledged lighthouse engineer at the age of twenty-six. Robert became obsessed with the vision of building a lighthouse on Bell Rock. However it took a huge storm in December 1799 with the loss of seventy ships, including a British warship, for the lighthouse to be requested by the Northern Lighthouse Board. In 1805 the building of the lighthouse was commissioned, but the head engineer at this time was not Robert Stevenson, but John Rennie. Robert had only built one lighthouse on his own before, so he was appointed assistant to Rennie. John Rennie could see Roberts potential and, having many other projects on the go, handed the building of Bell Rock over to him. Thus Robert Stevenson became Head Engineer for Bell Rock lighthouse in 1808, a year after the building started.

Building started in 1807, but there were only 14 ten-hour days available for construction that year, due to the tides. In 1808 the workers managed to get 22 days of construction with the tides and weather. All the custom-cut stone was shipped out and then joined using specially prepared Bell Rock mortar. This work programme continued until the light was finished on the first of February 1811.

34

Bell Rock

Fife and the Firth of Forth

Introduction

The 'Kingdom of Fife' has a long history, and when you paddle around its coastline you will see plenty of evidence of this. Bounded by the Firth of Tay to the north and Firth of Forth to the south, this coastline has a different feel about it. It is justifiably well known for its beaches that many travel from the nearby towns and cities to enjoy. St Andrews in the north of the area has history and culture oozing from every brick. As sea kayakers we gain a unique viewpoint of the cathedral and town, with its stunning beaches on either side.

The headland of Fife Ness marks the south coast of Fife and the entrance to the Firth of Forth. As a headland it is disappointing, yet as a landmark it is significant with views out to the historic North Carr Beacon and Bell Rock Light on a clear day. The beauty of the south Fife coastline lies in the numerous historic and beautifully maintained fishing villages, all with their characteristic red tile roofs. Whether it is Crail, Anstruther, Pittenweem, St Monas or Elie all will have you wanting to spend time to enjoy the village scenery, hospitality, food and drink. The famous Anstruther fish and chip shop being one particular eatery not to be missed.

The Firth of Forth is made all the more spectacular with the historic city of Edinburgh providing the dramatic backdrop. All of the paddles involve exploring the Forth's contrasting islands and discovering the wealth of history that is linked to them. The Isle of May is rightly often referred to as the 'jewel of the Forth', the cliffs and birdlife out on this island should not be missed.

A trip to Bass Rock should be made compulsory for all sea kayakers. This incredible outcrop of rock with its towering cliffs, topped with thousands upon thousands of gannets is just amazing. Lying more sheltered in the inner Firth the islands of Inchkeith, Inchcolm, Inchmickery and InchGarvie all provide fascinating trips. The history of these ranges from the historic St Colm's Abbey to quarantine hospitals and wartime defences. All these islands have the impressive Edinburgh skyline overlooking them, yet the paddler will always return having been amazed by the wildlife despite the seemingly urban location.

At the heart of the Firth of Forth lies the Forth Rail Bridge, an engineering masterpiece. It is futile trying to describe the experience, you will have to paddle beneath its towering structure yourself and enjoy being awed by its presence.

Tides and weather

This area is comparatively sheltered from wind and swell; however with many of the islands being a little offshore the wind needs to be taken into account. There is hardly any tidal movement to consider until the Inner Firth of Forth at Inchkeith and to the west. Here the tidal streams can prove quite significant, particularly on spring tides, and trips should be planned accordingly. The main consideration is around the flow as there are no tidal races or overfalls to speak of, although with wind against tide it can get quite rough.

© Landing at Seacliff beach, Bass Rock behind

St Andrews cathedral

St Andrews

No. 35 | Grade A | 13km | OS Sheet 59

Tidal Port	Leith
Start	△ St Andrews, West Sands (NO 505 173)
Finish	ⵔ Kingsbarns (NO 603 125)
HW/LW	HW/LW at St Andrews is around 15 minutes before Leith.
Tidal Times	Off St Andrews: The SE going stream starts about 5 hours and 40 minutes before HW Leith. The NE going stream starts about 1 hour and 50 minutes after HW Leith.
Max Rate Sp	0.5 knots along this section of coastline.
Coastguard	Aberdeen, tel. 01224 592334, VHF weather every 3 hours from 0730.

Introduction

The ancient town of St Andrews is a great place to visit, renowned for being the home of golf, having a distinctive cathedral, and of course its royal connections. Walking around this town full of amazing architecture and history is one thing, but paddling around it provides an opportunity to see it in all its glory from a unique vantage point. This along with some fantastic beaches along the way gives a pleasant day out.

Description

Launch at the small sandy beach alongside the Aquarium. As you leave the beach and head out amongst the low lying skerries that run along the coastline, the first ancient walls that are paddled by will belong to the castle that dates back to 1200. Alongside the small castle beach there is evidence of how this coastline with its fantastic beaches became a favourite Victorian holiday destination, in the form of the salt-water swimming pool. The journey round the town finishes with the most dramatic backdrop of all, the historic cathedral. Much of the medieval cathedral has sadly fallen down with the majority being destroyed in the Protestant Reformation. However what is left it truly breathtaking and the view from the sea is the best there is. The remains of the ornate east tower standing tall alongside St Rule's tower is the most obvious from a paddler's vantage point. The tower is part of the original church of St Andrews. It pre-dates the cathedral, and was built to house St Andrew's relics. It is hard to believe that such an impressive building could have been built in 1158. It is the largest church to have been built in Scotland and for a long time it was the largest building in the country.

To get to the launch site you will have driven past one of St Andrews worldwide attractions, the 'Old Course' that is the birthplace of golf. Over 600 years ago the game of golf started on 'The Links' that overlooks West Sands beach. Despite it being banned in 1457 by James II because it distracted men from archery practice and threatened the defence of the nation, it is still very much with us today, and St Andrews is a well known Mecca for all golf lovers.

As well as educating Prince William and providing the opportunity for him to meet his wife, Kate Middleton, St Andrews University has many other notable claims to fame. It is in fact the third oldest university in the English-speaking world, being founded in 1410. The first woman to enrol as a student did so here in 1862, a tradition Prince William will no doubt be glad continued!

After the old harbour entrance is passed East Sands will provide an opportunity for an early stop if required. The low-lying coastline that continues to Kingsbarns provides occasional landings and small skerries to weave between on route. At the Rock and Spindle there is a small stack and landing opportunity, with further landing options close to where the Kenly Water comes into the sea. Despite the lack of cliffs for any nesting birds on this section of coastline, there will still be plenty of sea birds around to share the journey with, as well as the occasional seal. If a stop on one of the areas famous sandy beaches is required, take the opportunity to enjoy your own more private one before arriving at the justifiably popular Kingsbarns beach.

Tides and weather

The tides are minimal along this section of coastline so planning the trip to take into account any wind is recommended. If there is any swell coming from the north or east than this can produce surf on the beaches which will affect launching or landing during the trip.

Additional information

There are plenty of amenities and places to eat and drink in St Andrews. At Kingsbarns there is only parking and toilets at the beach, but there is a pub in the village. There is a charge for car parking at the suggested launch site, and parking at East Sands (described below) is free.

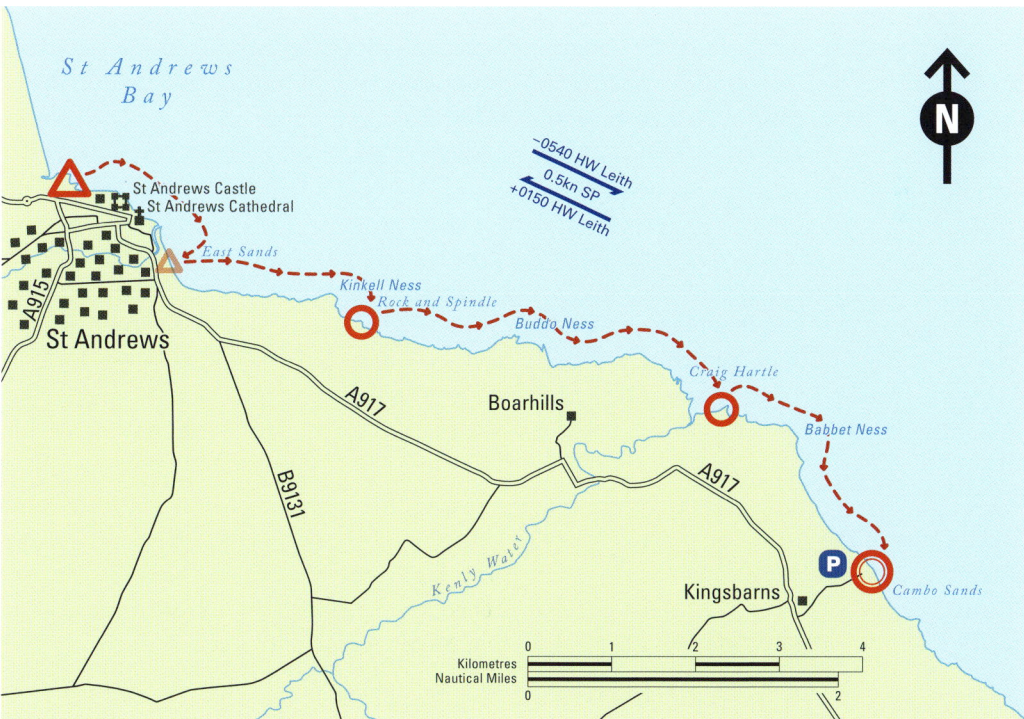

© Cambo Sands

35

Variations

To avoid a shuttle (or car parking fee) launching at East Sands (NO 517 163) and paddling out around the town to the start point described above and back works well. This can also allow a trip down the coast towards Kingsbarns and back if desired.

History

Legend says that a Greek monk brought the relics of St Andrew to the town. A shrine was built for St Andrew's relics in the church and pilgrims travelled from afar to pay their respects. Scotland has since adopted St Andrew as the patron saint and his saltire cross has become the nation's flag.

Crail harbour

Fife Ness 🌉🚗🌀

No. 36 | Grade B | 15km | OS Sheet 59

Tidal Port	Leith
Start	△ Kingsbarns (NO 603 125)
Finish	ⵔ Anstruther Easter (NO 568 033)
HW/LW	HW/LW at Anstruther Easter is around 10 minutes before Leith.
Tidal Times	Off Fife Ness: The SE and then SW going stream starts about 4 hours and 40 minutes before HW Leith. The NE and then NW going stream starts about 1 hour and 50 minutes after HW Leith.
Max Rate Sp	1 knot off Fife Ness.
Coastguard	Aberdeen, tel. 01224 592334, VHF weather every 3 hours from 0730.

Introduction

Fife Ness protrudes out into the sea forming the most eastern part of Fife, and is a key landmark for ships entering the Firth of Forth. Add to this the beautiful historic harbour at Crail and you have the ingredients for a fine day out.

The low lying coastline of Fife Ness

Description

36

Fife Ness

The beautiful sands at Kingsbarns provide a perfect launching spot, with a clear view of the low-lying coastline towards Fife Ness. There is plenty of parking here as well as public toilets, although the beach may be busy on a hot day. The journey towards Fife Ness, although not dramatic, will feel remote, with only the sea birds for company. Looking out to sea from Fife Ness you will see the notorious skerries marked by North Carr Beacon, and on a particularly clear day you should see Bell Rock Lighthouse in the far distance directly out to sea. Just before Fife Ness there is a fantastic sandy beach, and behind this is Constantine's Cave, so called because it was believed for many years that Pictish King Constantine II was killed here by the Vikings. Although this has since been proved inaccurate the cave still holds plenty of history with crosses carved on its walls from early Christians and Roman wine and oils jars being found here perhaps having been salvaged from a shipwreck 2,000 years ago.

With Fife Ness being such a major landmark you would be forgiven for anticipating an impressive lighthouse built by the Stevenson family standing proud looking out to sea, but unfortunately this is not the case. The modern small square shaped lighthouse was built in 1975 and behind it can be seen the coastguard station and houses. The light is there to warn ships of Fife Ness itself and more importantly the notorious North Carr rocks stretching out to sea. There is a convenient landing place at Fife Ness (easier at high water) by the remains of the harbour that was originally built for fishing and to export the stone from Craighead quarry that is situated close by. It is said that the high quality stone from this quarry was used to repair St Andrews Cathedral in 1455.

Having landed, spend the time to explore this area as you will find a rare example of a sea beacon construction yard (used to build North Carr beacon). There are also the remains of a tide mill that was built near to the harbour. This ingenious construction used a dam to trap the flood tide in a reservoir, which then could be discharged through the wheel after the tide had ebbed.

You may wish to paddle out to get a close look at the beacon at North Carr rocks, if not the journey continues into the Firth of Forth and towards Crail. Out to sea your eye will be drawn to the impressive cliffs of the Isle of May, a little island that guards the entrance to the Firth. Look out for the sandstone outcrop of rock marked as Kilminning Castle on route to Crail. The RAF used this as a target for bombing practice using bags of flour during World War II. A caravan site along the coastline marks the approach to the historic harbour of Crail. At low tide the harbour dries, but if you are feeling brave you can land outside the entrance and access the harbour by climbing up an iron ladder. Crail has a wealth of colourful old sandstone houses squashed in around the ornate harbour, many of which have been restored by the National Trust for Scotland. There are some lovely cafés close to the harbour as well as opportunities to buy freshly caught lobster from one of the colourful creel fishing boats in the harbour. So even if you have to climb the harbour walls to visit Crail, it is most definitely worth the effort.

The final part of this journey continues along low-lying coastline. Half way along look out for the sandstone outcrops and caves standing proud just above the shoreline. These are Caiplie Caves, known locally as 'The Coves'. This striking geological feature has carved symbols within the caves that suggest early Christian and Pictish use. Soon the colourful red tiled roofs of Cellardyke and Anstruther will come into view. Cellardyke harbour is locally known as Skinfast

Fife Ness

Haven and was built in about 1452. If paddling into the harbour for a closer look you will see from the different stone work how this harbour has had to be rebuilt many times over the years due to storm damage.

Anstruther Easter provides a perfect finish to this trip, with its sandy beach protected by the outer harbour walls. The only thing left to do is to load the kayaks and enjoy some world famous fish and chips at the Anstruther Fish Bar.

Tides and weather

There is little tidal movement on this trip so planning should focus on the wind, as this is clearly an exposed section on coastline. If there is any wind from the south-west then the trip should be paddled starting at Anstruther.

Additional information

There are no facilities other than toilets at Kingsbarns but there are excellent cafés and pubs at Crail and Anstruther, along with other local amenities.

Variations

It is well worth paddling out to North Carr rocks and the beacon as part of this trip and this is best done on route to the landing at Fife Ness.

Isle of May

No. 37 | Grade B | 22km | OS Sheet 59

Tidal Port	Leith
Start	△ Anstruther Easter (NO 568 033)
Finish	○ Anstruther Easter (NO 568 033)
HW/LW	HW/LW at Anstruther Easter is around 10 minutes before Leith.
Tidal Times	At 3.5 nautical miles west of the Isle of May: The NE going stream starts at about 1 hour after HW Leith. The SW going stream starts at about 5 hours before HW Leith.
Max Rate Sp	1 knot at the above point.
Coastguard	Aberdeen, tel. 01224 592334, VHF weather every 3 hours from 0730.

Introduction

The Isle of May, known as the 'Jewel of the Forth', is a National Nature Reserve. Over 200,000 seabirds come here to breed every year, with puffins being the most numerous. The cliffs of the west coast rise vertically out of the sea, with caves at their base. These cliffs are where guillemots and kittiwakes nest so densely that the black rock is painted white by the droppings of thousands of birds. During the breeding season there will be around 3,000 Atlantic grey seals on the island, making this the most important breeding ground for grey seals on the east coast of Scotland.

Description

Anstruther Easter provides the perfect starting point for this trip, with the Isle of May clearly visible out in the Forth. At the harbour there is a car park, just to the east of the lifeboat station that is right at the top of the sandy beach enclosed within the harbour. Anstruther Easter has long been an important port with ships sailing to the Mediterranean for wine and to the Baltic regions for timber. During the heyday of herring fishing there was a large fleet based here and today in the village you can visit the Scottish Fisheries Museum to discover more about the history of Anstruther.

The journey out to the Isle of May will not be a lonely one if you visit the island in early summer. Shortly after setting out you are likely to have puffins as companions, bobbing about on the sea in small groups, becoming more numerous as you get closer to the island.

For a sea kayaker there are more options for landing than are available to visitors coming over by boat, though from the warden's perspective it is probably better if you land in Kirkhaven at the south-east end of the island. This bay has a few skerries at its entrance and with swell coming in from the east it might not be that clear how to enter. Take your time and approach from the south-east. If this is too daunting try landing in East Tarbet or on the west coast at the north end of the island. The warden prefers to meet everyone who comes ashore, as that way information can be provided to visitors that helps make visits more interesting and also protects the wildlife from accidental disturbance. The island has a system of marked paths on which you should remain. A path will take you from the landing spot in Kirkhaven up to the small visitor centre and toilet. Here you can pick up a leaflet illustrating the path network and telling you about the island.

Puffins

It is hard not to fall in love with puffins, and along the Scottish coastline we are lucky to have some of Britain's main breeding colonies. Close up they are easily recognisable by their bright yellow, red and white striped beaks, and for this reason they are also sometimes called 'sea parrots'. From a distance they can still be recognised by their very fast wing beats as they skim the sea's surface. These birds spend their lives at sea, only coming to land between April and mid-August to breed. Living the rest of the time at sea in all conditions make them remarkably tough creatures. They are able to swim exceptionally well, feeding on fish and drinking sea water. When breeding they live in burrows, which are excavated in the soil found on top of the coastal cliffs. Puffins choose partners for life and each year will incubate one egg, returning to the same burrow annually. After hatching, the young will spend about forty-five days in the burrow before it heads out to sea to begin its life. It will spend two to three years at sea before returning to the same breeding area to start a family of its own.

In the late spring/early summer puffins will be all around. They nest in shallow burrows (42,000 are occupied) all over the island. This in part is why you must stay on the path, as it is easy to squash a burrow that might have a bird or egg inside. As well as the puffins, look out for three species of gull, two species of tern, eider ducks, shags and fulmars.

The second most common bird on the island is the guillemot with a tally of around 26,000 individuals. Guillemots nest on the western cliffs, which they share with up to 6,000 pairs of

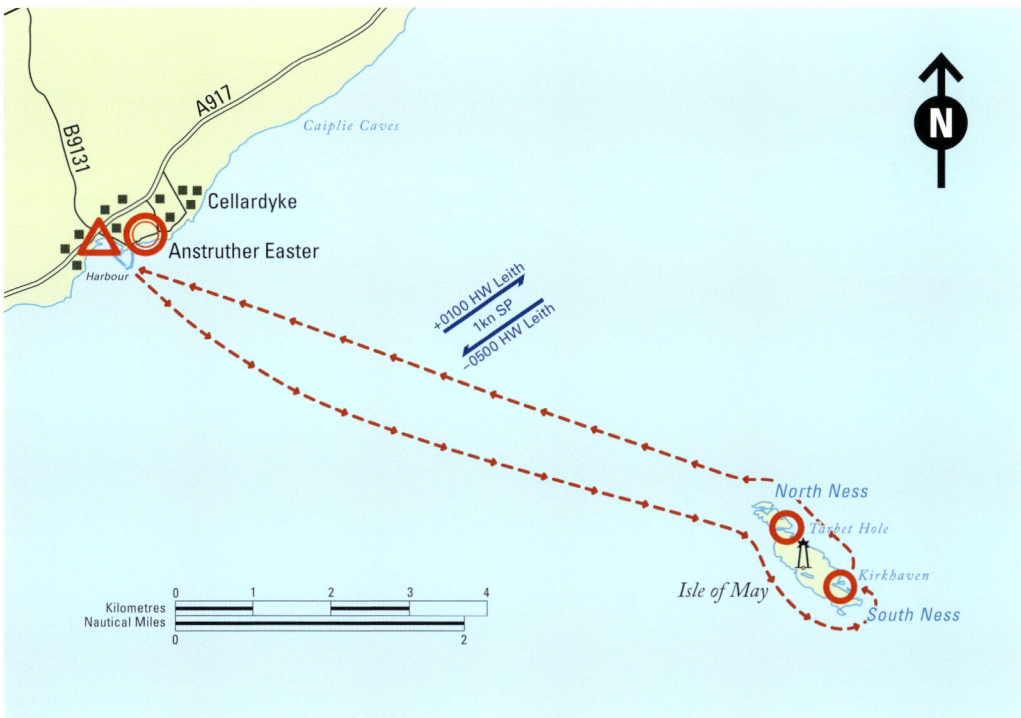

kittiwakes and 4,000 razorbills. It is a fantastic experience to kayak along the west side of the island surrounded by so many birds, but be careful not to go too close into the cliff as the birds might take fright and in the process of leaving their ledges the eggs could be knocked off the cliff.

On returning back to the harbour of Anstruther Easter you will be left with many amazing memories for this 'Jewel of the Forth'.

Tides and weather

The tidal streams do not flow that fast, so you should have little trouble doing the crossing and the wind should be the main consideration for this open stretch of water. At the NW and SE ends of the island expect to feel a little bit more tidal movement and associated rough water as it pushes past these prominent points.

With wind from the west there will be clapotis under the cliffs, and any swell from the east can make landings a bit more challenging on this coast.

Additional information

Anstruther Easter has a full range of local amenities and well as some good pubs and the famous Anstruther Fish Bar. Scottish Natural Heritage produce a leaflet describing the wildlife and history of the Isle of May, which you can pick up at the visitor centre on the island or by contacting SNH via their website www.snh.org.uk. The Scottish Fisheries Museum website can be found at www.scotfishmuseum.org and the Scottish Seabird Centre in North Berwick has a web cam

positioned on the Isle of May. Visit their website www.seabird.org for lots of information about seabirds as well as a glimpse of the Isle of May. It is possible for non-paddling friends to visit the island by one of the regular boat trips that leave from the harbour at Anstruther Easter.

Lights and cables

The Isle of May was the first place in Scotland to have a manned lighthouse. In the 17th century it was nothing more than a platform on which one ton of coal was shovelled each night. If it got windy and rainy the light became difficult to see, and in storms when it was needed most there was potentially no light to be seen. Robert Stevenson built a more reliable light in 1816, this is now a listed building and its unique gothic style castle is unlike any other lighthouse A additional smaller lighthouse known as 'the Low Light' was built in 1843 a few hundred metres from the main light. This was to provide a pair of lights that could be lined up by ships to help them to avoid the notorious Carr Rock off Fife Ness.

During the World War I the island was used as a signalling station to pass warnings of approaching enemy ships that might try to sail up the Forth. An improvement on visual observations was made in the 1930s when a cable was laid from the mainland out to the island. When ships passed over this cable, changes in magnetic field could be identified, so an enemy ship trying to sneak up the Forth under the cover of darkness could be identified and the necessary action taken.

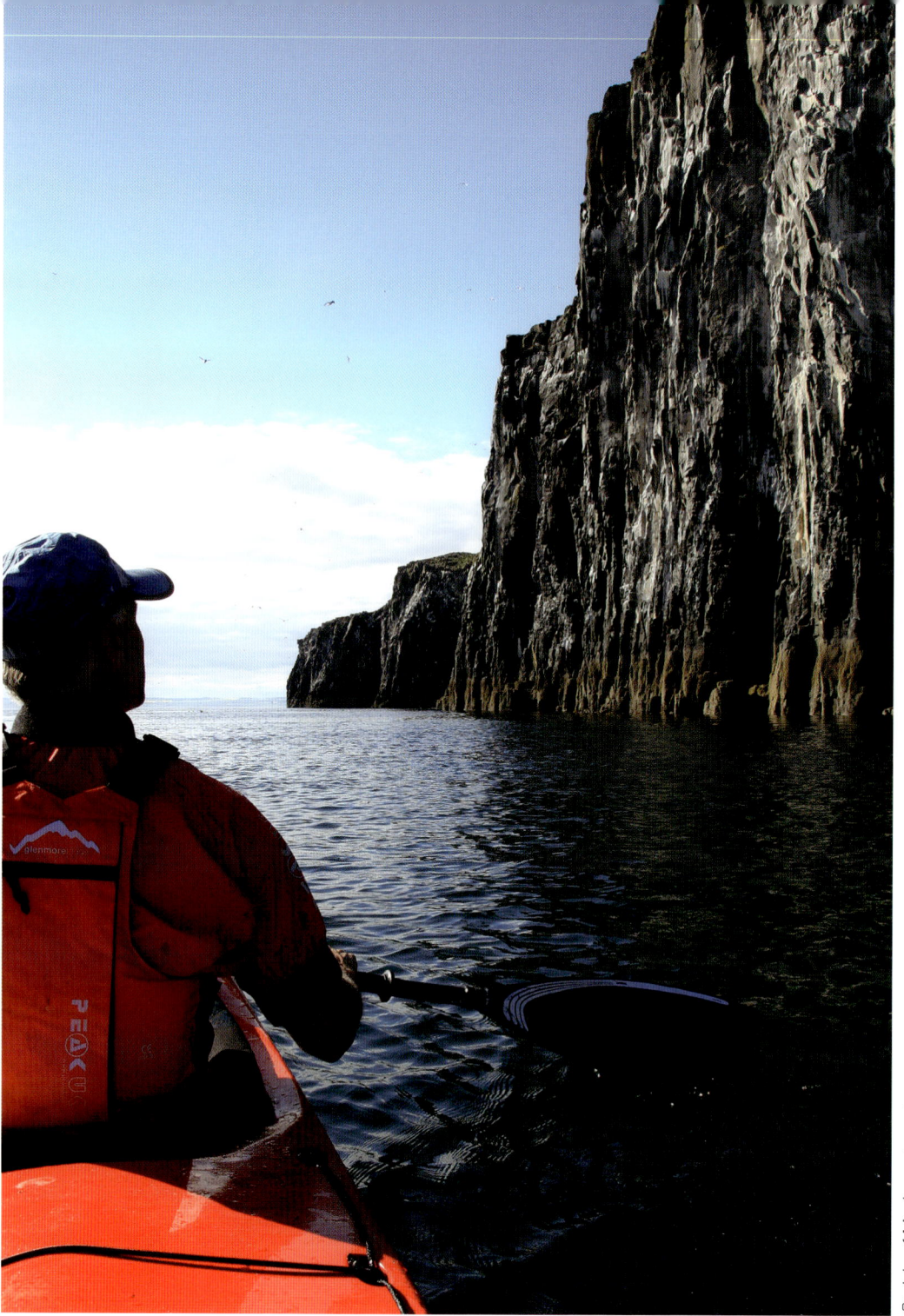

Isle of May's west coast

Anſtruther to Elie

No. 38 | Grade A | 10km | OS Sheet 59

Tidal Port	Leith
Start	△ Anstruther Easter (NO 568 033)
Finish	○ Elie (NT 497 996)
HW/LW	HW/LW at Anstruther Easter is around 10 minutes before Leith.
Tidal Times	Out from Anstruther Easter: The NE going stream starts at about 1 hour after HW Leith. The SW going stream starts at about 5 hours before HW Leith.
Max Rate Sp	1 knot along this section of coastline.
Coastguard	Aberdeen, tel. 01224 592334, VHF weather every 3 hours from 0730.

Introduction

Although not as dramatic as other trips on the east coast, this short journey provides constant variety with beautiful villages, cafés not to be missed and points of interest all coming in quick succession. Save this trip for a day where distance is not the focus, but appreciation of unrivalled fishing villages with fine food stops is.

38

Description

As you set off from the fine sandy beach at Anstruther Easter it will be the magnificent lifeboat station that will draw your attention. The station was set up in 1865, just forty-one years after the RNLI was first founded in 1824. Since then the RNLI's lifeboat crews have saved over 140,000 lives, with Anstruther playing a part in that, operating within the Firth of Forth. After leaving the shelter of the harbour the low-lying rocky coastline will lead you to the village of Pittenweem. Pittenweem was founded as a fishing village and it is still the most active of the fishing ports along this section of Fife coastline. This area was also well known for its rich trading links with Belgium and the Netherlands. Coal, wool, linen and salt would leave the Fife ports and on the return journey the ships' hulls would be filled with red pantiles as ballast. The locals soon found them to be excellent roofing material, hence the distinctive red roofs that are seen today. If you look closely you will see many of these pantiles on the oldest buildings are not all the same; that is because they were made over the knee of the tile worker, hence each tile worker ended up making their own unique set of tiles. There is not a particularly convenient landing in Pittenweem so it is worth continuing along the coastline towards the next village of St Monans.

The most striking view along the coastline ahead will be the windmill, not a common sight whilst sea kayaking. This windmill is part of the infrastructure that was used for salt production, and the remains of the saltpans can be seen just below the windmill. In 1771 nine saltpans were set up here and along with others in the Forth basin made this Scotland's main area for salt production for 800 years. It was the abundance of coal to fire the saltpan furnaces and the area's direct shipping links to Northern Europe that led to the development of salt production along this coastline. In 1611 salt was Scotland's third most important export, after wool and fish. The salt from this saltpan was transported by a wagonway to Pittenweem harbour, where it was then exported. Just after the windmill you will arrive at St Monans, and a stop is recommended.

St Monans takes its name from the legendary saint, St Monance, who was killed by invading Danes in 875. In this same raid St Aiden was killed on the Isle of May and it said some 6,000 Fife Christians were also slain. These days the village takes on a more cheerful atmosphere with its beautiful harbour, bright coloured boats and 17th to 19th century fisher and merchant houses in close surround. Planning to have lunch here is recommended as there are many good cafés and restaurants, in particular the East Pier Smokehouse overlooking the harbour.

As you head along the final section of coast to the finish at Elie, you will be rewarded great views across the Firth of Forth with the Isle of May and Bass Rock. The coastline will have some wildlife to provide interest with seals hauled out on some of the low-lying platforms as well as eider ducks weaving in and out of the rocks. There are a couple of ruined castles along this section, Ardross Castle dating back to the 14th century. The most dominant landmark you will see is the tower standing tall on the headland just before Elie. This is known as 'Lady's Tower' and it was Lady Janet Anstruther who built this beautiful building as her summerhouse and changing room for when she went bathing in the sea. When bathing she sent a bell-ringer around the town to warn the townsfolk to keep away! There is a handy little landing spot next to the tower to get out and have a look at it and the view back along the coastline.

As you round Elie Ness and its small white tower for a lighthouse you enter Wood Haven bay, which provides a sandy beach landing to finish the trip. If you wish to paddle a bit further it is well worth continuing on to Kincraig Point, returning back the same way. This will take you past the ruined chapel that was built for pilgrims on route to the shrine at St Andrews. They came

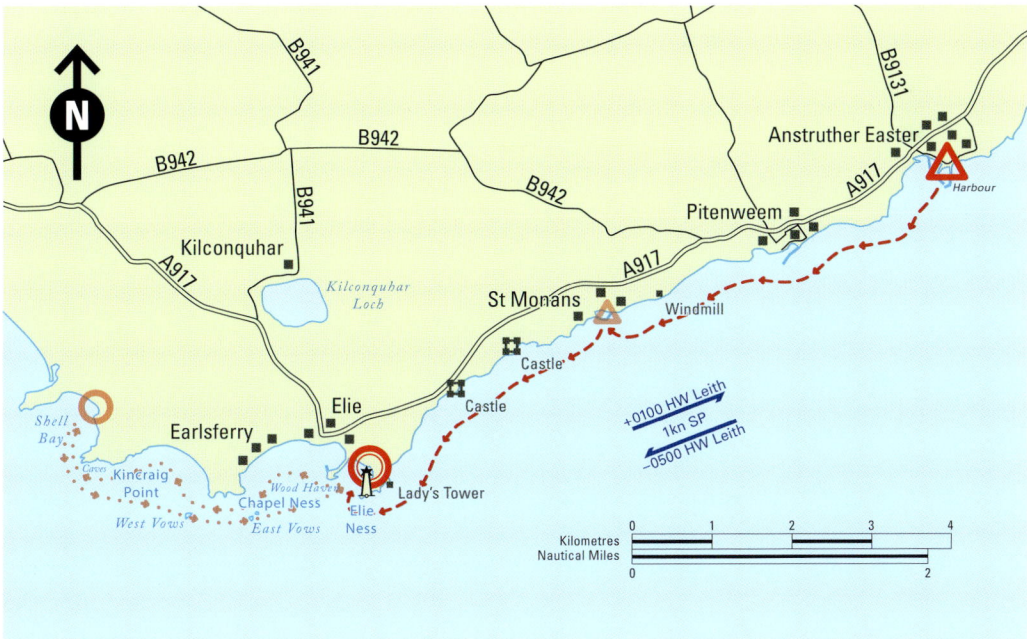

across on a ferry that was instituted for them by the Earls of Fife, running from North Berwick to Earlsferry, hence the naming of the village. The skerries just off the chapel headland are all named appropriately, East Vow having a beacon on it. When you get to Kincraig Point you will be under the largest cliffs on the north coastline of the Firth of Forth. Look out for the chains and occasionally carved out steps that make up the 'Chainwalk' running along the cliffs close to the shoreline. This adventurous walk/scramble was made in 1923, when a group of locals raised money for a blacksmith to put chains and rock steps along the shoreline cliffs. This allowed them to access the interesting rocks and plant life on the cliffs beyond Macduff's cave inlet. Returning to Elie you will be spoilt for choice, spending time exploring this village and of course the associated cafés and pubs, or to go and do the 'Chainwalk'.

Tides and weather

There are very little noteworthy tidal streams along this section of coastline, so plan the trip to make best use of any prevailing winds.

Additional information

The start and finish points on this trip have plenty of parking, toilets and local amenities. There is limited parking and less convenient launching at St Monans and at Pittenweem there is no convenient launching. If thinking of doing the 'Chainwalk' be aware that it is affected by the tides and will require good footwear, so care should be taken.

Variations

Extending the trip to include a trip out and back to Kincraig is the main variation. For a longer paddle it is possible to link this trip with the trip around Fife Ness. There is limited vehicle access at Crail, so it is not recommended to use this as a launching or landing spot to extend the trip.

Inchkeith ⊙◿◿

No. 39 │ Grade B │ 11km │ OS Sheet 66	
Tidal Port	Leith
Start	△ Kinghorn (NT 265 862)
Finish	◯ Kinghorn (NT 265 862)
HW/LW	HW/LW at Kinghorn is around the same as Leith.
Tidal Times	Between Kinghorn and Inchkeith: The W going stream starts about 5 hours and 55 minutes before HW Leith. The E going stream starts about 5 minutes after HW Leith.
Max Rate Sp	2 knots between Inchkeith and Kinghorn.
Coastguard	Aberdeen, tel. 01224 592334, VHF weather every 3 hours from 0730.

Introduction

This trip provides a short open crossing to Inchkeith, an island in the Firth of Forth packed with historical ruined buildings, alongside a beautiful hidden sandy beach. The beach can often be covered with seals and will be overlooked by numerous birds. All this with the dramatic backdrop of Edinburgh and its castle, makes for a unique day out.

Description

The harbour at Kinghorn is the ideal starting point, with plenty of parking and fairly easy launching. As you leave the harbour and the sandy beach behind the journey across to the northern tip of Inchkeith is obvious. There is a handy bright red mid channel buoy to make use of as a transit, as well as being a halfway mark for the crossing. The tide can run at a reasonable rate in the channel so making use of a transit is advisable.

It is possible to land on a stony beach at the north end, or continue the paddle along the east coast. The military remains will be obvious, as will the lighthouse that stands on top of the island (established in 1804 by Thomas Smith and Robert Stevenson). For an island covered in ruined buildings and surrounded by busy shipping, a city and towns, the number of birds and seals is just incredible. At the southern tip of the island an idyllic sandy beach appears from out of nowhere, and to top that off there may well be numerous seals resting on it. If the beach is seal free it provides the perfect stopping point to pull ashore, take in the views and perhaps carefully explore some of the wartime remains. If the seals have got there first, try not to disturb them and continue to the islands harbour on the west side.

The harbour on the west coast is obvious. Keep an eye out for the seals that may be hauled out on the skerries just out from the island. Edinburgh castle should be clearly visible beyond them as will the Forth Rail Bridge.

With such a varied history that has had war and death at the heart of it you will no doubt leave Inchkeith and head back to the mainland with mixed emotions. Hopefully, the more positive future for this unique island in the heart of the Firth of Forth is as a refuge for the abundant wildlife that has made it its home.

Quarantine

If you choose to take a walk and do some exploring, the buildings hold the stories of far more than just military history. Inchkeith has been used as a quarantine place on several occasions during its long history. In 1497 it was used as an isolated refuge for victims of a contagious disease called 'Grandgore'. When they boarded a ship in Leith to go to the island they were told that they were "there to remain till God provide for their health". It can only be assumed that the majority died on the island. In 1589 the island was again used as quarantine for a plague-ridden ship, as it was for plague victims from the mainland in 1609. The island saw more death again in 1799 when Russian sailors who died of an infectious disease were buried there.

Tides and weather

In the channel between Kinghorn and Inchkeith the tide can flow at up to 2 knots, so making use of transits will aid the crossing. As with any open crossing if the wind picks up, particularly if it is against the flow, rough water can develop quickly.

Timing the trip to arrive at the island towards low water will allow better sightings of the seals that make the surrounding skerries and beaches their home.

Additional information

There are no amenities at the harbour, though Kinghorn itself has plenty. If exploring any of the ruins on the island, do so with extreme care as they are not maintained or managed at all.

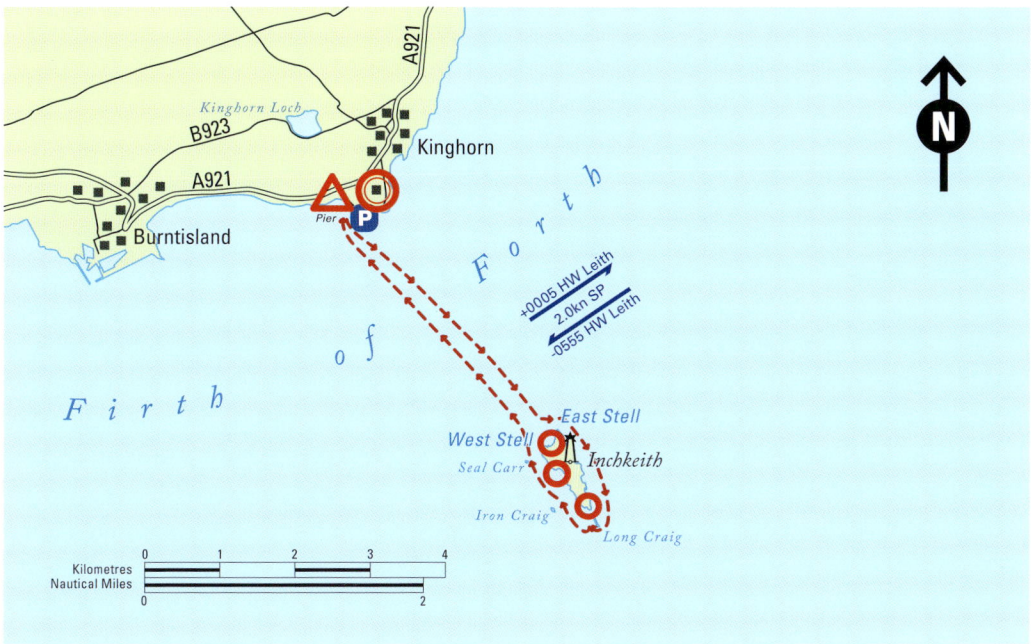

39

Inchkeith

History

On Inchkeith there are numerous ruined buildings of all shapes and sizes. The most obvious of these are the military installations that surround the entire coastline. This provides clear evidence of this islands key position in the defence of the inner Firth of Forth. The first fortifications date back to the early 16th century when a victorious English general ordered a fort to be built on the island, on the site of the current lighthouse. In 1549 a joint Scottish and French force took over the island and proceeded to build a larger fort. In 1564 Mary Queen of Scots inspected this fort and a commemorative stone inscribed 'M.R. 1564' can still be seen in a wall next to the lighthouse. The fortifications continued to be renewed and rebuilt over time and during World War 2 there were around 160 troops stationed here. It is these fortifications and associated buildings for housing the troops that are most obvious today. Military occupation ended in 1957 and the Northern Lighthouse board took over ownership. After this the island was farmed for a while, however is now left unworked.

Firth of Forth

No. 40 | Grade A | 20km | OS Sheet 65 & 66

Tidal Port	Leith
Start	△ South Queensferry (NT 136 784)
Finish	○ South Queensferry (NT 136 784)
HW/LW	HW/LW at Crammond Island is around the same time as Leith.
Tidal Times	Between the Forth Bridges: The E going stream starts about 30 minutes after HW Leith. The W going stream starts about 5 hours and 30 minutes before HW Leith. Beyond Oxcars: The W going stream starts about 5 hours and 55 minutes before HW Leith. The E going stream starts at about HW Leith.
Max Rate Sp	4.5 knots under the Forth Bridges. 2.5 knots in Mortimer's Deep. 3 knots between Oxcars and Inchcolm.
Coastguard	Aberdeen, tel. 01224 592334, VHF weather every 3 hours from 0730.

Introduction

Launching your sea kayak and looking up to the Forth Rail Bridge is an amazing experience, and definitely the best view of this historical monument. Once afloat you will have started a journey

40

Firth of Forth

that will take you to islands that are rich in history, support a surprising amount of wildlife, and have strong tidal streams. All this provides a unique paddling experience with Edinburgh City and its Castle as the backdrop.

Description

The launch site under the Forth Road Bridge is shared with Inchcolm Ferry, which is well sign-posted from the main roads. This gives plenty of parking and stunning views of both the road and rail bridges. It is also the site of the historical Hawes Inn. On leaving the launch site, head out under the rail bridge to the first island of the day, Inch Garvie.

At Inch Garvie the remains of the fortified defences are easily seen, these were maintained during World War II to defend the bridge. Earlier fortifications on Inch Garvie are said to have repelled an attack by Cromwell. Over the years these same fortifications have been used as a state prison as well as a quarantine hospital for those with infectious diseases. From Inch Garvie head on past the tanker berth and on towards Inchcolm. This area is regularly used by large shipping, so keep an eye out for these ships and keep outside the main buoyage for additional peace of mind. Keep a look out for porpoises and whales as, surprisingly enough, they are all seen in this area. On Inchcolm, there should be plenty of common seals around. The sandy bays on the north side of the island give the most sheltered landing, as well as great views of St Colm's Abbey.

Look left and right before crossing the main shipping lane past Oxcars light and on to Inchmickery. The remnants of World War II fortifications are said to have been built to look like the outline of a warship at anchor, and earns Incmickery its nickname 'Battleship Island'. The last island of the day, Cramond Island, can be reached from the mainland at low water. It is a useful place to stretch the legs before the final section of the journey. The paddle up the Forth gives a great view of Edinburgh and the Castle on your left, Inchcolm Abbey on the right and the Forth Rail and Road Bridges ahead. All that is left are the refreshments waiting for you in the Hawes Inn; watch out for the whisky Sir Benjamin Baker warned about!

The Forth Rail Bridge

Paddling under the rail bridge gives a real sense of scale to this incredible structure; even in this day and age it is hard to comprehend the effort that went into building it. It took 4,600 workers seven years to build it, starting the mammoth task in 1882. In this period 57 died and over 500 were injured, and this was considered a good safety record at the time. When asked about these accidents the bridge engineer Sir Benjamin Baker is reputed to have said, "Many would have escaped had it not been for the whisky of the Hawes Inn". The Forth Rail Bridge opened in 1890 as the largest cantilever bridge in the world. Being the largest does have its drawbacks though, because when it needs a new coat of paint it takes nine years to complete and uses 7,000 gallons of paint!

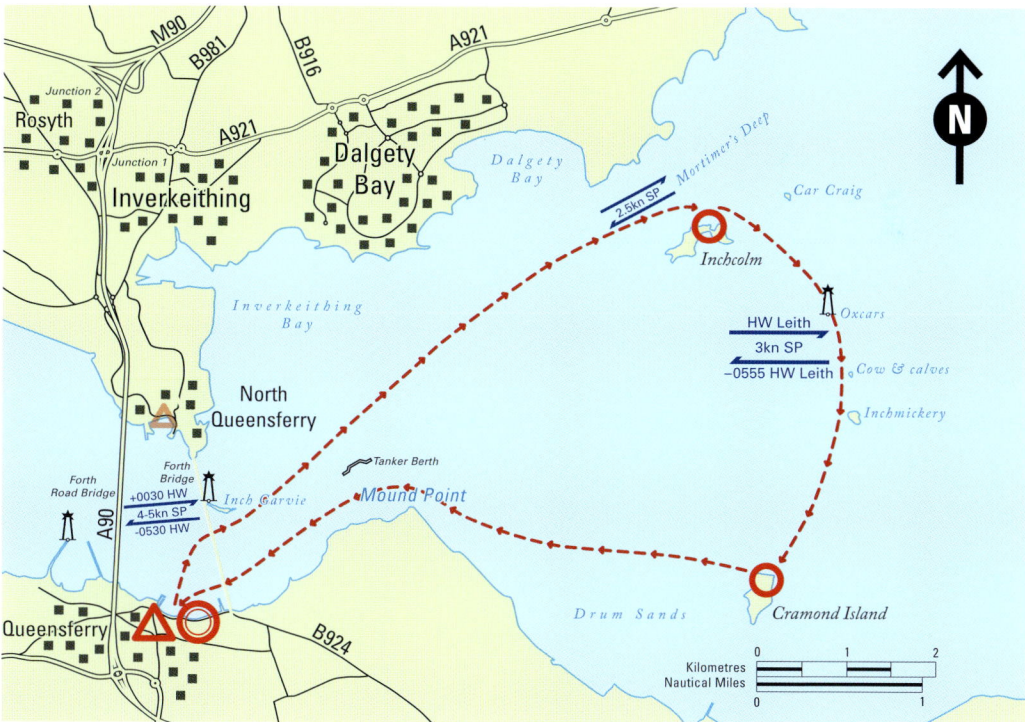

Firth of Forth

Tides and weather

The tidal streams in this area are very strong. If there is any wind against the tide it can produce very rough water, which can come as a surprise considering its relatively sheltered location.

The most efficient way, and on a spring tide the only way, to kayak this trip is to go out to Inchcolm making use of the east-going stream, and then return from Inchmickery on the west-going stream.

Additional information

South Queensferry and its beautiful cobbled streets offers plenty of options for eating out. If you would like further information about visiting Inchcolm Island, Historic Scotland manage the island and their website is as follows: www.historic-scotland.gov.uk

Variations

An alternative start and finish from North Queensferry is also possible, starting at (NT 122 803) and may be more convenient if you are travelling from the north.

The Iona of the East

Inchcolm is known as the 'Iona of the East'. The island was named after St Columba who visited in 567, and Alexander I founded the abbey in 1123. The Abbey is still remarkably well preserved and is a great place to explore. In the summer months there are boat trips out to the island and a custodian lives there managing the Abbey and shop. Historic Scotland asks visitors to the island during these months for a fee that goes towards the maintenance of the Abbey. The island has also been a site of many battles over the years, because its strategic position in the Firth of Forth and the riches that the Abbey held. In the 10th century Macbeth defeated invaders and for a large price of gold allowed the invaders to bury their dead on the island.

Fidra ⟲ 🛶 🏄

No. 41 | Grade A | 13km | OS Sheet 66 & 67

Tidal Port	Leith
Start	△ North Berwick (NT 563 853)
Finish	◯ North Berwick (NT 563 853)
HW/LW	HW/LW at North Berwick is around the same time as Leith.
Tidal Times	Off Fidra: The W going stream starts about 5 hours and 55 minutes before HW Leith. The E going stream starts about 5 minutes after HW Leith.
Max Rate Sp	0.5 Knots off Fidra
Coastguard	Aberdeen, tel. 01224 592334, VHF weather every 3 hours from 0730.

Introduction

This is a magic little trip that provides fantastic views of all that the Firth of Forth has to offer, as well as some great little islands to explore along the way.

Description

41

Fidra

The east beach of Milsey Bay in North Berwick is a perfect launch spot and the 19th century houses that line the seafront provide a grand backdrop throughout the paddle. For 500 years the 12th century harbour provided a key link to Earlsferry across the Firth, with a ferry that provided passage for the pilgrims on route to St Andrews.

The first island you head across to is Lamb, which off to the west is watched by its two sheep dogs, 'North and South Dog'. These are two small skerries either side of Fidra. Like the other islands off North Berwick, Lamb was formed by volcanic activity millions of years ago. This volcanic rock can be seen clearly at Lamb with its dark black colour and basalt column shapes. Another short crossing will take you to the island of Fidra, an RSPB reserve like nearby Bass Rock. There are remotely operated cameras on the island monitoring the birds, and these can be watched at the Scottish Seabird Centre in North Berwick. The island has a ruined chapel on it that was dedicated to St Nicholas in 1165 as well as a lighthouse and jetty. Despite the lighthouse it is not the Stevenson lighthouse engineers that Fidra is associated with, but the novelist of the family Robert Louis Stevenson. He often used to visit this area and in particular the beaches of Yellowcraigs opposite Fidra, and it is said that in his famous book he based his map of Treasure Island on the shape of Fidra. Paddling around the island you can try to imagine where the treasure is hidden, my guess would be at the back of the small cave next to the arch in the sheltered bay on the north side of the island. Depending on the height of the tide landing can be awkward on the island so you may want to consider paddling the short distance across to the lovely sandy beaches at Yellowcraigs for a rest.

Witch trials

North Berwick also became well known for its 'Witch Trials'. One of the most famous took place in 1591 when a woman named Agnes Sampson was accused of making a potion to summon up a storm as King James V1 of Scotland returned home from Denmark with his new wife. The King himself attended the trial and Sampson was tortured to confess and then burned at the stake, a fate that beheld so many other innocent women in this period.

The return to North Berwick is best done passing to the north of Lamb and then on to Craigleith. On this longer open water section of the paddle Bass Rock dominates the view, and out to the north is the Isle of May which guards the entrance to the Firth. North Berwick and its grand 19th century houses looks stunning from the sea and rising proudly behind is North Berwick Law, a 613-foot volcanic hill. On the summit of this hill there are the ruins of lookouts dating back to the Napoleonic Wars. A whale's jawbone has stood there since 1709, only nowadays it is a fibreglass replica which was put up in 2008 after the last real one collapsed in 2005 having been there since 1933.

At Craigleith it is worth paddling around the craggy north and east coasts on route back to the beach at Milsey Bay. This island used to be a rabbit warren where the animals were bred for food, until myxomatosis wiped them out in the 1950s and puffins took over. Unfortunately a plant called tree mallow then invaded, choking the puffins' burrows and preventing them from nesting. The Scottish Seabird Centre has been working hard to rid the island of the plant and it appears the puffins may be returning. So while enjoying the views while paddling under the cliffs of Craigleith before the final short crossing back to the starting point at the beach, keep a close eye out to see how the puffins are doing.

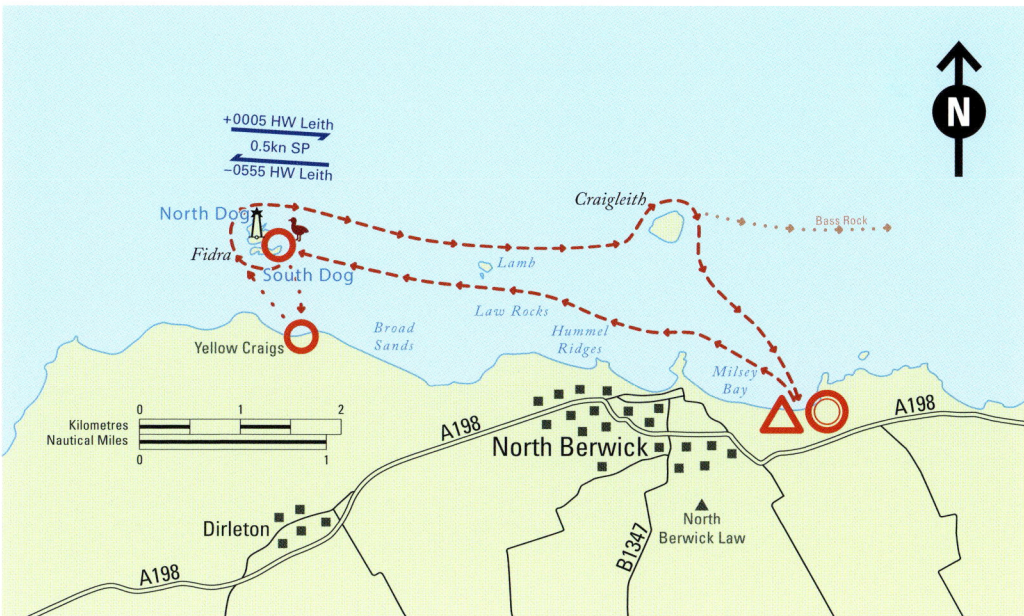

Tides and weather

There are no noteworthy tidal streams in this area, so the main consideration when planning this trip should be the wind. Be aware that in this outer part of the Firth of Forth any swell from the north or east will create an awkward sea state around the island and skerries.

Additional information

Parking in North Berwick can be difficult during the holiday season so it's worth starting early to get a parking space convenient to carry the sea kayaks from. At the east end of Milsey Bay beach there is a bigger parking space that works well. The Scottish Seabird Centre is well worth a visit and their website is www.seabird.org provides plenty of information about the seabirds and islands.

Variations

The trip can be made shorter by exploring fewer of the islands, or longer by continuing out to Bass Rock. Be aware that there are no easy landings on any of the islands so plan appropriate stops on one of the many lovely beaches on the mainland to the south.

Bass Rock

No. 42 | Grade B | 14km | OS Sheet 67

Tidal Port	Leith
Start	△ North Berwick (NT 563 853)
Finish	⬤ North Berwick (NT 563 853)
HW/LW	HW/LW at North Berwick is around the same time as Leith.
Tidal Times	At a point 3 nautical miles north-east of Bass Rock: The E going stream starts at about the same time as HW Leith. The W going stream starts about 6 hours before HW Leith.
Max Rate Sp	0.75 knots at the above point.
Coastguard	Aberdeen, tel. 01224 592334, VHF weather every 3 hours from 0730.

Introduction

This trip should be top of the list for all sea kayakers. The steep cliffs of Bass Rock tower above as you paddle past. The gannets, who are the guardians of the rock, circle above in their thousands and nest on the rock in such quantities they turn it white. The trip then continues on to a magnificent castle beside perfect beaches. What more could you ask for? It's just amazing!

Description

42

The popular beach of Milsey Bay in the picturesque town of North Berwick is the starting point. Parking can be busy here on a summer's weekend, so arriving early is a good idea. Once on the water Bass Rock will dominate the view, and from this distance it will look as if it is topped with white icing sugar. It is home to one of the biggest gannet colonies in Scotland with as many as 40,000 pairs of gannets coming here every year. Bass Rock is so significant the bird is named after it, as the Latin name for gannet is 'Sula Bassana'. As you head out to the rock you will have great views across to the Isle of May on the other side of the Firth of Forth. Bass Rock itself will become more and more impressive as you draw closer. Long before arriving you will hear the thousands of gannets, and soon you will smell them as well! It appears as if the whole rock is moving as the masses of white birds are constantly coming and going. The sky above will be filled with gannets circling and you will be treated to the most spectacular sight of all … the gannets diving for food.

The lighthouse was constructed in 1902 and vertical rock walls surround the entire island, so there are no landing places. Bass Rock used to be an ancient volcano, and what you see now is the plug of harder rock that formed in the centre while the softer rocks around have been worn away. The rock has plenty of caves to explore, some extending deeply into the heart of this impressive volcanic plug.

You will leave Bass Rock with a sensory overload of noise, smell and sights, so the idyllic beach of Seacliff to the south will be the place to head to for a rest. Explore the rocks to the west of the beach and discover the unique harbour. Blasted out of the red sandstone cliffs in 1890 the entrance measures just two metres across and is the smallest harbour in the UK. The beach was also used as a staging post for various raids on nearby Tantallon Castle, which you will paddle past on route back to North Berwick. This impressive castle was originally built in the 14th century and forms an impregnable fortress with three of its sides being protected by the steep cliffs rising up from the sea. In 2009 a psychology professor released a photograph showing a ghost looking out from the castle, this photograph has been confirmed by experts not to be manipulated, so if you feel you are being watched as you paddle by you know whom it may be!

On your way to the trips finish and you will pass Canty Bay, another fine beach to land on if time allows. Before pulling into the beach at North Berwick make sure you take one last look over your shoulder at the unforgettable Bass Rock.

History

Bass Rock has seen many uses over the years and it has had religious connections for a long time. The chapel was built around 1491 and is named in memory of St Baldred, an Irish missionary who is thought to have been the first inhabitant as far back as the 6th century. Since then it has often served as a prison, at one time keeping political and religious prisoners in a dungeon where many of them died. Up until the World War I the rock was used to graze sheep, collect eggs and harvest young gannets, known as guga. The practice of killing and eating young gannets is no longer done here, but once a year, on the Hebridean island of Lewis, the locals still travel out to the remote island of Sula Sgeir to harvest the guga. As you pass along the base of the cliff the gannets will be sitting on their nests unperturbed and confident. Getting this close to these amazing birds is fantastic, yet it is clear to see how easy it would have been to harvest them.

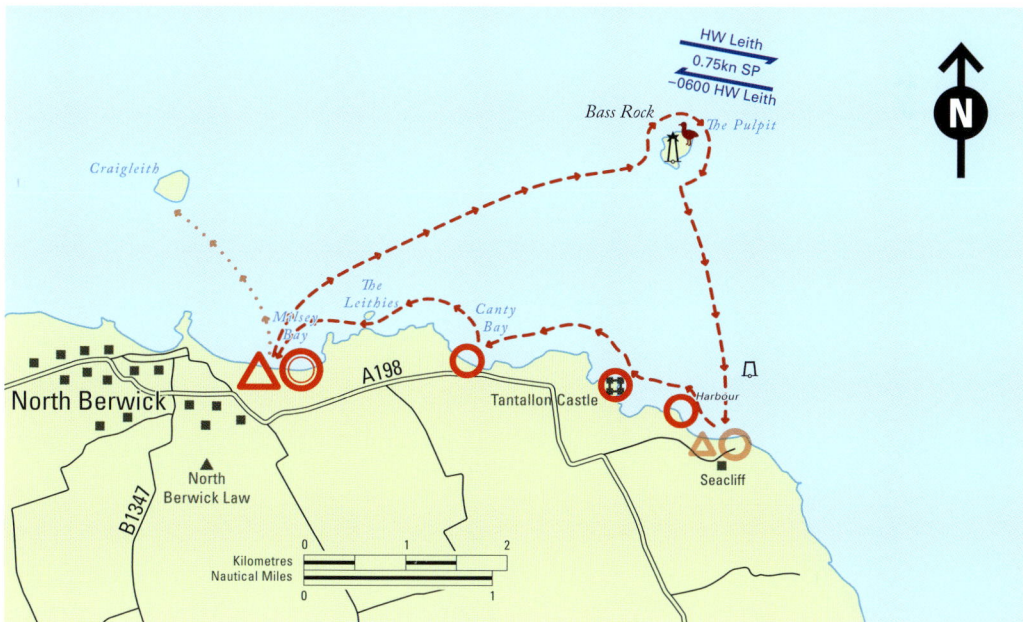

221

© Tantallon Castle

Tides and weather

There are no notable tidal streams on this trip, however the water forced around Bass Rock does move a bit faster than elsewhere. The north-east corner of the island is exposed to any swell or sea state from the North Sea and therefore care should be taken as rougher conditions are often experienced here.

Additional information

Sightseeing craft as well as big ships use the water between Bass Rock and the mainland, therefore keep a close eye out for them when crossing to or from the island. North Berwick provides a good range of amenities as well as being home to the Scottish Seabird Centre. The centre has cameras set up to monitor the gannets on Bass Rock and is well worth a visit. Its website also has plenty of useful information about the seabirds as well as webcams: www.seabird.org Tantallon Castle is looked after by Historic Scotland. Visit their website www.historic-scotland.go.uk to find out more about the castle.

Variations

Seacliff beach can provide an alternative starting point for this trip; it is reached down a rough private road and a small fee is asked for to access. This will provide a slightly shorter paddle out to Bass Rock and back. For a longer trip, continuing on to Craigleith and Fidra islands as described in the previous chapter is recommended.

Gannets

Gannets are one of the largest European seabirds and some of the biggest breeding colonies are found around the Scottish coastline. Seen high above the sea they are masters of flight, and in even the strongest of winds they manoeuvre effortlessly. They are instantly recognisable by their dazzling white plumage with black wing tips and creamy yellow head. In some areas there are huge colonies on rocky offshore islands, Bass Rock being one of the more famous. The gannets are probably best known for their spectacular feeding method of diving for fish from up to 30m above the sea's surface. They gather amazing speed with their wings folded back as they dive towards their prey. As they hit the water, split-second timing prevents wings being snapped and a strengthened skull along with air sacks protects the bird's brain from concussion. They can reach speeds of up to 100 km/h as they dive and strike the water.

42

Bass Rock

Cliffs and gannets of Bass Rock

The Borders

Introduction

Scotland's final section of coastline on the east coast is almost a short summary of all that has gone before, and should not to be overlooked. Beautiful sandy beaches have been a key feature of the north and east coastlines, and the borders will not disappoint. Dunbar, Pease Bay and Coldingham are all home to such beaches, and there are plenty more along the way.

Lighthouses have been a constant feature along the coastline and Barns Ness provides a towering structure, whilst St Abb's Head has its light towering high on the cliff top. The north coast started with a power station at Dounreay and the east coast will finish with one at Torness. Castles have never been far away from north to south and in the Borders there is the historic Dunbar Castle and its harbour, along with Fast Castle and of course the fortified town of Berwick-upon-Tweed just across the border in England.

Fishing has proven to be the life support of the east coast over the years, and from this beautiful historic harbours have grown. Whether it is the smallest harbour in Britain at Seacliff or at Cove, St Abbs or Burnmouth, all will tell their story and provide a idyllic place to stop. The villages of the border coastline will continue to provide places to eat and drink with hospitality assured, Dunbar, St Abbs and Eyemouth in particular. The borders coastline finishes with one last great headland, the home of thousands of birds and riddled with caves and geos; St Abb's Head. The cliffs continue beyond here though, and do so until the Scottish border is crossed and the English town of Berwick-upon-Tweed is arrived at. The coastline will tower above along this section, with caves, a stunning sea stack and a final grand sea arch 'Needles Eye' providing a fitting finish to the incredibly varied and east coast of Scotland.

Tides and weather

St Abb's Head provides the only tidal flows of note along this section of coastline with the flow generally being insignificant elsewhere. Facing slightly north into the North Sea it is the swell that will have the greatest effect on paddling the coastline, often making it unwise to head out, and landing or launching will be a challenge. A swell forecast should always be considered when planning trips, and any swell from the north through to the east will have an effect. A lot of the coastline is fairly shallow close into shore with numerous reefs, this again adds to the challenge when there is swell forecast. As this coastline is linear in nature there is no hiding from the swell or the wind and this can make the trips very committing in anything other than good conditions.

The Borders

225

© Needles Eye, Berwick-upon-Tweed

Barns Ness 🚣🚗〰️

No. 43 | Grade B | 18km | OS Sheet 67

Tidal Port	Leith
Start	△ Dunbar (NT 663788 or NT 682789)
Finish	◯ Pease Bay (NT 795710)
HW/LW	HW/LW at Dunbar is around 5 minutes before Leith.
Tidal Times	Off Dunbar: The W going stream starts about 5 hours and 55 minutes before HW Leith. The E going stream starts about 5 minutes after HW Leith.
Max Rate Sp	0.5 knot along this section of coastline.
Coastguard	Aberdeen, tel. 01224 592334, VHF weather every 3 hours from 0730.

Introduction

This is a trip of great contrasts. It starts with an ancient castle, goes on to pass a nuclear power station, sandy beaches and the dramatic lighthouse of Barns Ness itself, finishing with an ornate sandstone arch and a beautiful old harbour. This part of the East Lothian coastline also boasts the driest and sunniest climate in Scotland!

Sandstone arch with Torness Nuclear Power Station behind

Description

43

Barns Ness

Belhaven Bay to the west of Dunbar is the preferred start to this trip, however it will need to be towards high tide to avoid a very long walk to the water. On a lower tide the alternative put on is at the beach within Dunbar itself, just along from the harbour. If launching from this alternative site take some time to paddle around to Dunbar's ancient castle and beautiful harbour before heading off on the rest of the journey. Leaving Bellhaven Bay you will soon pass under the red cliffs of Long Craigs, and arrive at the ancient castle of Dunbar.

Take the time to explore the remains of the castle, and you should find the fantastic little natural arch that forms part of the castle walls just next to the harbour entrance. Dunbar has had a prominent harbour for many years due to its key location for trade and fishing. The current Victorian harbour was built in 1842 when a large breach had to be made through the original castle walls to accommodate an entrance. Further improvements were made in 1858 and this allowed up to 800 boats to use the harbour, this being the key period for herring fishing. The harbour is as spectacular as they come these days, and the way its entrance is guarded by the ancient castle walls is a key part of this. The gun battery of Lammer Island is clear to see as you paddle along the harbour walls. This was built to ward off potential French or Spanish invasions during the 18th century. The battery mounted sixteen guns and remained there until after the Napoleonic wars, however it never fired a shot in anger. After its decline it became an isolation hospital and a military hospital during World War I. Just along from the battery beyond where the harbour walls finish you will find a small sandy beach that is the alternative put on.

As you leave Dunbar be sure to look over your shoulder as there is a fantastic view of the town with the dramatic red bricked church overlooking the houses and beach below. The low-lying coastline leads you to the beautiful beach of White Sands, a place well worth earmarking for a food stop. As with many of the beaches along this trip it is popular with surfers, so if not looking for too much excitement when landing avoid days when there is any north or easterly swell. Beyond White Sands is the dramatic lighthouse of Barns Ness, which overlooks the low-lying yet treacherous reefs at its foot (take care if there is any swell). Built in 1901 by David Stevenson it stands thirty-seven metres tall, but these days its light no longer shines brightly as it was deactivated in 2005.

Dunbar Castle

There is very little remaining of this great and strategic castle these days, although there has been a castle here since at least the Iron Age period in the 2nd century. The castle has stood up to many battles over the years, particularly during the Middle Ages when Scotland was frequently under attack from England. One of the most notable battles was in 1338 when the countess of Dunbar 'Black Agnes' defended it for many weeks against a large English army led by two great generals. During this time when the castle was under siege supplies that had come from Bass Rock were smuggled in from the sea, and eventually the English generals gave up and left the castle to its Scottish defenders.

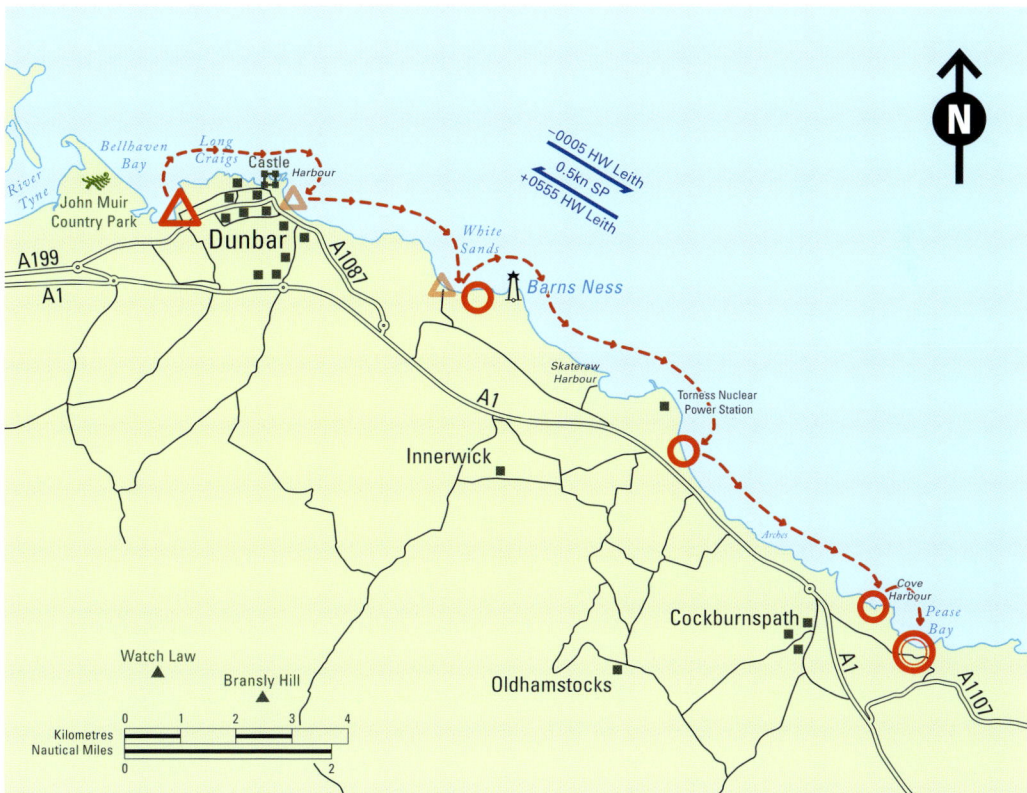

© Torness Nuclear Power Station

Torness nuclear power station

It took eight years to build and opened in 1988, the last of the UK's second-generation nuclear power plants. It can supply up to 1.5 million homes with electricity and currently is due to be decommissioned in 2023. In 1999 it had a lucky escape when an RAF Tornado jet crashed into the North Sea less than 1km away. The two crew members were commended for their airmanship in ensuring the jet was beyond the power station before abandoning it. Less dramatic than this the power plant had to shut in 2011 when a large mass of jellyfish reduced the flow of seawater at the intakes, thus potentially not allowing the reactors to cool sufficiently. The warm water from the outflow attracts fish and there will be plenty of people fishing there at a weekend.

Torness nuclear power station cannot be described as a beautiful view, and many would of course say it should not be there at all. However, paddling towards it you cannot be anything other than amazed by its size and shape.

Just beyond the power station is another large beach which provides a stopping opportunity. Beyond the beach stay close in to shore as there as some great shapes in the small red sandstone cliffs, such as the ornate sandstone arches that are seen here. On an exceptionally high tide you will be able to paddle pretty close to them, at other times it is worth a walk for a closer look. Another small sandy beach provides a clue that the hidden harbour of Cove is just

around the corner. At higher water Cove provides a great place to land with a sandy beach at the back of the beautiful harbour, so it is worth planning to spend some time soaking up the history of this unique little harbour, as well as the views back to Torness with Barns Ness and Bass Rock beyond.

The trip finishes just on from Cove at the beach and associated caravan park of Pease Bay, with more small red cliffs guiding you in. Sadly the caravan park somewhat spoils the view as you land, but looking on down the coast to the remote Fast Castle Head will fuel the mind with future paddling plans.

43

Barns Ness

Cove

This hidden harbour and its associated buildings are all listed as structures of architectural and historic interest, and of these the most interesting are perhaps the tunnels and cellars leading from the harbour. These were built in the 1700s with the cellars originally for the storage of fish. However, due to its hidden nature (secret cellars and caves only accessible at low tide) it soon became a prime place for smugglers to secrete their ill-gotten goods. As with so many of these harbours the herring fishing was a key source of income. However, this was declining in the late 1800s, and losing three out of its four boats and eleven out of its twenty-one men in the east coast fishing disaster meant the end of fishing in Cove.

Tides and weather

There is minimal tidal flow along this section of coastline so wind should be the key considera-tion when planning the trip. It can be paddled in either direction as the wind dictates. Ensure that the swell forecast is checked as all the landings are well known for their surf and could cause an unprepared sea kayaker a problem.

Additional information

When landing at Pease Bay vehicles will have to be left outside the caravan park entrance. It is a long carry with the kayaks so it is worth considering using a trolley if available. Dunbar has lots of lovely cafés, pubs and sites of interest. If thinking about using alternative launch sites at White Sands or Skateraw Harbour, be aware that there are 2.1 metre height restrictions.

Variations

The trip can be made shorter using alternative launch sites at White Sands or Skateraw.

St Abb's Head

No. 44 | Grade B | 19km | OS Sheet 67

Tidal Port	Leith
Start	△ Pease Bay (NT 795 710)
Finish	○ Coldingham (NT 917 665)
HW/LW	HW/LW at St Abbs is around 15 minutes before Leith.
Tidal Times	For St Abb's Head: The SSW going stream starts about 3 hours and 5 minutes before HW Leith. The NNW going stream starts about 3 hours and 45 minutes after HW Leith.
Max Rate Sp	1–2 knots off St Abb's Head and Fast Castle Head.
Coastguard	Aberdeen, tel. 01224 592334, VHF weather every 3 hours from 0730.

Introduction

The rock architecture and wildlife of this east coast headland is enough to impress any sea kayaker. It is a remote and committing section of coastline that has all the ingredients for a great day out. Kayaking amongst the bird life nesting on the imposing cliffs at the St Abb's Head Nature Reserve is a magical experience and one not to be missed.

233

The red cliffs of St Abb's Head

Description

The holiday park of Pease Bay is a launch site that is in stark contrast to what lies beyond. It is quite a walk to the sea from the parking area, so a trolley is recommended. Soon you will leave the busy beach and head towards the imposing headland of Fast Castle Head, with its grey sedimentary cliffs rising up to 160 metres above the sea below. Here you come across some of the first caves of the trip. There are very few landing spots, however at Hirst Rocks you may be able to pull in on a bouldery beach. There are the remains of some ruined fishing houses and a cableway that was used to carry the fish up the hillside, a clear reminder at how hard it was to earn a living for the east coast fishermen in times gone by. By now you should be able to make out the ruined walls of Fast Castle high up on the headland. There is little left of this dramatic castle that was first in recorded use in 1333. In those days it could only be accessed by a drawbridge over a narrow ravine with access to the sea via a pulley system with basket.

Paddling round Fast Castle Head the view behind will take in Torness nuclear power station and Bass Rock in the far distance. Ahead, the red volcanic cliffs of St Abb's Head will be making an appearance. Look out for the slender thumb of rock called 'Wheat Stack' which has been climbed by climbers, and then the bay of Souter with its old zigzag path that would have been used by fishermen of the past still evident. The sedimentary folds of rock and steep grassy hillside provide a unique beauty to this inaccessible section of coastline, there will be only the nesting kittiwake colonies to keep you company here. If conditions allow, there is a dramatic stopping point with a great view of St Abb's Head on a rocky beach with a waterfall cascading down onto it (marked on the map just past Heathery Carr). If you are unable to land here, the only real

44 — St Abb's Head

guaranteed place for a stop before St Abbs is the disused historic harbour of Pettico Wick. The harbour was built in 1862 to service the lighthouse, before the present day road was built. In 1880 a salmon fishery was also established here and the harbour thrived for many years.

The next few kilometres of coastline after Pettico Wick will provide some of the most breathtaking scenery on the east coast. The red cliffs are a maze of rock gardens, hidden geos, sea stacks, and through routes to tempt the inquisitive sea kayaker. The shapes of these rock formations are just amazing, being topped off with St Abb's lighthouse itself (built by the Stevenson brothers in 1862). This whole area is a National Nature Reserve, primarily due to its importance as a seabird-nesting site with over 60,000 birds making these dramatic cliffs their home. Kittiwakes and guillemots are the most numerous alongside plenty of razorbills, shags, fulmars and puffins. During the March – July nesting season these will all be lining the cliffs and making an incredible noise. In these periods be sure to keep a reasonable distance from the cliffs to avoid undue disturbance. Even so you will have plenty around you as you paddle along and keep a wary eye out for any crash landing seabirds as they launch themselves from the cliffs!

The quaint village and harbour of St Abbs, with its lifeboat station in the heart of the harbour, is a beautiful harbour with a handy café. As you may well have noticed this whole area is a mecca for scuba divers, with its particularly clear waters and spectacular underwater scenery. So much so that in 1984 it became Britain's first voluntary marine reserve, which was established by David Bellamy. Just around the corner from St Abbs the trip finishes at the sandy beach of Coldingham Bay. This final bit of coastline will allow some more rock hoping to top off an amazing trip, before landing at the beach with its bright beach houses that will provide a colourful contrast to the rest of this great day out.

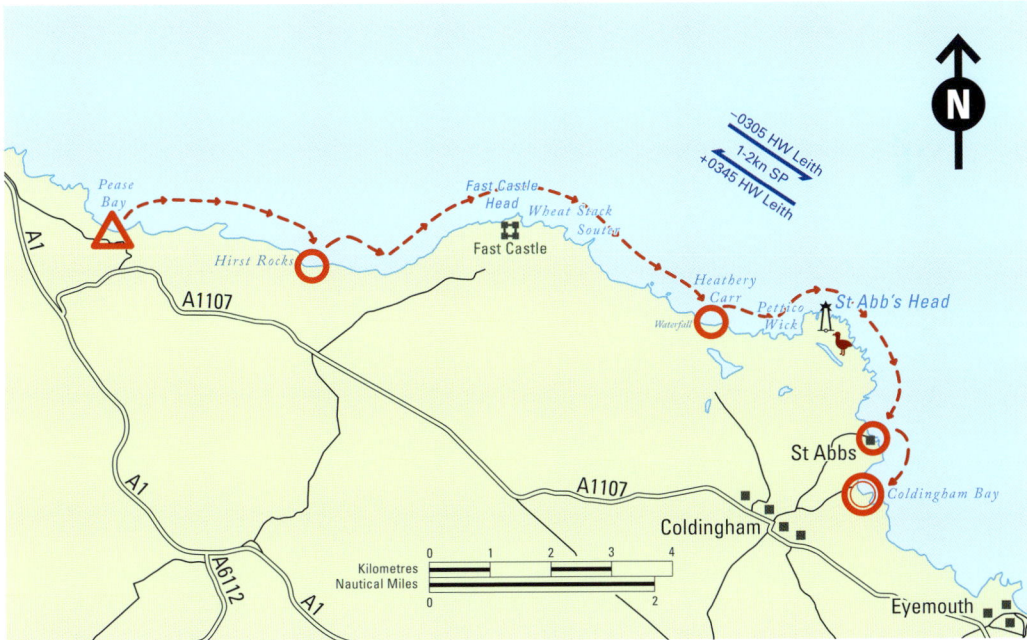

Tides and weather

Try and plan the trip so that you leave Pease Bay at the start of the south going stream. If this is not possible or it is better to make use of a tailwind you can paddle against the tide at all points with relative ease, making use of eddies where possible. The coastline provides limited landing opportunities, with both start and finish beaches having the potential for large surf. With this considered a day with limited swell is recommended.

Additional information

There is plenty of parking at the start and finish, and at Coldingham it is usually possible to drop the kayaks off at the beach and then park in the large car park. There is limited parking at St Abb's harbour, which is usually busy with divers so it is not recommended to use this as a launch site. If you do then there is a car park charge as well as a launching fee. It is also worth considering visiting the St Abb's Head Nature Reserve on foot or to drive out to the lighthouse for a small toll fee, these both offer a great view of the paddle to finish the day off.

Variations

To avoid the need for a shuttle start and finish at Coldingham Bay. Heading around St Abb's Head to Pettico Wick and back provides the best that this coastline has to offer, and can be enjoyed twice!

The waiting fishing wives

The waiting fishing wives

On October 14th 1881 a ferocious hurricane hit the south east coast and devastated the fishing fleet that was working out to sea off this coastline of Scotland. It was the cause of the worst fishing disaster in Scotland's history, and the date that will never be forgotten became known as Black Friday. In total 189 lives were lost on this terrible day. In the fishing villages of Eyemouth, Burnmouth, St Abbs and Cove this left many woman widowed and children fatherless, the communities were devastated. In these four villages you will find small poignant sculptures that have been placed as a reminder to us all of how these villages suffered from Black Friday. Each sculpture depicts the exact numbers of woman widowed and their children looking out to sea for their loved ones that never returned.

© Coldingham Bay

Eyemouth 🏕️ ⛴️ 🚗 🚌 🌀

No. 45 | **Grade B** | **19km** | **OS Sheet 67 & 75**

Tidal Port	Leith
Start	△ Coldingham (NT 917 665)
Finish	⭕ Berwick upon Tweed (NU 007 526)
HW/LW	HW/LW AT Coldingham is around 15 minutes before Leith.
Tidal Times	Along this section of coastline: The SE going stream starts about 2 hours and 45 minutes before HW Leith. The NW going stream starts about 3 hours and 5 minutes after HW Leith.
Max Rate Sp	0.5 knot along this section of coastline.
Coastguard	Aberdeen, tel. 01224 592334, VHF weather every 3 hours from 0730.

Introduction

This is a wild bit of coastline that offers big cliffs, ornate sea stacks and a grand sea arch. There are few escape routes and the coastline is exposed to whatever the North Sea wants to throw at it. In the right conditions it provides a fantastic trip, and it's not every day you can say you've paddled to England!

45

Eyemouth

Description

Coldingham Bay is a popular venue for surfing and has plenty of parking and a picturesque beach to start this journey from. Just before the sandy bay and harbour of the traditional fishing town of Eyemouth you will pass under Fort Point, where in 1547 the first trace italienne or star fort style of fortification was built in Britain. It is easy to land at the beach that forms Eyemouth's sea front and there are plenty of amenities. However this early in the trip you may want to continue to the next village of Burnmouth for a break. The coastline leading to Scout Point has some interesting low-lying rock gardens to explore and beyond this lays the towering Fancove Head with its 100-metre cliffs. There are deep caves, sea stacks and sea gullies to explore on this section as the cliffs tower above you all the way to Burnmouth, the last village in Scotland.

Burnmouth nestles at the foot of the steep hillside with a single row of houses clinging to the shoreline. You can pull ashore either at the stony beach south of the harbour at higher water, or within the harbour. On a higher tide you see this lovely village at its best, but at low tide you will see the remarkable parallel lines of serrated rocks that head out into the sea. This place is fully exposed to the ravages of the sea and it is hard to conceive what it must be like in a big northerly gale. As with other fishing villages on this coast, Burnmouth was affected by the east coast fishing disaster in 1881, and the small commemorative statue of the wives and children looking out to see can be found on the harbour wall. Heading on from Burnmouth look out for the ornate sea stack with a needle like hole through it as you pass Ross Point. This sandstone formation is known as Maiden's Stone and at high water it can be paddled around. This marks the start of some great sandstone features that are enjoyed for the rest of the trip. Just on from here you will pass Lamberton beach and a possible rocky landing; look out for the little stone shelter build into the hillside here with old winch alongside. This also is the marker for the last kilometres worth of paddling in Scotland, so have your passport ready as England is just around the corner!

As you arrive in England the imposing Marshal Meadows Bay will meet you, and if you're lucky you might see the otters that I have seen playing in this area. Beneath the towering cliffs of this sandstone amphitheatre there is a beach that can be landed on at most states of the tide. You may notice a rickety old ladder up the steep slope. This leads to a dark tunnel that was built by Victorians to access the beach, but nowadays it brings you out in the caravan park that sits high on the cliff top. The final section of coastline takes in some fantastic small red sandstone

cliffs, which at high water can provide plenty to explore. Of particular note is the grand sea arch of Needles Eye and its surrounding caves. Soon the small cliffs will subside and the Berwick Holiday Park will take over. This leads to the sands of Meadow Haven Beach, next to the pier on the north side of the river mouth. This is an easy landing place with car parking not too far away. All that will be left to do is to find one of the many lovely cafés in Berwick-upon-Tweed and reflect of a great day before escaping back north of the border.

Tides and weather

There is little tidal movement along this coastline, so plan the trip taking into consideration the prevailing wind. This coastline is very exposed to any swell from the north or east, and along it there are numerous hidden reefs and few landing places.

Additional information

The most challenging navigation on this trip will be finding the car park for Meadow Havens Beach, allow time for this. The ancient town of Berwick-upon Tweed, with its walls and ramparts surrounding it, is well worth spending the time to explore. The Eyemouth Maritime Centre (www.worldofboats.org) is also worth a visit.

Variations

If you would like to use the bus service for a shuttle, I would recommend starting in Berwick-upon-Tweed and finishing at Eyemouth, leaving the vehicle at the start. This works well as the bus is right next to the get out at Eyemouth. There are cafés/pubs to wait in if required and then it is a short walk from the bus stop in Berwick to the start point through the town's ramparts. Using Burnmouth as an alternative start or finish can also give an option of a shorter trip.

Appendix A – HM Coastguard and Emergency Services

In UK waters, HM Coastguard co-ordinates rescues and emergency services. They also broadcast weather forecasts and inform water users about potential hazards in their area. They monitor VHF channel 16 and you should use this channel to make initial contact; you will then be directed to a working channel. Note the times here are for UT. During the UK summer months remember to add 1 hour.

There are two HM Coastguard stations that fall within the scope of this book.

HMCG	Area	Telephone	Weather announced on CH16 (UTC)
Shetland	Cape Wrath to Brora, including the Pentland Firth.	01595 692 976	0110, 0410, 0710, 1010, 1310, 1610, 1910, 2210
Aberdeen	Brora to English Border	01224 592 334	0130, 0430, 0730, 1030, 1330, 1630, 1930, 2230

Appendix B – Weather Information

The weather is the most discussed topic within the communities that make up the UK coast-line. The north and east coasts of Scotland offer less protection to the weather and associated conditions than many other areas within the UK, and therefore the weather needs to be paid particular attention to. The Met Office (www.metoffice.gov.uk) was founded in 1854 to provide information about the weather to marine communities. It was not until 1922 that forecasts were first broadcast by BBC radio, a tradition that still remains today.

The Met Office website provides detailed predictions for the weather all over the UK but if you are away from computer or phone with web access you should still be able to get a forecast on LW radio.

RADIO

BBC RADIO 4 (92.5 – 94.6 FM AND 198 KHZ LW)

0048 – Shipping and inshore waters forecast, coastal station reports

0520 – Shipping and inshore waters forecast, coastal station reports

BBC RADIO SCOTLAND (92–95 FM AND 810 MW)

1904 (Mon – Fri) – Outdoor conditions, including inshore waters forecast

0704 (Sat & Sun) – Outdoor conditions, including inshore waters forecast

2204/2004 (Sat/Sun) – Outdoor conditions, including inshore waters forecast

WEB

Met Office – www.metoffice.gov.uk

BBC Weather – www.bbc.co.uk/weather

XC Weather – www.xcweather.co.uk

Windfinder (includes swell forecast) – www.windfinder.com

Magic Seaweed (surf forecasts) – www.magicseaweed.com

Appendix C – Mean Tidal Ranges

Tidal Port	Mean Spring Range (metres)	Mean Neap Range (metres)
Dover	6.0	3.2
Ullapool	4.5	1.8
Aberdeen	3.7	1.8
Leith	4.8	2.4

Appendix D – Glossary of Gaelic Words

Before the advent of maps and charts the Scottish fishermen navigated the waters by local knowledge. To help them with this they used to descriptively name many of the coastal features; this way they could describe to each other where they went or how to get there. When translating the Gaelic names around the coastline these days you will learn a lot about the area from these very descriptive names. The fishermen only used to fish a relatively small area near to their crofts, and therefore would just name all the features in that area. The next area's fishermen would then name the features in their area independently. It follows that you will see lots of repetition in the Gaelic names as each area would have its own 'black rock' that it named, and so on. Here is a list of some of the more common Gaelic names you will find while kayaking the Scottish coastline. A lot of the original mapmakers would have been non-gaelic speaking, which is why you'll find variations of spelling. To make matters more complicated, 'local' names, particularly for wildlife, can vary from area to area!

COASTAL FEATURES

Acairseid	Anchorage
Aiseag	Ferry
Ard or Aird	Promontory or Height
Bàgh	Bay
Bodha	Rock over which waves break
Bogha	Arch
Cabhsair	Causeway
Cala	Port
Camus	Bay/Inlet
Caol or Caolas	Narrows or Kyle/Firth/Strait
Carraig	Rock/Cliff
Ceann	Headland/Point
Cladach	Shore/Stony Beach

Cleit	Rocky Ridge
Coire	Whirlpool
Cuan	Ocean
Eilean	Island
Geò or Geodha	Chasm/Rift
Innis	Island or Meadow/Pasture
Long	Ship
Mol	Shingly Beach
Maol	Promontory
Muir/Mara	Sea/of the sea
Oitir	Sandbank
Port	Harbour
Poll	Fishing Bank
Rinn or Roinn	Point or Promontory
Rubha, Rubh or Ru	Point/Headland
Sgeir	Skerry/Reef
Sròn	Nose/Point
Sruth	Current
Taobh	Coast
Traigh	Tidal Beach
Uamh	Cave

LAND FEATURES

Abhainn	River
Aill	Steep river bank
Allt	Stream
Aonach	Moor/Plain/a desert place
Bàrr	Top/Summit
Bealach	Pass
Beinn	Mountain
Bidean	Pinnacle
Bruthach	Steep Place/Brae
Bun	River Mouth/Source/Root/Base
Caisteal	Castle
Cill or Ceall	Church or Burial Place
Clach	Stone
Clais	Ditch
Cnap	Hillock
Coille	Wood/Forest
Creag	Crag/Cliff
Dùn	Fortress/Castle
Eas or Easan	Waterfall
Fraoch	Heather
Glac	Hollow
Inbhir	River Mouth
Linn	Pool
Meall	Rounded Hill/Mound

Ord	Steep Hill
Sgùrr	Large Conical Hill
Slochd	Hollow
Tigh	House

COMMON DESCRIPTIONS FOR THESE FEATURES

Ard	High
Bàn	Pale/White
Beag or Bheag	Small
Buidhe	Yellow
Dearg	Red
Dubh	Black/Dark
Domhain	Deep
Donn	Brown
Fada	Long
Garbh	Rough/Thick
Geal	White
Geàrr	Short
Glas	Pale/Grey
Gorm	Green/Blue
Liath	Grey/Blue
Mor or Mhor	Big/Large
Naomh	Saint
Ruabh	Red/Brown
Uaine	Green

WILD LIFE

An Leumadair	Dolphin
Buthaid	Puffin
Caora	Sheep
Coinneanach	Rabbit
Cù	Dog
Eun-mara	Seabird
Faoileag	Black Headed Gull
Gille-Brìghde	Oyster Catcher
Gobhar	Goat
Iasg	Fish
Iolaire	Eagle
Madadh	Wolf/Dog
Muc-mhara	Whale (pig of the sea)
Puthag	Porpoise
Ròn	Seal
Sgarbh	Cormorant
Sùlaire	Gannet
Trilleachan	Sandpiper

Thanks to Anne Martin for technical comment.

Glossary of Gaelic Words

Appendix E - Trip Planning Route Card - User's Guide

The trip planning route card is designed to be used in conjunction with the information supplied in each route chapter in the book. In addition to this you will also require a set of relevant tide timetables. If the blank route card is photocopied, all the information for your route to be paddled can be worked out on it. This way it will help you plan your paddle as effectively as possible, and then allow you to have all the information you need on a handy piece of paper. This can be displayed in your map case on your kayak for easy reference. To help you use the card please refer to the following example and guidelines:

Trip Name & Number	*Noss Head (No.14)*

Page Number	*83*	VHF Weather	*0730, 1030, 1330, 1630*
Date	*27th April 2013*	Weather Forecast	
Coastguard Contact	*Aberdeen, 01224 592334*	*Fair, visibility good, wind W F2-3*	

- Fill in the name, number and page of your chosen trip for easy future reference.
- When choosing the date of the trip, check in the chapter's 'Tide & Weather' section as to whether it will need specific tides that will dictate the date.
- Obtain a weather forecast using information supplied in Appendix B.
- Coastguard contacts can be found in the introductory info for each trip and in Appendix A.

TIDAL INFORMATION

Tidal Port *Aberdeen*		Mean Sp Range *3.7m*			Local Port *Ackergillshore*		
		Mean Np Range *1.8m*					
Tidal Port Tide Times (UT)	Height in Metres	Tidal Range in Metres	HW/LW	+1 Hr for BST?	Local Port HW/LW Time Difference	Local Port HW/LW	Sp or Np Tides
0154	*4.4*	*3.9*	*HW*	*0254*	*-0220*	*0034*	*Sp*
0757	*0.5*	*3.9*	*LW*	*0857*	*-0220*	*0637*	*Sp*
1416	*4.4*	*3.9*	*HW*	*1516*	*-0220*	*1256*	*Sp*
2021	*0.5*		*LW*	*2121*	*-0220*	*2101*	*Sp*

Trip Planning Route Card

- Identify Tidal Port from the chapter introductory information.
- Identify Mean Spring and Neap Ranges from tide timetable or see Appendix C. These will help identify Spring or Neap Tides and Estimated Maximum Speed.
- Local Port is also found in the chapter introductory information.
- Obtain the Tidal Port Times and Height in Metres from your tide timetables. Usually four times and heights, but occasionally three.
- To work out the Tidal Range in Metres subtract the LW heights from the HW heights.

- Add 1 Hr for BST? Add an hour to your Tidal Port Times if you are in British Summer Time.
- The Local Port HW/LW Time Difference can be found in the chapter introduction.
- To work out Sp or Np Tides compare your Tidal Range to the Mean Sp and Np Ranges.

Location	Direction of Tidal Stream	Tidal Stream Time Diff.	Tidal Port HW (BST?)	Tidal Stream Start Time	Tidal Rate	Est. Max Speed
Noss Head	S	+0530	0254	0824	2kn	2kn
	N	-0040	1516	1436		

Location	Direction of Tidal Stream	Tidal Stream Time Diff.	Tidal Port HW (BST?)	Tidal Stream Start Time	Tidal Rate	Est. Max Speed

Location	Direction of Tidal Stream	Tidal Stream Time Diff.	Tidal Port HW (BST?)	Tidal Stream Start Time	Tidal Rate	Est. Max Speed

- Use the Location as indicated in the chapter introductory and tidal information.
- For the Direction of Tidal Stream there are generally four periods of tidal movement every 24 hours. Direction for the Tidal Stream Start Time soonest after 0000 hours in the first box.
- The Tidal Stream Time Difference is found in the chapter introductory and tidal information.
- Tidal Port HW can be transposed from above converting to BST if appropriate.
- The Tidal Stream Start Time is worked out by subtracting/adding the Tidal Stream Difference from/to the Tidal Port HW time.
- Tidal Rate is the average spring speed for the tidal stream, found in the chapter introduction.
- Estimate Maximum Speed based on whether it is Spring, Neap or in between tides.
- If it is Springs use the speed given in the chapter's introductory and tidal information.

- On Neap Tides halve this spring rate.
- When in between springs and neaps use the average of the spring and neap speeds.
- Note that speeds given are average spring rates. If paddling on a spring tide look to see if your Tidal Range in Metres is bigger or smaller than the Mean Sp Range. If it is bigger the speeds will be faster than average spring rates given.

	Location	Notes	ETA	ETD
Start	Ackergillshore	Do not park at the slipway turning area		0930
1st	Castle Sinclair	Landing place in hidden inlet east of castles	1015	1130
2nd	Noss Head	Paddling under cliffs, beware of tidal movement	1145	1145
Finish	Staxigoe	Beware of breaking waves if there is swell	1245	

- When choosing Locations for the Route Plan use places that have tidal importance and where you may want to stop.
- When working out ETD (Estimated Time of Departure) or ETA (Estimated Time of Arrival) enter key times which need to be met for the best use of tidal stream first, as recommended in Tide & Weather. Work out other times around these.
- To work out the times an average paddling speed of 6km/h or 3 knots can be used. This can be adjusted to suit your needs, or time added for coastal exploration if desired.

Please feel free to photocopy the blank Trip Planning Route Card on the page overleaf. An A4 downloadable version is available on our website.

For this and other resources go to www.pesdapress.com, follow the links to resources/downloads/printables.

www.pesdapress.com

Trip Planning Route Card

Trip Name & Number	
Page Number	VHF Weather
Date	Weather Forecast
Coastguard Contact	

Tidal Port			Mean Sp Range			Local Port		
			Mean Np Range					
Tidal Port Tide Times (UT)	Height in Metres	Tidal Range in Metres	HW/LW	+1 Hr for BST?	Local Port HW/LW Time Difference	Local Port HW/LW	Sp or Np Tides	

Location	Direction of Tidal Stream	Tidal Stream Time Diff.	Tidal Port HW (BST?)	Tidal Stream Start Time	Tidal Rate	Est. Max Speed
Location	Direction of Tidal Stream	Tidal Stream Time Diff.	Tidal Port HW (BST?)	Tidal Stream Start Time	Tidal Rate	Est. Max Speed
Location	Direction of Tidal Stream	Tidal Stream Time Diff.	Tidal Port HW (BST?)	Tidal Stream Start Time	Tidal Rate	Est. Max Speed

	Location	Notes	ETA	ETD
Start				
1st				
2nd				
3rd				
4th				
5th				
Finish				

Trip Planning Route Card

Index

A

Aberdeen 167, 168
Aberdeen Coast 151
Aberdeen Harbour 170
Aberdour Bay 142, 145, 146
Achastle-shore 94
Ackergillshore 85, 86, 88
Ackergill Tower 86
An Dun 98, 102
An Garbh-eilean 16, 17
Anstruther 195, 196, 198, 200,
203, 204, 205
Anstruther Easter 193, 196, 197,
198, 200, 201, 204
Anstruther Fish Bar 196, 200
Anstruther Lifeboat Station 204
Arbroath 177, 180, 181, 182, 183,
184
Arbroath Signal Tower Museum
181, 185
Ardersier 119
Ardmore Point 36
Ard Neackie 25, 26, 28
Ardross Castle 205
Armadale Bay 38, 47
Auchmithie 180, 181, 182

B

Balintore 103, 105, 106, 107, 108,
110, 111
Balnakeil 20
Balnakeil Bay 15, 16, 18, 21, 22,
24
Banff 137, 139, 140, 141
Banff Bay 140, 142
Barns Ness 227, 229
Barns Ness Lighthouse 229
Bass Rock 216, 219, 220, 221,
222, 223, 229
Belhaven Bay 228
Bell Rock 180, 181, 183, 184,
185, 186
Bell Rock Lighthouse 181, 183,
186
Ben Hope 23, 34
Berriedale 97, 99, 100, 102

Berriedale Castle 99
Bervie, River 174
Berwick Holiday Park 242
Berwick-upon-Tweed 239, 242
Bettyhill 32, 35, 36
Bettyhill Fishing Station 34
Bighouse Lodge 44, 45
Black Score 82
Blowup Nose 168
Boars of Duncansby 76
Boddam 160, 162, 166
Boddam Harbour 159
Borders, The 225
Borve Castle 35, 36
Boursa Island 38
Bow Fiddle Rock 129, 130, 131,
132
Boyne Bay 137
Brawl 38
Brims Castle 51
Brims Ness 51
Broad Haven 164
Broch 83
Brough 57, 59
Buchan Ness Lighthouse 160
Bucholie Castle 82
Buckie 130
Bullers of Buchan 159, 161
Burghead 125, 126, 127
Burnmouth 240
Burwick 72

C

Cadboll 105
Caiplie Caves 195
Cairnbulg 147, 150, 153, 154,
157
Cairnbulg harbour 150
Cairnbulg Point 150, 154
Caithness Broch 84
Canty Bay 221
Caol Beag 30
Cape Wrath 15, 16, 17, 18, 20
Cape Wrath Lighthouse 18
Castlecraig 110, 116
Castle Geo 82

Castlesea Bay 180
Catterline 173, 175
Ceannabeinne 24
Cellardyke 195
Chainwalk 206
Chanonry Point 11, 117, 118,
120, 121
Chanonry Point Lighthouse 118,
120
Clach Bheag 23
Clach Mor na Faraid 23
Clashach Cove 126
Clashach Quarry 127
Cleit an t-Seabhaig 27
Cleit Dhubh 17
Cleit Mhor 95
Clo Kearvaig 17, 18
Clo Mor 16, 17
Coldingham 233, 236, 239
Coldingham Bay 235, 240
Collieston 163, 165, 166
Colsea Yawn 168
Constantine's Cave 194
Cove (Aberdeen) 167, 168, 170
Cove (Barns Ness) 230, 231
Covesea 128
Covesea Lighthouse 127
Covesea Lookout Tower 127
Covesea Skerries 127
Cowie Chapel 169
Craig Head 130
Craighead quarry 194
Craigleith 217, 222
Crail 193, 195, 196, 206
Cramond Island 213
Crathie Point 131
Crawton 172, 173
Creag Ruadh 34, 36
Cromarty 113, 114, 116
Cromarty Firth 108, 109, 115,
116
Crooked Haven 173
Crosskirk Bay 50
Crovie 144
Cruden Bay 162, 164
Cullen 131, 132, 138
Cullykhan Bay 142, 146

Cummingston 126
Cummingston Cliffs 128

D

Deil's Heid 180
Deveron, River 140
Dolphins 11, 111, 116, 121, 122
Doonie Point 169
Dounreay Nuclear Power Plant 46, 50
Downies 168
Duke's Candlesticks 99
Dunbar 227, 228, 232
Dunbar Castle 229
Dunbeath 93, 95, 96, 97, 100, 102
Dunbeath Castle 98
Dunbeath Harbour 95, 98
Dunbuy Island 161
Duncansby Head 69, 73, 75, 76, 77
Duncansby Stacks 74
Dunnet 58
Dunnet Head 55, 56, 59, 60
Dunnottar Castle 172, 175
Dunrobin Castle 104
Durness 20, 22, 24
Durness Old Church 22
Dwarwick 56, 58, 59
Dwarwick Pier 55

E

East Sands 191, 192
East Tarbet 198
Eathie 114
Eathie Salmon Station 115
Edinburgh 207, 212, 213
Edinburgh Castle 212, 213
Eilean Choraidh Island 26
Eilean Hoan 24
Eilean Iosal 31
Eilean nan Ron 27, 28, 29, 30
Elie 203, 205, 206
Elie Ness 205
Ethie Haven 179
Eyemouth 239, 240, 242
Eyemouth Maritime Centre 242

F

Fancove Head 240
Faraid Head 18, 21, 22, 23, 28

Farr Bay 34, 35
Farr Point 32, 33, 35
Fast Castle 234
Fast Castle Head 234
Ferryden 178, 181
Fidra 215, 216, 222
Fife 187
Fife Ness 185, 193, 194, 196, 201, 206
Findlater Castle 131
Findochty 130, 132
Firth of Forth 187, 211, 214
Fort George 117, 118, 119, 120
Forth Rail Bridge 211, 213
Forth Road Bridge 212, 213
Fort Point 240
Fowlsheugh 172
Fraserburgh 148, 150, 157
Fraserburgh Bay 150
Fraserburgh Castle 149
Fraserburgh Harbour 149
Freisgill 24, 26
Fresgoe 46, 50
Fresgoe Harbour 43
Fresgoe Inn (Fresgoe House) 46
Freswick Bay 77, 82, 84

G

Gallow Hill 114
Gardenstown 139, 141, 143, 144, 146
Gardenstown Harbour 144
Garran 173
Garron Point 169
Gaylet Pot 180
Geodha Brat 27
Geodha nan Aigheann 27
Geodha na Seamraig 18
Geodh' Ruadh 38
Gills Bay 55, 57, 58, 59, 66, 67, 68, 70, 71, 72
Girdle Ness 170
Girnigoe 86
Girnigoe Castle 86
Gloup, The 64
Gow's Castle 127

H

Halladale, River 44
Halliman Skerries 127
Hare Craig 161
Haven, The 91, 92

Hawes Inn 212, 213
Head of Garness 140
Hell's Lum 145
Hells Mouth 69
Helmsdale 97, 99, 100, 101
Hirst Rocks 234
Holborn Head 49, 51, 52
Hopeman 126, 127, 128
Hopeman Harbour 126
Horses Head, The 130

I

Inchcolm 212, 214
Inchcolm Abbey 213, 214
Inchcolm Ferry 212
Inch Garvie 212
Inchkeith 207, 208, 209, 210
Inchmickery 212
Inverallochy 150
Inverbervie 171, 173, 174, 175
Iona of the East 214
Isle of May 195, 197, 198, 200, 201
Isle of May Lighthouse 201

J

Jewel of the Forth 197
John o' Groats 61, 62, 65, 66, 71, 72, 73, 76, 77

K

Kearvaig 16, 17, 20
Keiss 77, 81, 83, 84
Keiss Castle 81, 83
Keiss Pier 81
Kenly Water 191
Kessock Bridge 119
Kilminning Castle 195
Kincraig Point 205, 206
Kinghorn 207, 208, 209
Kingsbarns 189, 191, 193, 194, 196
King's Cave 108
Kinlochbervie 20
Kinnaird Head 147, 148, 149, 150, 186
Kinnaird Head Lighthouse 149
Kinneff Church 173, 175
Kirkhaven 198
Knee, The 75
Knock Head 137, 138

Index of Place Names

Kyle of Durness 16
Kyle of Tongue 27

L

Lady's Tower 205
Lamberton Beach 240
Lamb Island 216
Lammer Island 228
Latheronwheel 93, 96
Lidel Eddy 72
Links Bay 138
Lions Head 144
Little Skerry 68, 69
Loch Eriboll 26
Logie Head 131
Long Craigs 228
Long Haven 161
Lossiemouth 125, 127
Lunan Bay 179
Lybster 89, 92, 93, 94, 96
Lybster Oil Field 96

M

Macduff 140, 141
Maiden Kame 172
Maiden's Stone 240
Maiden, The 26
Marshal Meadows Bay 241
McFarquar's Cave 114
Meadow Haven Beach 242
Meall Thailm 31
Mell Head 64
Melvich 44, 47
Melvich Bay 44
Merry Men of Mey Tidal Race
56, 57, 58
Mestag Castle 64
Mey 71
Mey Castle 56, 57, 59
Mid Clyth 92
Milsey Bay 216, 217, 218, 220
Mol Mor 31
Mol na Coinnle 30
Montrose 177, 178, 181
Montrose Basin 178
Moray Firth 117
Moray Firth - North 79
Moray Firth - South 123
More Head 140, 141
Muckle Skerry 69, 71
Muckle Skerry Lighthouse 69,

70
Murdoch Head 161

N

Navermouth 34
Naver, River 34
Neave Island 30, 34, 36
Needle E'e (Scurdie Ness) 180
Needles Eye (Eyemouth) 242
Ness of Litter 51
Ness, River 118
Nethertown 68
Nethertown Pier 62, 68
Newtonhill 168
Nigg 109, 110
Nigg Ferry 107
North 116
North Berwick 215, 216, 217,
218, 219, 221
North Berwick Law 217
North Carr Beacon 194, 195, 196
North Carr Rocks 194, 195, 196
North Haven 161
North Queensferry 214
North Sutor 107, 109, 110, 111
Noss Head 85, 86, 87, 88
Noss Head Lighthouse 87
Nybster 82, 83

O

Occumster 92
Old Man of Hoy 46, 56
Old Slains Castle 164
Old Wick Castle 90
Ord Point 99
Oxcars Light 212
Oyster Catcher, Portmahomack
106

P

Pease Bay 227, 231, 232, 233, 234
Pennan 145, 146
Pentland Firth 13, 59, 64, 68, 69,
70, 74, 75
Pentland Skerries 67, 68
Pentland Triangle 72
Peterhead 156, 157
Pettico Wick 235
Pittenweem 204, 206
Pole, The 90
Port a' Chinn 33, 36, 37, 38, 41,

47
Port Allt a'Mhuillinn 38
Port an Righ 108
Port Erroll 159, 162, 163, 164,
165
Portessie 129, 130, 132
Portknockie 131, 132
Portlethen 168
Portlethen Shore 168
Portmahomack 103, 104, 106
Port Mor 36
Port of Brims 51, 53
Portskerra 37, 39, 40, 43, 44, 47
Portsoy 137, 138
Portsoy Harbour 136
Prail Castle 179
Priest Craigs, The 130
Puffins 199

R

Rabbit Islands 27, 28, 31, 32
Rattray Head 153, 154, 156, 157
Rattray Head Lighthouse 153,
154
Reay 47, 52
Red Head 179
Redhythe Point 135, 138
Rock and Spindle 191
Rockfield 105, 106
Rosehearty 143, 145, 146
Rosemarkie 113, 114, 116, 117,
118, 120
Round Tower 161

S

Sandend 129, 131, 132, 135, 136,
138
Sandhaven 147, 148, 150
Sandside 47
Sandside Bay 41, 46, 49, 50
Sandside Head 43, 46
Sandwick 105
Sandwood Bay 20
Sango Bay 23, 24
Sangobeg 24
Sango Sands 21
Sannick Bay 70, 76
Sarclet 91
Scarfskerry 57
Scartan Bay 69
Sclaites Geo 75

Scotland's Haven 57
Scotstown 153, 156, 157
Scottish Fisheries Museum 198, 200
Scottish Lighthouse Museum 150
Scottish Outdoor Access Code 10
Scottish Primrose 41
Scottish Seabird Centre 200, 216, 217, 218, 222
Scout Point 240
Scrabster Lighthouse 52
Sculptures Cave 127
Scurdie Ness 177, 178, 181
Scurdie Ness Lighthouse 178
Seacliff 220
Seacliff Beach 222
Seanachaisteal 23
Sgeir an Oir 31
Shandwick 108, 110, 111
Shandwick Stone 111
Sinclair Castle 86
Sinclair's Bay 86
Skares, The 164
Skateraw Harbour 232
Skerray 30, 31, 32
Skerray Harbour 30, 32
Skerray Pier 29
Skirza 74, 77, 82, 84
Skirza Head 74
Skirza Pier 73, 81
Skuas 53
Skullomie 31
Slains Castle 162
Smoo Cave 22, 23
Souter Bay 234
South Queensferry 211, 214
South Ronaldsay 72
South Sutor 110
St Abbs 235, 236
St Abb's Head 233, 234, 236
St Abb's Head Nature Reserve 233, 236
St Abb's Lighthouse 235
St Andrews 189, 190, 191, 192
St Andrews University 190
Staxigoe 85, 87, 89, 90
St Bennet's Well 114
St Catherine's Dub 165, 166
St Colm's Abbey 212

St Combs 154
St John's Church 141
St John's Head 58, 59
St John's Point 56, 57, 59
St Mary's Chapel 50
St Monans 204, 205, 206
Stocked Head 141
Stonehaven 167, 169, 170, 171, 172, 174, 175
Stonehaven Harbour 169
Strathan 27
Strathmarchin Bay 137
Strathy Bay 37, 39, 40, 41, 47
Strathy Point 36, 37, 38, 39, 47
Strathy Point Lighthouse 39
Stroma Island 61, 62, 65, 68, 71, 72, 76, 77
Sutors Stacks 113, 114, 115, 116
Swilkie Point 61, 65, 66
Swilkie, The 64
Swiney Castle 94
Swona Island 59, 64, 66, 72

T

Talmine 25, 27, 28, 32
Tantallon Castle 221, 222
Tarbat Ness 103, 104, 105, 106
Tarbat Ness Lighthouse 104
The Broch, Burghead 126
The Links 190
Thirle Door 75
Three Kings 108
Thurso 49, 51, 52, 53
Todd's Hole 179
Todhead Lighthouse 173
Tongue 32
Torness Nuclear Power Station 230
Torrisdale Bay 34, 36, 41
Traigh Alt Chailgeag 24
Traigh Bhuidhe 99
Tree Geo 62, 65
Tronach Head 130
Troup Head 142, 143, 144, 146
Twa Haven 162

U

Usan 179

W

Well of Health 111
Wester Haven 57
West Sands Beach 190
Whaligoe 89, 91, 92
Wheat Stack 234
Whitehills 135, 137, 138
Whiten Head 18, 24, 25, 26, 28
White Sands 229, 232
Wick 92
Wick Bay 90
Wife Geo 74
Windmill (St Monans) 204
Wine Tower, The 148
Wood Haven Bay 205

Y

Yellowcraigs 216

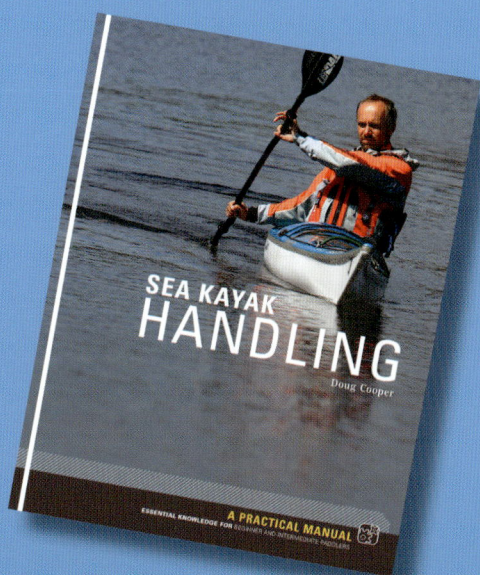